AMA Handbook of Poisonous and Injurious Plants

AMA
Handbook of Poisonous and Injurious Plants

Dr. Kenneth F. Lampe
Mary Ann McCann
Division of Drugs and Technology

American Medical Association
Chicago, Illinois

ISBN: 0-89970-183-3

Library of Congress Cataloging in Publication Data
Lampe, Kenneth F.
  AMA Handbook of Poisonous and Injurious Plants.

  Includes bibliographies and index.
  1. Poisonous plants—Toxicology—Handbooks, manuals,
etc.   2. Skin—Inflammation—Handbooks, manuals, etc.
3. Poisonous plants—United States—Handbooks, manuals,
etc.   4. Poisonous plants—Canada—Handbooks, manuals,
etc.   5. Poisonous plants—Caribbean Area—Handbooks,
manuals, etc.   I. McCann, Mary Ann.   II. American Medical
Association.   III. Title.
RA1250.L27   1985   615.9'52   84-28532
ISBN 0-89970-183-3

Distributed by Chicago Review Press, Chicago

Contents

Preface

The purpose of the *AMA Handbook of Poisonous and Injurious Plants* is to provide physicians and other health care professionals with an easily used reference for the management of plant intoxications. The format also makes it useful as a field guide for the recognition of dangerous and injurious plants.

There is a brief introduction on the epidemiology of plant poisoning, general principles for the management of intoxications, and botanical nomenclature. Section I discusses native or cultivated plants of the United States, Canada, and the Caribbean that produce systemic intoxications in man. Section II and III discuss plant dermatitis and mushroom poisoning. The plants in Section II are limited to those most frequently encountered as producing dermatitis or those illustrative of a specific type of dermal response. Because the identification of mushrooms from photographs is uncertain, Section III depends upon description of the symptom complex for differential diagnosis and suggested management.

Acknowledgements

Our particular appreciation is extended to Gary Lincoff and
to the Library of the New York Botanical Garden and to
Nina Woessner and other staff members of the Fairchild
Tropical Garden in Miami. We are grateful to Michael
Ellis of the Poison Control Center of the University of Texas
Branch at Galveston and David Spoerke of the Rocky
Mountain Poison Center in Denver. We wish to acknowledge
James Ackerman and Arlee Montalvo of the University of
Puerto Rico, Lynn Brady of the University of Washington in
Seattle, and Elizabeth McClintock of San Francisco who
provided assistance in finding specimens for photography
as well as many others who supplied us with photographs
and information. We wish to thank Charles Bailey and
Marjorie King of the Department of Medical Photography
at the University of Miami for their help. We also wish
to thank the many individuals and plant nurseries who gave
us permission to photograph their plants.

We are indebted to Sandra McVeigh, our editor, and for the
help and expertise of the Department of Creative Services.
We wish to thank Patti Fitzgerald and Mary Marks for the
preparation of the manuscript copy, and Mary Danaher for
technical assistance. Without the considerable assistance
of the librarians at the AMA and the University of Miami
School of Medicine, the preparation of this Handbook
would have been immeasurably more difficult.

In addition to the resources of the American Medical
Association, the preparation of this manuscript was
supported, in part, by a contract from the Division of Poison
Control, Bureau of Drugs, Food and Drug Administration
(HEW-PHS-FDA 221-78-0091) and by a grant provided by
the National Library of Medicine (R01-LM-01655).

Photo
Credits

Charles M. Bailey (Lake City, FL): 82, 83, 116, 268, 269

Lynn Brady (Seattle, WA): 36, 144, 304, 316, 351

Paul Consroe (Tuscon, AZ)/reprinted with permission from *Arizona Medicine:* 223

William Crawford (Manchester, IA): 29, 329

Thomas J. Duffy (Walnut Creek, CA): 425

Michael Ellis (Galveston, TX): 216, 227, 354, 355, 369

William T. Gillis (deceased): 37, 123, 206

George Grimes (Denver, CO): 433, 437

Roger Hammer (Goulds, FL): 338

Annie Hannan (Ann Arbor, MI): 50

George Hatfield (Ann Arbor, MI): 213, 229, 431, 432

William L. Hearn (Miami, FL): 436

George James (Brookville, MD): 150, 151

Marjorie King (Miami, FL): 2, 24, 28, 103, 104, 108, 115, 117, 138, 159, 161, 172, 205, 263, 264, 288, 291, 337, 347, 367

John Kohout (LaGrange, IL): 40

Kitty Kohout (LaGrange, IL): 16, 100, 285, 322, 325

Evelyn Lampe (Chicago, IL): 283

John Lewis (Lisle, IL): 239

Library, New York Botanical Garden: 71, 90, 128, 143, 160, 192, 200, 226, 236, 293, 315, 320, 371, 397

Gary Lincoff (New York, NY): 233, 314, 352, 408

Elizabeth McClintock (San Francisco, CA): 386, 422

Nancy McGivney (Naperville, IL): 156

Sturgis McKeever (Statesboro, GA): 278

Charles T. Mason Jr. (Tucson, AZ): 368

Lawrence T. Mellichamp (Charlotte, NC): 60, 258, 259, 260

Arlee M. Montalvo (San Juan, PR): 38, 183, 287, 348, 398

Lauri Nieminen (Turku, Finland): 430

Eloy Rodriguez (Irvine, CA): 295

Catherine B. Scates (Post Falls, ID): 423, 424, 434, 435

Harry Smith Horticultural Photographic Collection (Hyde Hall, Rettendon, Chelmsford, Essex, England): 11, 54, 409

David Spoerke (Denver, CO): 75
Leo J. Tanghe (Rochester, NY): 426
D. Jesse Wagstaff (Washington, DC): 421
Jonathan Wasserberger (Los Angeles, CA): 209
Robert Weeks (Gainesville, FL): 20
Frances Welden (New Orleans, LA): 84
Nina Woessner (Miami, FL): 97, 210, 301
Thomas A. Zanoni (Santo Domingo, Dominican Republic):
    201, 225, 350

All photographs not listed above are by Kenneth F. Lampe.

Introduction

General Management of Plant Poisoning

General Management of Plant Poisoning

Calls to Poison Control Centers concerning plants constitute about 10% of inquiries, but only a small fraction of these calls report symptoms. Most of these calls concern children under age 3 years; children less than 1 year have access only to plants in the home, and the dominant symptom-producing plants are thus members of the family Araceae, primarily the dumbcane (*Dieffenbachia*) and a philodendron (usually *P. scandens*) (see Table 1). Older preschool children may ingest plants and mushrooms in the yard or playground but rarely are seriously poisoned except in subtropical areas (see Table 2). A number of intoxications associated with presumably harmless plants may be due to chemical contamination by pesticides, herbicides, and fertilizers. Foraging by teenagers and adults for wild edible plants occasionally results in serious, sometimes fatal, intoxications. Fatalities in adults usually result from eating amatoxin-containing mushrooms, species of *Cicuta* mistaken for wild parsnips, or use of leaves of the tree tobacco (*Nicotiana glauca*) in salad.

Whenever possible, the plant should be identified by direct examination. The trivial name of the plant, although useful as a starting point, may be inaccurate and is subject to wide geographical variation.

Observation usually is recommended for asymptomatic children who have ingested an unidentified plant. However, when it is known that a potentially dangerous plant or an uncultivated mushroom has been eaten, vomiting should be induced. Ipecac is more effective for removing plant material from the stomach than gastric lavage. The dose of syrup of ipecac for children over 1 year is three teaspoonsful. *The administration of syrup of ipecac to infants 6 to 12 months old should be conducted under medical supervision and not in the home*. For children age 6 to 9 months, the dose is 5 ml; for those 9 to 12 months, the dose is 10 ml. Ipecac should be administered with a glass of water. It should never be

1

given when the gag reflex is depressed, there is diminished consciousness, or convulsive movements are observed, since aspiration may occur. The child should be made ambulatory or held in a "spanking position" to protect the airway. Emesis usually occurs in 20 minutes; if not, the dose may be repeated once. If emesis is not induced or there is inadequate recovery from the stomach, lavage should be performed through a large bore orogastric tube. Saline or half normal saline should be employed as the lavage fluid to minimize electrolyte derangement. Activated charcoal (young children, approximately 20 g; adults, 100 g) with water should be administered after emesis has ceased or can be instilled at completion of lavage before the tube is removed. When the delay following ingestion makes evacuation of the stomach contents of doubtful practicality, the administration of activated charcoal and water is advised.

If spontaneous emesis occurred after plant ingestion with adequate return of stomach contents, syrup of ipecac or gastric lavage usually is unnecessary. The victim, especially the young child, should be monitored for fluid and electrolyte disturbances after profuse and protracted vomiting and diarrhea because hypovolemic shock can develop rapidly.

There are relatively few specific antidotes for plant poisoning. In general, the recommended management depends upon the course and severity of the intoxication in the particular patient. The amount and nature of the toxins in any plant species may vary widely with geographic location (suggesting genetic strains), growing conditions, maturity, and the plant part ingested. Often, too little material will be consumed to cause systemic intoxication. Good clinical judgement must prevail. Often, hurried plant identifications are in error. As an example, some cases of presumed honeysuckle poisoning turned out, on closer examination, to be due to the berries of a poisonous *Solanum* vine entwined with the honeysuckle plant.

Table 3 may be used to make a presumptive classification of a plant poisoning based on the early signs and symptoms. This may permit decisions concerning the institution of therapy while more information as to the specific plant, the condition of the patient, and the severity of the intoxication is obtained.

Because serious plant and mushroom intoxications are uncommon, the aid of a Poison Control Center should be sought. These Centers possess lists of consultants on particular aspects of plant and mushroom poisoning.

Table 1.
Inquiries to the Rochester, New York, Poison Control Center Concerning Ingestion of Plants By Children 1 Year of Age or Less By Frequency[1]

1. Philodendron
2. Jade Plant
3. Wandering Jew
4. Swedish Ivy
5. Spider Plant
6. Dieffenbachia and Rubber Plant
7. Asparagus Fern
8. Aloe
9. String-of-Pearls
10. Pothos

---

[1]Lawrence RA: Plant ingestions in infants under 1 year of age. Annual Meeting, American Academy of Clinical Toxicology, American Association of Poison Control Centers, and Canadian Academy of Clinical Analytical Toxicology. Chicago, Illinois, October 18-20, 1978.

Table 2.

Inquiries to Poison Control Centers Concerning Plant Ingestions: Most Frequently Involved Species*

NCPCC[1] (Data from all reporting centers)	Salt Lake City, Utah[2]	Rochester, New York[3]	Miami, Florida[4]
1. Philodendron	1. Philodendron	1. Yew	1. Brazilian Pepper
2. Pokeweed	2. Pyracantha	2. Nightshade	2. Dieffenbachia
3. Holly Berries	3. Apricot & Other Pits	3. Honeysuckle	3. Rosary Pea
4. Pyracantha	4. Dieffenbachia	4. Philodendron	4. Pencil Tree Cactus
5. Poinsettia	5. Poinsettia	5. Poinsettia	5. Ficus
6. Dieffenbachia	6. Honeysuckle	6. Pokeweed	6. Oleander & Philodendron
7. Nightshade	7. Wandering Jew	7. Wandering Jew	7. Ixora & Allamanda
8. Elder	8. Horse Chestnut	8. Dieffenbachia	8. Poinsettia
9. Jerusalem Cherry	9. Sweet Pea	9. Jade Plant	9. Coral Plant
10. African Violet	10. Creeping Charlie	10. Coleus	10. Balsam Pear, Angel's Trumpet, & Bischofia
11. Elephant Ear Plant	11. Jimson Weed & Schefflera		11. Hibiscus, Sea Grape, Crown-of-Thorns, "Croton," & Bottle Brush
12. Begonia	12. Oregon Grape & Tulip		

Table 2. (cont.)
Inquiries to Poison Control Centers Concerning Plant Ingestions: Most Frequently Involved Species*

National Data Collection System for 1983.[5] Reporting areas: Mass, Washington DC, West Va, western Va, sw Pa, Ga, Ala, La, Minn, western Iowa, N Dak, S Dak, Nebr, Colo, Mont, Wyo, se Idaho, Utah, Ariz, Oregon, San Diego.

1. Philodendron	16. Aloe
2. Dumbcane	17. Asparagus fern
3. Poinsettia	18. Weeping fig
4. Jade plant	19. Climbing nightshade
5. Pyracantha (Firethorn)	20. Poison Ivy
6. Holly	21. Rhododendron, Azalea
7. Schefflera	22. Pittosporum
8. Pokeweed	23. Oregon grape
9. Spiderplant	24. Oak (acorn)
10. Honeysuckle	25. Oleander
11. Rubber plant	26. Chrysanthemum
12. Arrowhead vine	27. Jerusalem cherry
13. Decorative pepper	28. Mistletoe
14. Flame violet	29. Begonia
15. Pothos	30. Mountain Ash

*Only a few of these plants are considered harmful, see Section I.

[1]Bulletin, National Clearinghouse for Poison Control Centers, FDA, Bethesda, Maryland, (Apr) 1977.

[2]Spoerke DG, Temple AR: One year's experience with potential plant poisonings reported to the Intermountain Regional Poison Control Center. *Vet Hum Toxicol* 20:85-89, 1978.

[3]Lawrence RA, Schneider MF: Ten year study of plant ingestions, 1967-1977: Preliminary report. Annual Meeting, American Academy of Clinical Toxicology, American Association of Poison Control Centers, and Canadian Academy of Clinical Analytical Toxicology. St. Adele, Quebec, August 2-5, 1977.

[4]Fawcett NP: Pediatric facets of poisonous plants. *J Florida Med Assoc* 65:199-204, 1978.

[5]Veltri JC, Litovitz TL: 1983 Annual report of the American Association of Poison Control Centers National Data Collection System. *Am J Emerg Med* 2:420-443, 1984.

Table 3. Signs and Symptoms of Common and/or Serious Plant Intoxications*

		Dieffenbachia/Philodendron	Colchicum/Gloriosa	Euphorbia/Hippomane	Actaea/Anemone/Ranunculus	Convallaria/Digitalis/Nerium	Aconitum	Solanum	Pieris/Rhododendron/Veratrum	Conium/Laburnum/Nicotiana/Sophora	Cicuta	Taxus	Gelsemium	Brugmansia/Datura	Amaryllis/Narcissus/Wisteria	Ilex	Abrus/Ricinus	Prunus	Phytolacca	Podophyllum	Karwinskia
Mouth & Throat	Burning/Irritation	++	++	D	++	+	+	D	+	+											
	Increased Salivation	+		D	++		+		D	++	+										
	Dry Mouth											D	+	++							
	Dysphonia/Dysphagia	+		D			±					+	+	+							
Gastroenteric Tract	Nausea		+	+	+	+	±		D	+	+				+	+	DD				
	Vomiting		+	+	+	+	±		D	+	±	D			++	++	DD	D	++	+	
	Diarrhea		++	++	+	+		D	D	+					±	±	DD		D	+	
	Abdominal Pain		++	++		+		D	D			D			+		DD	D	+		
	Decreased Bowel Sounds									+				++						±	
Cardiovascular	Tachycardia													+							
	Bradycardia					+			++			D									
	Arrhythmias					±	++					D									
	Conduction Defects					++								+							
	Hypertension																				
	Hypotension								++			D									

6

Table 3. (Cont.)

Nervous & Neuromuscular												
Dizziness			±			+	+	+	+	+		
Weakness/Lethargy			±		+	+	+	D	+			D
Syncope			±									
Delirium/Psychosis			±			D±				+		
Tremors/Convulsions			±		D±	D	±	±	D±			±
Depression/Coma					D	+	D	+			D±	±
Headache					+	±	+	+				
Paresthesias			++		D							
Muscle Weakness/Paralysis	±		±		D	+	D	+			D±	±	DD
Visual												
Mydriasis			+		+	±	+	+	+			±
Visual Disturbances			+		D	+	+	++				
Cutaneous												
Increased Sweating					+	+	++				D	++
Dry Skin								++	+			
Flushing/Rash							D	+				
Cyanosis							D	D			D±	
Misc.												
Hyperthermia	+							+				
Painful/Bloody Micturition	+											

+ Commonly occurs   ++ Pronounced or persistent   ± Occasionally reported   D Delayed onset   DD Occurrence significantly delayed

*See text for additional details. The differential diagnosis of mushroom intoxications is given in Section III.

7

Botanical Nomenclature

A case report involving a plant should always include its botanical (binomial) name, eg, *Duranta repens*; both are italicized. *Duranta* is the name of the genus and *repens* is the particular species. A genus (plural: genera) may be composed of a single species or several hundred. Although not essential for medical reporting, a botanically complete name also includes that of the individual (often abbreviated) who named the plant. In this case, the full name would be *Duranta repens* L.; L. is the abbreviation for Carolus Linnaeus (1707-1778) and is not italicized. There is only one valid name for a plant. Previously employed names that have been changed for taxonomic reasons are known as synonyms. In this Handbook, the more common current synonyms are included in parentheses with an equal sign, eg, *Duranta repens* L. (= *D. plumieri* Jacq.). Some species are divided further into subspecies (ssp.), varieties (var.), and forms (forma), eg, *Philodendron scandens* C. Koch & H. Sello ssp. *oxycardium* (Schott) Bunt. In this instance, the plant was named *Philodendron oxycardium* by Heinrich Schott but was transferred to subspecies status by George Bunting. Hybrid names are indicated by an X, as in *Brugmansia* X *candida*. This is read *Brugmansia* hybrid species *candida*; the letter X is not pronounced. Horticultural names are not italicized but are capitalized and set in single quotation marks, eg, *Ilex glabra* cv. 'Compacta'; cv. is the abbreviation for cultivar.

Associations of like genera are placed in a family. The family name is not italicized, but the initial letter is always capitalized. Eight family names have been changed recently. In this Handbook, the older name has been conserved, but the new name is added in parentheses, eg, Umbelliferae (Apiaceae).

If a specific species cannot be found, it probably has toxicity similar to another member of that genus. To a lesser extent, such an association may apply to members of the same family (see Table 4).

The botanical nomenclature for cultivated plants conforms, for the most part, to that given in *Hortus Third*.

The names of indigenous species for the United States and Canada are taken, for the most part, from Kartesz and Kartesz. Names for West Indian species and Guam were selected from the floras listed in the references.

Care must be excercised when evaluating poison plant literature. In some instances, information on toxicity of plants in grazing animals has been extrapolated to man. Some plant lore without merit has passed through generations of textbooks. Even evaluations based on actual case reports in man, as in this Handbook, may be flawed by erroneous identification of the plants.

There are no rules for trivial or common names of plants. These have been included only to facilitate identification. Many names are no longer in use, but there is no way to make such a determination. The trivial names were obtained from many sources. In addition to floras, Hawaiian names are from Neal, Cuban names from Roig y Mesa, and Mexican names from Aguilar and Zolla. Many less common, older trivial names for plants in the United States were selected from Clute.

Table 4.
Plants Producing Systemic Poisoning Arranged by Family and Genus

Amaryllidaceae
Amaryllis
Clivia
Crinum
Galanthus
Hippeastrum
Hymenocallis
Lycoris
Narcissus
Zephyranthes

Anarcardiaceae
Schinus

Apocynaceae
Acokanthera
Adenium
Allamanda
Nerium
Thevetia
Urechites

Aquifoliaceae
Ilex

Araceae
Alocasia
Anthurium
Arisaema
Arum
Caladium
Calla
Colocasia
Dieffenbachia
Epipremnum
Monstera
Philodendron
Spathiphyllum
Symplocarpus
Xanthosoma
Zantedeschia

Araliaceae
Hedera

Asclepiadaceae
Calotropis
Cryptostegia

Berberidaceae
Caulophyllum
Podophyllum

Boraginaceae
Echium
Heliotropium

Calycanthaceae
Calycanthus

Campanulaceae
Hippobroma
Lobelia

Caprifoliaceae
Lonicera
Sambucus
Symphoricarpos

Celastraceae
Celastrus
Euonymus

Compositae (Asteraceae)
Senecio

Coriariaceae
Coriaria

Cornaceae
Aucuba

Corynocarpaceae
Corynocarpus

Cucurbitaceae
Momordica

Ericaceae
Kalmia
Leucothoe
Lyonia
Pernettya
Pieris
Rhododendron

Euphorbiaceae
Aleurites
Euphorbia
Hippomane
Hura
Jatropha
Manihot
Pedilanthus
Ricinus

**Guttiferae
(Clusiaceae)**
Calophyllum
Clusia

Hippocastanaceae
Aesculus

Iridaceae
Iris

**Leguminosae
(Fabaceae)**
Abrus
Baptisia
Caesalpinia
Cassia
Crotalaria
Gymnocladus
Laburnum
Leucaena
Pachyrhizus
Robinia
Sesbania
Sophora
Wisteria

Liliaceae
Allium
Aloe
Colchicum
Convallaria
Gloriosa
Ornithogalum
Schoenocaulon
Scilla
Urginea
Veratrum
Zigadenus

Loganiaceae
Gelsemium
Spigelia
Strychnos

Loranthaceae
Phoradendron
Viscum

Meliaceae
Melia
Swietenia

Menispermaceae
Menispermum

Myoporaceae
Myoporum

Oleaceae
Ligustrum

**Palmae
(Arecaceae)**
Caryota

Papaveraceae
Chelidonium

Phytolaccaceae
Phytolacca
Rivina

Polygonaceae
Rheum

Ranunculaceae
Aconitum
Actaea
Adonis
Anemone
Caltha
Clematis
Helleborus
Ranunculus

Rhamnaceae
Karwinskia
Rhamnus

Rosaceae
Eriobotrya
Malus
Prunus
Rhodotypos

Rutaceae
Poncirus

Sapindaceae
Blighia
Sapindus

Saxifragaceae
Hydrangea

Scrophulariaceae
Digitalis

Solanaceae
Atropa
Brugmansia
Capsicum
Cestrum
Datura
Hyoscyamus
Lycium
Nicotiana
Physalis
Solandra
Solanum

Taxaceae
Taxus

Thymelaeceae
Daphne
Dirca

**Umbelliferae
(Apiaceae)**
Aethusa
Cicuta
Conium
Oenanthe

Verbenaceae
Duranta
Lantana

Zamiaceae
Zamia

References

Hortus Third. New York, Macmillan Publishing Co, 1976.

Adams CD: *Flowering Plants of Jamaica*. Mona, Jamaica, University of the West Indies, 1972.

Aguilar Contreras A, Zolla C: *Plantas Tóxicas de México*. Mexico City, Instituto Mexicano del Seguro Social, 1982.

Barker HD, Dardeau WS: *La Flore d'Haiti*. Port-au-Prince, Department of Agriculture, 1930.

Clute WN: *American Plant Names*, ed 3. Indianapolis, Willard N Clute Co, 1940.

Correll DS, Correll HB: *Flora of the Bahama Archipelago*. Vaduz, Germany, J Cramer, 1982.

Gooding EGB, et al: *Flora of Barbados*. London, Her Majesty's Stationery Office, 1965.

Howard RA (ed): *Flora of the Lesser Antilles. Leeward and Windward Islands*. Jamaica Plain, Mass, Arnold Arboretum, Harvard University, 1974.

Kartesz JT, Kartesz R: *A Synonymized Checklist of the Vascular Flora of the United States, Canada, and Greenland*. Chapel Hill, University of North Carolina Press, 1980.

Leon Hermano (J Sauget): *Flora de Cuba*. Havana, Museum de Historia Natural del Collegio de La Salle, vol 1, 1946.

Leon Hermano (J Sauget), Hermano Alain (H Liogier): *Flora de Cuba*. Havana, Museum de Historia Natural del Collegio de La Salle, vol 2-4, 1951-1957.

Liogier A: *Flora de Cuba*. Rio Piedras, Editorial de Universidad, vol 5, 1962.

Liogier AH: *Flora de Cuba, Supplemento*. Caracas, Editorial Sucre, 1969.

Liogier AH: *Diccionario Botanico de Nombres Vulgares de la Españo*l. Santo Domingo, Jardin Botanico Dr. Rafael Moscoso, 1974.

Liogier HA, Martorell LF: *Flora of Puerto Rico and Adjacent Islands: A Systematic Synopsis*. Rio Piedras, Editorial de Universidad, 1982.

Miller OK Jr, Farr DF: *An Index of the Common Fungi of North America (Synonymy and Common Names)*. Vaduz, Germany, J Cramer, 1975.

Neal MC: *In Gardens of Hawaii*. Honolulu, Bishop Museum, 1965.

Roig y Mesa JT: *Diccionario Botanico de Nombres Vulgares Cubanos*. Havana, Ministry of Agriculture, Bull 45, 1953.

Scoggan HJ: *Flora of Canada*. Ottawa, National Museum of Natural Sciences, 4 volumes, 1978-1979.

Stone BC: Flora of Guam. *Micronesia* 6:1-659, 1970.

Tutin TG, et al (eds): *Flora Europaea*. New York, Cambridge University Press, 5 volumes, 1964-1980.

I.

Systemic
Plant
Poisoning

I.

Systemic Plant Poisoning

Abrus precatorius L.
Family: Leguminosae (Fabaceae)

Trivial Names: Rosary Pea; Crab's Eyes; Bead or Red
Bead Vine; Black Eyed Susan (Bahamas and Hawaii); Coral
Bead Plant; Graines d'église (Guadeloupe); Indian or
Wild Licorice or Licorice Vine; Kolales Halomtano (Guam);
Jumbo, Jumbi, or Jumbee Beads (Virgin Islands); Love
Pea or Bead; Ojo de Pájaro (Mexico); Ojo de Cangrejo
(Puerto Rico); Peonia (Cuba); Peroniás or Peronillas
(Puerto Rico); Prayer Beads; PUKIAWE-LEI (Hawaii);
Réglisse or Liane à Réglisse (Guadeloupe and Haiti);
Semilla de Culebra (Mexico); Seminole Bead; Weather
Plant or Vine

Description: The rosary pea is a slender, twining vine
with a woody base. It is supported generally on other
plants or a fence. The compound leaves have numerous
short leaflets, which are sensitive to light and droop at
night and on cloudy days. The inconspicuous flowers are
a pale reddish purple. The fruit, a pea-shaped pod
about 1.5 inches long, splits open as it dries to reveal
three to five hard-coated, brilliant scarlet, pea-sized
seeds with a small enamel-black spot at the point of
attachment (hilum). This hilar spot serves to distinguish
them from look-alike seeds from Mexican vines of the
genus *Rhynchosia*, in which the black and red colors
are reversed. Figure 1-2

Distribution: This weed is common in Florida, the
Caribbean, Hawaii, and Guam. The seeds are imported by
tourists as novelty jewelry and inside rattles and by
Mexican-Americans as good luck charms (buena suerte).

Toxic Part: Ingestion of a chewed or broken seed is
toxic. Because of its hard, water-impermeable coat, the
mature seed is considered harmless if swallowed whole.

17

Toxin: Abrin, a plant lectin (toxalbumin), inhibits protein synthesis in growing cells of the intestinal wall.

Symptoms: The onset of poisoning occurs after a latent period of many hours up to three days, depending on the number of seeds ingested and their degree of pulverization. Toxicity is characterized by nausea, vomiting, diarrhea, and, sometimes, ulcerative lesions in the mouth and esophagus. The entire gastric mucosa and the ileum at the site of gut-associated lymphoid tissue (Peyer's patches) become hemorrhagic. There is loss of intestinal function. Other effects reported probably are secondary to extensive fluid and electrolyte depletion.

Management: Hypovolemia and electrolyte disturbances should be corrected; if necessary, parenteral alimentation should be instituted. The ingestion of one well-chewed seed of this extremely toxic plant may be fatal despite intensive care.

References:

Davis J: *Abrus precatorius* (rosary pea), the most common lethal poisonous plant. *J Florida Med Assoc* 65:189-191, 1978.

Godal A, et al: Radioimmunoassays of abrin and ricin in blood. *J Toxicol Environ Health* 8:409-417, 1981.

Olsnes S, et al: Mechanism of action of the toxic lectins, abrin and ricin. *Nature* 249:627-631, 1974.

Olsnes S: Abrin and ricin: Two toxic lectins inactivating eukaryotic ribosomes, in Bernheimer AW (ed): *Perspectives in Toxinology*. New York, John Wiley & Sons, 1977, 121-147.

Olsnes S, Pihl A: Toxic lectins and related proteins, in Cohen P, van Heyningen S (eds): *Molecular Action of Toxins and Viruses*. Amsterdam, Elsevier Biomedical Press, 1982, 52-105.

Acokanthera **species**
Family: Apocynaceae

A. longiflora Stapf.
A. oblongifolia (Hochst.) Codd (= *A. spectabilis*

(Sond.) Hook. f.)
A. *oppositifolia* (Lam.) Codd

Trivial Names: Bushman's Poison, Poison Bush,
Poison Tree

A. *oblongifolia*: Wintersweet

Description: These dense evergreen shrubs or small
trees are native to Africa. The leaves are large, leathery,
and have smooth edges. The fragrant flowers are tubular
with a flat flare at the mouth and are borne in clusters.
The fruit resembles a small, ellipsoidal plum and turns
reddish to purple-black at maturity; it contains one to
two seeds. Injury to the plant causes exudation of
copious amounts of white latex. Figure 4

Distribution: These plants are grown fairly commonly,
often as hedges, in California, to a much lesser extent in
Florida and Hawaii, and as a greenhouse plant
elsewhere.

Toxic Part: The fruit pulp contains only traces of
toxin and, in some species, is considered edible. The
seeds contain the greatest concentration, but the toxin
is distributed in substantial amounts throughout the
plant, including the wood.

Toxin: Cardiac glycosides resembling ouabain

Symptoms: Pain in the oral cavity, nausea, emesis,
abdominal pain, cramping, and diarrhea develop after
ingestion. Digitalis glycoside toxicity has a variable
latent period that depends on the quantity ingested.
Toxicity is usually expressed as conduction defects
and sinus bradycardia. Hyperkalemia may be present.
Rhythm disturbances other than escape beats may
not occur.

Management: Gastric lavage or induced emesis may
be performed. Activated charcoal may be given and
repeated later. Saline cathartics also can be used.
Repeated electrocardiographic monitoring and serum
potassium determinations should be performed.
Conduction defects may require the use of atropine or
transvenous pacing. Phenytoin is the agent of choice
for rhythm disturbances. Dialysis and forced diuresis
are not useful.

19

References:

Ekins BR, Watanabe AS: Acute digoxin poisonings: Review of therapy. *Am J Hosp Pharm* 35:268-277, 1978.

Watt J, Breyer-Brandwijk M: *Medicinal and Poisonous Plants of Southern and Eastern Africa*, ed 2. Edinburgh, E & S Livingstone, 1962, 62-78.

Aconitum species
Family: Ranunculaceae

A. columbianum Nutt.
A. napellus L.

Trivial Names: Monkshood, Aconite, Friar's Cap, Helmet Flower, Soldier's Cap, Wolfsbane

Description: These perennial plants are usually erect, sometimes branched, 2 to 6 feet in height, and have tuberous roots. They resemble delphiniums. The characteristic helmet-shaped flowers grow in a raceme at the top of the stalk and appear in summer or autumn. The flowers are usually blue but may be white, pink, or flesh toned. The dried seed pods contain numerous tiny seeds. Figure 5-6

Distribution: Approximately 100 species of monkshood are native to the north temperate zone, including Canada and Alaska. Many species are in cultivation in all but the extreme temperature regions of the United States.

Toxic Part: The whole plant is poisonous, especially the leaves and roots.

Toxin: Aconitine and related alkaloids

Symptoms: A tingling, burning sensation of the lips, tongue, mouth, and throat occurs almost immediately after ingestion, followed by numbness and a feeling of constriction in the throat. Speech may be difficult, and salivation, nausea, and emesis may develop. Transient visual blurring with yellow-green vision and mydriasis also may occur. The patient is weak, dizzy, uncoordinated,

20

and may complain of paresthesias. Fatalities result from cardiac arrhythmias.

Management: Arrhythmias should be managed as indicated by electrocardiographic monitoring.

References:
Ffrench G: Aconite-induced cardiac arrhythmia. *Br Heart J* 20:140-142, 1958.

Fiddes F: Poisoning by aconite. *Br Med J* 2:779-780, 1958.

Actaea species
Family: Ranunculaceae
A. pachypoda Ell.
A. rubra (Ait.) Willd.
A. spicata L.

Trivial Names: Baneberry, Cohosh, Dolls Eyes, Herb-Christopher, Necklaceweed, Poison de Couleuvre or Pain de Couleuvre (Canada), Snakeberry

Description: The baneberries are perennial herbs that are 1 to 2 feet in height with large compound leaves. Small white flowers grow in terminal clusters in the spring. Berry-like fruit forms in the summer or early autumn; their color depends upon the species (*A. pachypoda*, white; *A. rubra*, red; and *A. spicata*, purplish black). Figure 7-9

Distribution: *Actaea* species grow throughout the north temperate zone: *A. pachypoda*, Nova Scotia to Georgia west to Minnesota and Missouri; *A. rubra*, Alaska to California east through Canada and the United States to the Atlantic and south through the Rockies to New Mexico; *A. spicata*, only in cultivation.

Toxic Part: Only the berries and roots are poisonous.

Toxin: Not known, reputedly protoanemonin (and a questionable hallucinogenic substance in *A. rubra*)

Symptoms: The juice exerts a direct irritant and vesicant action on the skin and mucous membrances. Upon ingestion, there is intense pain and inflammation of the mouth, tongue, and throat, often with blistering and ulceration. Salivation is profuse. Bloody emesis and diarrhea occur in association with severe abdominal cramping. Renal damage initially is associated with

21

polyuria, painful micturition, and hematuria followed by oliguria. About 30 minutes after ingestion, central nervous system involvement is manifested by dizziness, confusion, syncope, and, in severe cases, convulsions. Hallucinations were reported in one case after intentional ingestion of *A. rubra* berries.

Management: The irritant effect usually limits the amount ingested. If there is evidence that a substantial quantity was swallowed, the stomach should be lavaged, followed by instillation of demulcents, such as egg white in milk. Appropriate measures may be required to prevent fluid and electrolyte depletion, and renal function should be monitored.

References:

Bacon A: An experiment with the fruit of red baneberry. *Rhodora* 5:77-79, 1903.

Hegnauer R: Chemotaxonomie der Pflanzen. Basel, Birkhauser, 1962.

Lampe K, Fagerström R: *Plant Toxicity and Dermatitis*. Baltimore, Williams & Wilkins, 1968, 40-45.

Adenium species
Family: Apocynaceae

Trivial Names: Desert Rose, Mock Azalea

Description: These shrubs or trees are 6 to 10 feet in height with swollen trunk and branches and fleshy dark green leaves. Bright and showy funnel-form pink or purple flowers cluster at the branch tips. Figure 10

Distribution: *Adenium* are rarely cultivated but may be grown in hot dry areas of the United States and in Jamaica.

Toxic Part: The whole plant is poisonous.

Toxin: Digitalis-like glycosides

Symptoms: No human intoxications have been reported in the United States. See the discussion on *Digitalis* species.

References:
Watt J, Breyer-Brandwijk M: *Medicinal and Poisonous Plants of Southern and Eastern Africa*, ed 2. Edinburgh, E & S Livingstone, 1962, 78-80.

Adonis species
Family: Ranunculaceae

A. aestivalis L.
A. amurensis Regel and Radde
A. annua L.
A. vernalis L.

Trivial Names: Pheasant's Eye, Flor de Adonis (Cuba), Gota de Sangre (Cuba), Red Morocco

Description: These small perennial plants have conspicuous yellow or crimson spring flowers that are 2 to 3 inches across on short stems. Figure 11

Distribution: *Adonis* are primarily in cultivation, usually in rock gardens, in the north temperate zones of the United States. They are alpine plants from southern Europe, Asia Minor, and Asia.

Toxic Part: The whole plant is poisonous.

Toxin: Digitalis-like glycosides and possibly a protoanemonin-like irritant

Symptoms: Poisoning attributed to these plants has not been reported in North America.

Aesculus species
Family: Hippocastanaceae

A. californica (Spach) Nutt.
A. flava Soland (= *A. octandra* Marsh.)
A. glabra Willd.
A. hippocastanum L.

Trivial Names: Horse Chestnut, Buckeye, Bongay, Conquerors, Fish Poison, Marronnier or Marronnier d'Inde (Canada)

Description: There are about 13 species of *Aesculus*, mostly large trees. These plants have compound leaves and showy clusters of flowers, which may be white, white blotched with red and yellow, pink, yellow and red, or red. The seed pod is leathery and smooth or warty. The common name, buckeye, is derived from the seed, which is glossy brown with a white scar. Figure 12-15

Distribution: These plants occur primarily in the central and eastern temperate zone to the Gulf Coast and California, southern Ontario, southwestern Quebec, and Newfoundland.

Toxic Part: The nuts and twigs are poisonous.

Toxin: A mixture of saponins, known collectively as aescin, is cytotoxic.

Symptoms: The saponins are poorly absorbed and intoxication is limited to severe gastroenteritis; other symptoms are secondary to excessive fluid loss and electrolyte imbalance. Most serious or fatal cases result from frequent multiple exposures.

Management: Fluid and electrolyte replacement, demulcents, and general therapy for gastroenteritis should be instituted.

References:

Anisimov M, et al: Mechanism of cytotoxic action of some triterpene glycosides. *Toxicon* 16:207-218, 1978.

Hardin J, Arena J: *Human Poisoning From Native and Cultivated Plants*, ed 2. Durham, NC, Duke University Press, 1974, 101-104.

Hoppe W, et al: Structure of the principal aglycone of horse chestnut saponin. *Angew Chem*, *Int Ed* 7:547-548, 1968.

Lampe K, Fagerström R: *Plant Toxicity and Dermatitis*. Baltimore, Williams & Wilkins, 1968, 21-24.

Mathies H; The chemistry, pharmacology and clinical aspects of the horse chestnut. *Planta Medica* 2:129-138, 148-158, 1954. (In German)

Aethusa cynapium L.
Family: Umbelliferae (Apiaceae)

Trivial Names: Fool's Parsley, Dog Parsley, Dog Poison, False Parsley, Fool's Cicely, Lesser or Small Hemlock

Description: This carrot-like plant is 8 to 24 inches high. The leaves resemble parsley but have a glossy shine on both sides and an unpleasant garlic-like odor. The white flowers and seed pods are inconspicuous and mounted on the stem tips. Figure 16

Distribution: *Aethusa* is naturalized from Europe and grows in waste places in the extreme northern United States from Minnesota to Maine and south to Delaware, Pennsylvania, and Ohio and in southwestern British Columbia, Ontario, Quebec, New Brunswick, and Nova Scotia.

Toxic Part: The whole plant is poisonous.

Toxin: Unsaturated aliphatic alcohols (eg, aethusanol A) closely related to cicutoxin (from *Cicuta* species) and traces of coniine

Symptoms: Intoxication produces primarily nausea, emesis, sweating, and headache that resemble poisoning from *Cicuta* species, but the concentration of toxin is probably insufficient to cause serious effects.

Management: Establish a patent airway and assist respiration. If indicated, persistent convulsions may be relieved by administration of intravenous diazepam or another rapid-acting anticonvulsant.

References:

Bohlmann F, et al: Polyenes from *Aethusa cynapium* L. *Chem Ber* 93:981-987, 1960. (In German)

Lampe K, Fagerström R: *Plant Toxicity and Dermatitis*. Baltimore, Williams & Wilkins, 1968, 107-117.

Aleurites species
Family: Euphorbiaceae

A. cordata (Thunb.) R. Br.

A. fordii Hemsl.
A. moluccana (L.) Willd.
A. montana (Lour.) E.H. Wils.
A. trisperma Blanco

Trivial Names:

A. cordata: Japan Oil Tree

A. fordii: **Tung Nut** or Tung Oil Tree, Aceite Chino
(Cuba), Chinawood Oil Tree

A. molluccana: **Candlenut or Candleberry;** Avellano
(Dominican Republic); Country Walnut, Indian Walnut,
Jamaican Walnut, Otaheite Walnut, or Walnut (Virgin
Islands); KUKUI (Hawaii, Guam); Lumbang (Guam);
Nogal de la India (Cuba); Noix de Bancoul, Noix des
Molluques, or Noisette des Grands-Fonds (Guadeloupe);
Nuez de la India, Nuez Nogal, or Palo de Nuez
(Puerto Rico); Raguar (Guam)

A. montana: Mu or Mu Oil Tree

A. trisperma: Banucalad (Hawaii)

Description: These medium-sized trees have a milky
latex. The large simple leaves are often lobed. Flowers
occur in large clusters and are white or white with red
or orange veins. The fruit of *A. fordii* is green turning to
brown at maturity; the capsule is 2 to 3 inches long
and contains three to seven hard seeds with a white flesh.
The unhulled seed resembles an unshelled hickory
nut; the hulled seed looks like a chestnut. Figure 20-24

Distribution: *Aleurites* species grow in the West
Indies, states bordering the Gulf of Mexico, Hawaii,
and Guam.

Toxic Part: The whole plant is poisonous, but seeds are
involved most often in human intoxications.

Toxin: A derivative of the irritant, phorbol

Symptoms: A feeling of discomfort, warmth, and
nausea develops shortly after ingestion of the seed, followed
by emesis, severe colic, and diarrhea. Other symptoms
may result from dehydration and electrolyte imbalance.

Management: Replacement of fluids, correction of
electrolyte losses, and other therapy for severe

gastroenteritis, including analgesics if indicated, should
be administered.

References:

Balthrop E, et al: Tung nut poisoning. *J Florida Med
Assoc* 40:813-820, 1954.

Okuda T, et al: The toxic constituent of the fruits of
Aleurites fordii. Chem Pharm Bull (Tokyo)
22(4):971-972, 1974. (In English)

Palmer H: Are the seeds of tung oil tree poisonous
when eaten by man or animal? *J Florida Med Assoc*
20:13-15, 1933.

Allamanda cathartica L.
Family: Apocynaceae

Trivial Names: Allamanda or Yellow Allamanda, Canario
or Cautiva (Puerto Rico), Flor de Barbero (Cuba),
LANI-ALI'I or NANI-ALI'I (Hawaii)

Description: This ornamental sprawling shrub or
woody climber has large yellow flowers and opposite
lance-shaped leaves that are 4 to 6 inches long. *A.
cathartica* usually is propagated by cuttings, which do
not fruit. *A. neriifolia* Hook., cultivated in the same
geographical area, is a bush with more diminutive leaves
and flowers; it frequently fruits. Figure 25-28

Distribution: *Allamanda* is a common cultivated plant
in the West Indies, Florida, and Hawaii.

Toxic Part: Bark, leaves, fruit, seeds, and sap are poisonous.

Toxin: Unidentified cathartic

Symptoms: Poisoning usually is manifested as self-limited
mild catharsis. Ingestion of decoctions of this plant
may cause severe, persistent diarrhea.

Management: Usually no treatment is required. Fluid
replacement may be necessary, particularly in young
children, if dehydration develops.

27

Allium species
Family: Liliaceae

Trivial Names:

A. canadense L.: Wild Garlic, Ail du Canada (Canada), Meadow Garlic, Meadow Rose Leek, Onion Tree, Wild Onion

A. cepa L.: **Onion,** Cebolla, 'AKA'AKAI (Hawaii), Zongnon (Haiti)

A. sativum L.: **Garlic,** Ajo, 'AKA'AKAI-PILAU (Hawaii), Clown Treacle, Lai (Haiti), Poor Man's Treacle

A. vineale L.: **Field Garlic,** Crow Garlic

Description: There are about 400 species of *Allium*; the species listed above are most often implicated in human toxicity. These plants may be distinguished from many *Allium* look-alikes by the characteristic onion or garlic odor when bruised. Figure 29-31

Distribution: There are many cultivated and native species of *Allium* throughout the United States including Hawaii and Alaska. *Allium canadense* may be found from Minnesota to Ontario south to Texas east to Quebec and western New Brunswick and south to Florida.

Toxic Part: Bulbs, bulblets (Fig. 29), flowers, and stems are poisonous.

Toxin: N-propyl sulfide, methyl disulfide, and allyl disulfide

Symptoms: Gastroenteritis is common in young children who ingest parts of *A. canadense*. Chronic ingestion of the bulblets diminishes iodine uptake by the thyroid, which may become significant in areas lacking natural sources of iodine.

Management: No specific therapy for gastroenteritis is indicated other than measures to prevent dehydration.

References:

Van Etten C: Goitrogens, in Liener I (ed): *Toxic Constituents of Plant Foodstuffs*. New York, Academic Press, 1969, 103-142.

Willis JH Jr: Goitrogens in Foods, in *Intoxicants Occurring Naturally in Foods*. Pub. 1934, Washington, DC,

National Academy of Sciences/ National Research Council, 1966, 3-17.

Alocasia species
Family: Araceae

Trivial Names: Elephant's Ear; AHE POI or 'APE (Hawaii); Cabeza de Burro, Malanga de Jardín or Malanga Cara de Chivo (Cuba); Chine Ape; Papao-Apaka or Papao-Atolong (Guam); Taro

Description: These erect perennials have single, long-stemmed, spearhead-shaped leaves that are prominently veined and often varicolored. Flowers appear on a greenish spathe similar to *Colocasia*. Individual plants may develop from runners (rhizomes). Figure 32-33

Distribution: The *Alocasia* are popular house plants throughout the United States and are hardy in tropical and subtropical areas. *A. macrorrhiza* (L.) G. Don is cultivated for food.

Toxic Part: The leaves and stems are injurious.

Toxin: Calcium oxalate raphides are the primary injurious substances, but it is speculated that irritant proteins may be present also.

Symptoms: Chewing of a plant part causes a painful burning sensation of the lips, mouth, tongue, and throat. An acute inflammatory reaction occurs, sometimes accompanied by blistering and edema of the injured tissues. Hoarseness, dysphagia, and difficulty with speech develop. Due to the rapid onset of pain, these plants are rarely swallowed.

Management: The pain and edema of the oral cavity recede slowly without therapy. Cool liquids or demulcents held in the mouth may bring some relief. Analgesics sometimes are indicated. The insoluble oxalates in these plants do not cause systemic poisoning in man.

References:
Mitchell J, Rook A: *Botanical Dermatology*. Vancouver, Greengrass, 1979.

Plowman T: Folk uses of new world aroids. *Econ Bot* 23:97-122, 1969.

Sakai WS, Hanson M: Mature raphid and raphid idioblast

structure in plants of the edible Aroid genera *Colocasia*, *Alocasia*, and *Xanthosoma*. *Ann Bot* 38:739-748, 1974.

Aloe species
Family: Liliaceae

Trivial Names: Aloe; Laloi (Haiti), PANINI-'AWA'AWA or Star Cactus (Hawaii), Sábila (Cuba, Puerto Rico), Sempervivum or Sinkle Bible (Jamaica), Zábila (U.S.-Mexican Border, Dominican Republic), Závila (Puerto Rico)

Description: There are about 250 species of *Aloe*, which are perennial herbs. The leaves usually appear in compact rosettes and are thick, hard, pointed, and may have teeth or spines on the margins. The flowers are usually red or yellow. Seed pods split on drying. Figure 34

Distribution: Aloes are cultivated extensively in the West Indies, Florida, southern California, Hawaii, Guam, and elsewhere as a summer planting or house plant.

Some aloes, for example *A. barbadensis* Mill. (*A. vera* (L.) Webb & Berth.), known as Barbados Aloe, Curacao Aloe, Medicinal Aloe, or Unguentine Cactus, are grown commercially for the cathartic glycosides in the latex and for their mucilaginous gel, which is employed as a skin moistener.

Toxic Part: The latex beneath the skin is poisonous.

Toxin: Barbaloin, an anthraquinone glycoside

Symptoms: A pronounced purgative action occurs 6 to 12 hours following ingestion of a cathartic aloe due to an irritant effect on the large intestine. Anthraquinones color alkaline urine red; excessive doses may cause nephritis.

Management: Usually no therapy is required, but fluid replacement may be indicated.

References:

Morton JF: Folk uses and commercial exploitation of aloe leaf pulp. *Econ Bot* 15:311-319, 1961.

Spoerke DG, Elkins BR: *Aloe vera*--fact or quackery. *Vet Human Toxicol* 22:418-424, 1980.

Amaryllis species
Hippeastrum species (*Amaryllis* species of
horticulture except *A. belladonna* L. are species
of *Hippeastrum*.)
Family: Amaryllidaceae

Trivial Names: Amaryllis, Azucena de Mejico
(U.S.-Mexican border), Barbados Lily, Belladonna Lily,
Cape Belladonna, Lirio, Naked Lady Lily, Tararaco or
Tararaco Doble (Cuba)

Description: *Amaryllis* and *Hippeastrum* have
variously colored flowers but shades of red or pink with
white are most common. Bulbs usually extend partly
above ground. Figure 35, 200

Distribution: These plants occur as cultivated
ornamentals only. They are extremely popular as a summer
garden plant in temperate zones and as a potted plant
throughout the year.

Toxic Part: Bulbs are poisonous.

Toxin: The emetic, lycorine, and small amounts of related
alkaloids

Symptoms: Ingestion of large quantities may produce
nausea and persistent emesis with some diarrhea.

Management: Human poisonings are infrequent because
of the small concentration of alkaloids. Fluid replacement
may be required if dehydration develops. See *Narcissus*.

References:
Jasperson-Schib R: Toxic Amaryllidaceae. *Pharm Acta
Helv* 45:424-433, 1970. (In German)

Anemone species
Family: Ranunculaceae

A. canadensis L.

A. nuttalliana DC.
A. patens L. (= *Pulsatilla patens* (L.) Mill.)
A. pulsatilla L. (= *Pulsatilla amoena* Jord.,
P. vulgaris Mill.)

Trivial Names: Pasque Flower, Anemone, April Fools,
Cats Eyes, Gosling, Hartshorn Plant, Lily of the Field,
Lion's Beard, Nightcaps, Nimble Weed, Prairie Crocus,
Prairie Hen Flower, Prairie Smoke, Thimbleweed, Wild
Crocus, Windflower

Description: These perennial herbs are often used
in rock gardens because they are usually no more than
1 foot high. The divided flowers appear singly on the
stem and may be showy yellow, red, white, or purple.
Figure 39-41

Distribution: There are many species of *Anemone* in
Canada, Alaska, and the north temperate zone of the
United States. *A. patens* and *A. pulsatilla* are of
European origin.

Toxic Part: The whole plant is poisonous.

Toxin: Protoanemonin

Symptoms: The direct irritant and vesicant actions of
the toxin on the skin and mucous membranes often
produce blisters. Chewing of plant parts causes acute
inflammation and occasional ulceration of the mouth and
throat. Ingestion, although rare, is associated with
severe gastroenteritis including bloody emesis and diarrhea.
See *Actaea* species.

Management: The irritant effects usually limit the amount
ingested. If there is evidence that a substantial quantity
has been ingested, the stomach should be lavaged followed
by administration of demulcents.

References:
Aaron T, Muttitt E: Vesicant dermatitis due to prairie
crocus (*Anemone patens* L.). *Arch Dermatol*
90:168-171, 1964.

Anthurium **species**
Family: Araceae

Trivial Names: Anthurium, Anturio, Flamingo Flower,

Flamingo Lily, Flor de Culebra (Puerto Rico), Guinda (Puerto Rico), Hoja Grande (Cuba), Lenguna de Vaca (Cuba, Puerto Rico), Lombricero (Cuba), Pigtail Plant, Tail Flower

Description: *Anthurium* grow about 2 feet high and have dark green, heart-shaped, leathery leaves. The "flower" has a persistent scarlet, white, or green spike, which may be followed by colorful showy berries. Figure 42-45

Distribution: These plants are native to tropical America. They are house plants in most areas, but may be grown in gardens in south Florida and Hawaii.

Toxic Part: Leaves and stems are injurious.

Toxin: Calcium oxalate raphides and possibly unidentified proteins

Symptoms: Painful burning of the lips, mouth, tongue, and throat may develop. Acute inflammatory reactions are sometimes associated with blistering and edema of tissues. Hoarseness, dysphonia, and dysphagia occur. Due to the rapid onset of pain, plant material is rarely swallowed.

Management: The pain and edema of the oral cavity recede slowly without therapy. Cool liquids or demulcents held in the mouth may bring some relief. Analgesics may be indicated. The insoluble oxalates in these plants do not cause systemic poisoning in man.

References:

Mitchell J, Rook A: *Botanical Dermatology*. Vancouver, Greengrass, 1979.

Plowman T: Folk uses of new world aroids. *Econ Bot* 33:97-122, 1969.

Arisaema species
Family: Araceae

A. dracontium (L.) Schott
A. triphyllum (L.) Schott (includes *A. atrorubens* (Ait.) Blume and *A. stewardsonii* (Britt.) Huttl.)

Trivial Names:

A. dracontium: **Green Dragon,** Dragon Arum, Dragon Root, Dragon Tail, Dragons Head, Jack-in-the-Pulpit

A. triphyllum: **Jack-in-the-Pulpit,** Bog Onion, Brown Dragon, Cuckoo Plant, Indian Jack-in-the-Pulpit, Memory Root, Pepper Turnip, Petit Prêcheur (Canada), Priests Pentle, Small Jack-in-the-Pulpit, Starchwort, Three Leaved Indian Turnip, Wake Robin

Description:

A. dracontium has a single 3-foot stalk with 7 to 13 leaflets at the tip. Several inches below the leaflets, a single green "flower" (spathe) up to 3 inches long emerges from the stalk. This spathe has a slender funnel-shaped, protruding hood that extends backward. The spike-like, erect spadix inside extends for several inches. Berries are orange-red. Figure 46

A. triphyllum has two leaves branching from the stalk with three lance-shaped leaflets at the end. The spathe appears between the branching of the two leaves and may be green, green striped with brown, or brown. It is shaped like a pulpit with a long pointed hood extending over the short blunt spadix. Berries are red. Figure 47-49

Arisaema bloom from late spring to early autumn.

Distribution: *Arisaema* grow in damp shady areas from Quebec to Florida west to Ontario and southwest to Minnesota and Texas.

Toxic Part: The whole plant is injurious.

Toxin: Calcium oxalate raphides and, possibly, other unidentified irritants

Symptoms: A burning, biting sensation of the lips, mouth, and throat occurs in association with inflammation, edema, and salivation.

Management: Symptoms rarely require treatment. The pain and edema recede slowly. Cool liquids or demulcents held in the mouth may bring some relief. The insoluble oxalates in these plants do not cause systemic poisoning in man.

References:

Mitchell J, Rook A: *Botanical Dermatology*. Vancouver, Greengrass, 1979.

Plowman T: Folk uses of new world aroids. *Econ Bot* 23:97-122, 1969.

Arum species
Family: Araceae

A. italicum P. Mill.
A. maculatum L.
A. palaestinum Boiss.

Trivial Names:

A. italicum: Italian Arum

A. maculatum: Adam and Eve, Cuckoopint, Lords-and-Ladies

A. palaestinum: Black Calla, Solomon's Lily

Description: Arums are stemless plants with 8-to 10-inch ovate leaves and tuberous roots. The showy "flower," a spathe, is generally dullish purple in the above species and encloses a spike (spadix) on which brilliant red fruits form. Figure 53-54

Distribution: These common house plants are hardy outdoors in the South. All of these species originated in Europe and the Near East.

Toxic Part: The whole plant is injurious.

Toxin: Calcium oxalate raphides and a questionable volatile irritant (aroin).

Symptoms: Burning and irritation with edema of the lips, mouth, tongue, and pharynx occur. Plant material is seldom ingested but can cause gastroenteritis. Contact dermatitis may be caused by the root juices.

Management: No treatment is required unless swelling of the oropharynx produces mechanical obstruction.

Cool liquids or demulcents held in the mouth may provide some relief.

References:

Mitchell J, Rook A: *Botanical Dermatology*. Vancouver, Greengrass, 1979.

Plowman T: Folk uses of new world aroids. *Econ Bot* 23:97-122, 1969.

Schwartz L, et al: *Occupational Diseases of the Skin*, ed 3. Philadelphia, Lea & Febiger, 1957.

Atropa belladonna L.
Family: Solanaceae

Trivial Names: Deadly Nightshade, Belladonna, Black Nightshade, Nightshade, Sleeping Nightshade

Description: These perennial plants are about 3 feet high. The stems are much branched with 6-inch ovate leaves. Solitary flowers, which emerge from the leaf joints, are blue-purple to dull red and about 1 inch long. The berry is nearly globular, about 0.5 inch in diameter, and is purple to shiny black when mature. The root is a thick rhizome. The sap is reddish. Figure 56-57

Distribution: *Atropa* is in cultivation only. It is native to Eurasia and North Africa.

Toxic Part: The whole plant is toxic.

Toxin: Atropine and other belladonna alkaloids

Symptoms: Ingestion causes dry mouth with dysphagia and dysphonia, tachycardia, and dry skin. Elevation of body temperature may be accompanied by rash. Mydriasis, blurred vision, and urinary retention also may develop. Hallucinations are more common in children.

Management: If the severity of the intoxication warrants intervention (hyperthermia, delirium), a slow intravenous administration of physostigmine is repeated until symptoms abate or cholinergic effects appear. The initial pediatric dose is 0.5 mg; for adolescents and adults, 2 mg. The duration of action of the belladonna alkaloids is longer than that of physostigmine; therefore, administration of the latter may have to be repeated.

References:

Rumack B: Anticholinergic poisoning: Treatment with physostigmine. *Pediatrics* 52:449-451, 1973.

Aucuba japonica Thunb.
Family: Cornaceae

Trivial Names: Japanese Aucuba, Japanese Laurel

Description: This evergreen usually is grown as a large bush. The opposite leaves are about 7 inches long and coarsely toothed. There are numerous horticultural varieties that differ in leaf shape and color. Purple flowers are borne in panicles at the ends of branches. The fruit is scarlet, matures in early winter, and contains a single pit. Figure 58

Distribution: This plant is cultivated as an ornamental in the Atlantic Gulf states from Texas to Washington, D.C. and along the Pacific coast.

Toxic Part: Although the toxin is present in every part of the plant, all reported intoxications have involved the fruit.

Toxin: The acid-labile glycoside, aucubin

Symptoms: Ingestion of the fruit does not always cause symptoms, but moderate digestive upset with vomiting and fever may result.

Management: Unless emesis is persistent, therapeutic intervention is not required.

References:

Chang IM, et al: Toxicological studies in aucubin (I). Acute toxicities and effects on blood serum enzymes. *Korean J Pharmacognosy* 14:95-101, 1983. (In English)

Inouye H, et al: Purgative activities of iridoid glucosides. *Planta Medica* 25:285-288, 1974.

Leveau AM, et al: Concerning the toxicity of the fruit of *Acuba japonica* (Cornacees). *Plantes Med Phytotherap* 13:199-204, 1979. (In French)

Trim AR, Hill R: Preparation and properties of aucubin, asperuloside and some related glycosides. *Biochem J* 50:310-319, 1952.

Baptisia species
Family: Leguminosae (Fabaceae)

Trivial Names: Wild Indigo, Cloverbloom, False Indigo, Horse Flea Weed, Horsefly, Horsefly Weed, Prairie Indigo, Rattlebush, Rattleweed, Shoofly

Description: There are about 30 species of *Baptisia*. These herbs grow to about 3 feet and have oval leaves. The sweetpea-like flowers are blue, yellow, or white and grow in racemes. The fruit is a pea-like pod. Figure 59-60

Distribution: *Baptisia* are native throughout the United States from Texas, Missouri, and Minnesota east to the Atlantic coast south to Florida and north to Massachusetts. In Canada, it occurs only in southern Ontario.

Toxic Part: The entire plant is toxic.

Toxin: Numerous alkaloids, of which cytisine is probably the most important intoxicant

Symptoms and Management: No intoxications have been reported in humans. Ingestion of clinically significant quantities of this plant is improbable.

If symptoms occur (eg, nausea, sweating), management should be as for *Laburnum anagyroides*.

Blighia sapida K. König
Family: Sapindaceae

Trivial Names: Ackee, Akee, or Aki; Arbre Fricassé (Haiti); Seso Vegetal (Cuba, Puerto Rico)

Description: The ackee is a tree growing about 30 to 40 feet in height. It has compound leaves with five pairs of leaflets; the longest is about 6 inches at the tip. There are small, greenish white flowers. A conspicuous reddish fruit pod splits at maturity to reveal three shiny black seeds embedded in a snowy white waxy aril.
Figure 61-62

Distribution: *Blighia* grows in the West Indies, Florida, and Hawaii.

Toxic Part: The pink raphe attaching the aril to the seed and the arils in the immature fruit are poisonous. The arils become edible when the fruit is ripe and are used in cooking.

Toxin: Hypoglycin A (a cyclopropyl amino acid)

Symptoms: Poisoning occurs almost exclusively on the island of Jamaica, where it may reach epidemic proportions during the winter months under the name of "vomiting sickness." The intoxication may take two forms: In the first, there is emesis followed by a remission period of eight to ten hours, then renewed emesis, convulsions, and coma. The second type is characterized by convulsions and coma at the onset. Six hours or more elapse between ingestion and onset of symptoms. Severe hypoglycemia develops. Diarrhea and hyperpyrexia are absent.

Management: Intoxication is associated with high mortality. Therapy consists of fluids, glucose, electrolyte correction, and, since sensitivity may occur primarily in patients with a pre-existing nutritional deficit, vitamin supplements.

References:

Hill K, et al: Acute hypoglycemia occurring in the vomiting sickness of Jamaica. *West Indian Med J* 4:91-104, 1955.

Kean E (ed): *Hypoglycin*. New York, Academic Press, 1975.

Tanaka K: Jamaican vomiting sickness, in Vinken PJ, Bruyn GW (eds): *Handbook of Clinical Neurology*. New York, North-Holland, vol 37, 1979, 511-539.

Caesalpinia species
Family: Leguminosae (Fabaceae)

C. bonduc (L.) Roxb. (= *C. crista* of several authors;
C. bonducella Flem.)
C. drummondii (T. & G.) Fisher
C. gilliesii (Wallich ex Hook.) Barth. (= *Poinciana gilliesii* Wall.)
C. mexicana Gray
C. pulcherrima (L.) Sw. (= *Poinciana pulcherrima* L.)
C. vesicaria L.

Trivial Names:

C. bonduc: Brier (Bahamas), Grey Nicker or Nickal, Guacalote Amarillo (Cuba), Haba de San Antonio (Puerto Rico), Horse Nicker, Mato Azul (Puerto Rico), Mato de Playa (Puerto Rico)

C. drummondii: There are no common names in our geographical area.

C. gilliesii: **Bird of Paradise,** Espiga de Amor (Puerto Rico)

C. mexicana: There are no common names in our geographical area.

C. pulcherrima: **Barbados Pride, Dwarf Poinciana,** Carzazo (Dominican Republic), Clavellina (Puerto Rico), Doddle-Do (Puerto Rico), Dul-Dul (Puerto Rico), Flor de Camarón (Mexico), Flower Fence, Francillade (Haiti), Guacamaya (Cuba), Maravilla (Mexico), 'OHAI-ALI'I (Hawaii), Spanish Carnation, Tabachín (Mexico)

C. vesicaria: Brasil (Cuba), Brasiletto (Bahamas), Indian Savin Tree (Jamaica)

Description: There are about 150 species of *Caesalpinia* distributed throughout the world.

C. bonduc: This scrambling shrub rarely grows erect. The stems have numerous prickles, and the leaves are doubly compound. Yellow flowers grow in racemes. Fruit pods are dark brown, 3 inches long and 1.5 inches wide, covered with prickles, and contain two flattened, globular seeds about 1 inch in diameter.

C. drummondii: This shrublet grows about 8 inches high. Fruit pods are slightly less than 1 inch long and contain one or two seeds.

C. gilliesii: This shrub is 15 feet tall and has no spines. The leaves are compound. The yellow flowers have bright red, protruding filaments. The fruit pod is about

4 inches long, 0.75 inches wide, and contains six to eight seeds.

C. mexicana: This small, spineless tree has yellow flowers. The fruit is a flat pod about 2.5 inches long. Figure 66

C. pulcherrima: This upright shrub has scattered prickles and yellow flowers with red streaks that grow in terminal racemes. The fruit is a flat pod about 4 inches long containing five to eight shiny brown, flat, bean-like seeds about 3/8 inch long. Figure 67

C. vesicaria: This small tree has an aromatic odor. Its trunk and branches are prickly. Yellow flowers are streaked with red and form in terminal racemes. The fruit is a flat pod about 4 inches long and less than 1 inch wide. Figure 68-69

Distribution:

C. bonduc: This weed-like plant is common in the West Indies from the Bahamas to Barbados.

C. drummondii: This rare species is a native of southern Texas and Mexico.

C. gilliesii: Bird of Paradise plants are cultivated extensively in Florida and the Gulf coast states to Texas and in Arizona.

C. mexicana: This ornamental is cultivated in southern Texas and Mexico.

C. pulcherrima: Barbados Pride is cultivated extensively in the West Indies from the Bahamas to Barbados and in Hawaii, Guam, and frost-free areas of Florida, Texas, and Arizona.

C. vesicaria: This tree is native to the Bahamas, Cuba, Jamaica, and Haiti. It is not found in Puerto Rico.

Toxic Part: The seeds are poisonous. The immature seeds of some species, eg, *C. pulcherrima*, are edible; roasting the seeds of some other species, eg, *C. bonduc*, abolishes toxicity.

Toxin: Tannins

Symptoms: After a latent period of 30 minutes to six hours, nausea followed by profuse and persistent vomiting develops; diarrhea appears later. Recovery usually is complete within 24 hours.

Management: Treatment is as for simple gastroenteritis. Fluid replacement may be necessary in young children.

References:
Toxicity studies of Arizona ornamental plants. *Arizona Med* 15:512-514, 1958.

Bayley I: Bush teas of Barbados. *J Barbados Mus Hist Soc* 16:103-112, 1949.

Jouglard J, et al: Accidental intoxications from ingestion of seeds of "Mimosa du Japon." *Bull Med Leg Toxicol* 16:55-58, 1973. (In French)

Caladium species
Family: Araceae

C. bicolor (Ait.) Vent.

Trivial Names: Caladium, Angel Wings, Caladio (Puerto Rico), Cananga, Capotillo (Mexico), Couer Saignant (Haiti), Corazón de Cabrito (Cuba), Elephant's Ear, Heart-of-Jesus; Lagrimas de Maria, Mother-in-Law Plant, Paleta de Pintor (Puerto Rico)

Description: Caladiums have showy, variegated, prominently veined, heart-shaped leaves. Coloration may vary from white to orange or red depending on species. Figure 70

Distribution: These plants may be cultivated in gardens year round in subtropical climates and during the summer in temperate zones. They are popular house plants.

Toxic Part: The whole plant is injurious.

Toxin: Calcium oxalate raphides

Symptoms: In most cases, symptoms are limited to burning and intense irritation of the lips, mouth, and oropharynx.

Management: Pain and edema subside slowly without therapy. Cool liquids or demulcents held in the mouth may bring some relief. Analgesics are sometimes indicated. The insoluble oxalate in these plants does not cause systemic poisoning in man.

References:

Mitchell J, Rook A: *Botanical Dermatology*. Vancouver, Greengrass, 1979.

Plowman T: Folk uses of new world aroids. *Econ Bot* 23:97-122, 1969.

Calla palustris **L.**
Family: Araceae

Trivial Names: Water Arum, Female Water Dragon, Water Dragon, Wild Calla

Description: This small plant has heart-shaped leaves that are 4 to 6 inches long and borne on 10-inch stems. The spathe is about 2 inches long, inconspicuous, green on the outside, and white on the inside. Red berries form on the spadix in thick clusters. Figure 71

Distribution: This plant is found in wet, boggy areas from Quebec to Alberta to north central Alaska and south central Yukon south to Colorado, Texas, and Florida.

Toxic Part: The whole plant, particularly the root, is injurious.

Toxin: Calcium oxalate raphides

Symptoms: Chewing any part of the plant produces a painful burning of the lips, mouth, tongue, and throat. Due to the rapid onset of pain, plant material is rarely swallowed. Contact dermatitis is common.

Management: The pain and edema recede slowly without therapy. Holding cool liquids or demulcents in the mouth may give some relief. The insoluble oxalates do not produce systemic poisoning in man.

Calophyllum inophyllum L.
Family: Guttiferae

Trivial Names: Mastwood, Alexandrian or Indian Laurel, Beautyleaf, KAMANI (Hawaii), Laurelwood, María Grande (Puerto Rico)

Description: This low-branched tree grows to 40 feet or more. The trunk is covered by light gray bark with a pink inner bark. The paired leaves are shiny green and leathery with a prominent midrib. They are 3 to 8 inches long and elliptical with a slight notch at the tip. The flowers form small clusters resembling orange blossoms and are fragrant. The fruit is globose, 1.25 to 1.5 inches in diameter, and becomes yellowish brown at maturity. It contains one large seed with a bony shell. The plant has a cream-colored, resinous latex.
Figure 72-73

Distribution: This tree is native to India and the Malay Peninsula. It is a commonly planted ornamental in the West Indies, south Florida, Hawaii, and Guam.

Toxic Part: The seed kernel is poisonous.

Toxin: A number of constituents (inophyllum A-E, calophylloide, calophynic acid) have been identified structurally but their pharmacologic activity has not been determined.

Symptoms: Nausea and persistent vomiting result from poisoning. The latex is used in a number of home remedies in the West Indies and the Pacific and appears to be nontoxic, although it may cause keratoconjunctivitis on contact with the cornea.

Management: Care should be taken to prevent dehydration, particularly in young children.

References:

Morton JF: *Plants Poisonous to People in Florida and Other Warm Areas*, ed 2. Miami, published by the author, 1982, 59-60.

Quisumbing E: *Medicinal Plants of the Philippines*. Dept Agric Nat Res Tech Bull 16, Manila, Bureau of Printing, 1951, 616-620.

Calotropis species
Family: Asclepiadaceae

C. gigantea (L.) Ait. f.
C. procera (Ait.) R.Br.

Trivial Names:
C. gigantea: **Crown Flower,** Giant Milkweed,
PUA KALAUNU (Hawaii)

C. procera: **Small Crown Flower,** Algodón de Seda (Cuba,
Puerto Rico), French Jasmine, Giant Milkweed, Mudar,
Tula (Puerto Rico)

Description: These tree-like shrubs have ovate or
elliptical thick, rubbery, opposite leaves. The flowers
appear in clusters along the branches; they have a
prominent crown with recurved petals and a sweet pleasant
odor. Colors vary from creamy white to lilac, mauve,
and purple. The seeds have silky attachments (like other
types of milkweed seeds), which emerge from pods as
they split on drying. The two species differ in size
(*C. gigantea* to 15 feet, *C. procera* generally under
6 feet); *C. procera* has more diminutive plant parts.
Figure 74

Distribution: Crown flowers are cultivated in south
Florida and Hawaii; *C. procera* is a weed in the West
Indies.

Toxic Part: The latex has a vesicant action on mucous
membranes, particularly the eye. Skin reactions to this
plant may be due to allergy rather than to a direct
irritant action. All parts of the plant contain a cardiac
glycoside.

Toxin: A proteolytic enzyme, calcium oxalate, an
unidentified allergen, and a mixture of cardioactive
glycosides with digitalis-like activity

Symptoms: Ingestion produces intense burning,
irritation, and swelling of the mucous membranes.
Substantial quantities are rarely swallowed, even by
animals, due to the acrid taste. Corneal exposure results
in severe keratoconjunctivitis.

Management: The ingestion of significant quantities
may produce digitalis-like disturbances, which are
managed according to the electrocardiographic assessment.

References:

Crout DHG, et al: Cardenolides, Part VI. Uscharidin, calotropin, and calotoxin. *J Chem Soc* 2187-2194, 1964.

Grant WM: *Toxicology of the Eye*, ed 2. Springfield, Illinois, Charles C Thomas, 1974, 331-332.

Caltha species
Family: Ranunculaceae

C. leptosepala DC.
C. palustris L.

Trivial Names: Marsh Marigold, Bull Flower, Cowslip, Gools, Kingcup, May or Horse Blob, Meadow Bright, Populage, Soldier's Buttons, Souci d'Eau (Canada), Water Goggles

Description: These plants are perennial herbs of the marshy wetlands. Their large, kidney-shaped leaves are about 7 inches wide. The stems are 8 to 24 inches long, smooth, hollow, and furrowed. *C. palustris* blooms in April or early May; the bright yellow flowers are about 2 inches in diameter. These are followed by short, flat, many-seeded pods. *C. leptosepala* is an alpine bog plant, which often blossoms at the lower edge of the retreating snow line in spring. Figure 75-76

Distribution: *C. palustris* grows in Alaska, Canada to the Arctic, and in the southeastern United States into North Carolina and Tennessee. *C. leptosepala* is found in Montana, Washington, British Columbia, Alberta, and Alaska. Other species, some with white flowers, also may be found in the northwestern states.

Toxic Part: All parts of the mature plant are poisonous and have a direct irritant and vesicant action on the skin and mucous membranes. Prior to flowering, the immature plant may be boiled and eaten as greens.

Toxin: Protoanemonin

Symptoms: Chewing plant parts causes acute inflammation and occasional ulceration of the mouth and throat. Ingestion, although rare, is associated with severe gastroenteritis including bloody emesis and diarrhea. See *Actaea* species.

Management: The immediate irritant action usually limits the quantity ingested. If there is evidence of substantial consumption, the stomach should be lavaged, followed by administration of demulcents.

References:

Fyles F: *Principal Poisonous Plants of Canada*. Ottawa, Canadian Department of Agriculture, 39 (Second Series), 1920, 37-38.

Calycanthus species
Family: Calycanthaceae

C. fertilis Walt.
C. floridus L.
C. occidentalis Hook. & Arn.

Trivial Names: Carolina Allspice; American Allspice; Calycanth; Pineapple Shrub; Spicebush; Strawberry Bush or Shrub; Sweet or Sweet-Scented Shrub; Sweet Bettie, Bubbie or Bubby Blossoms, or Bubby Bush

Description: *Calycanthus* grows as a shrub up to 12 feet in height. These plants have opposite leaves that are up to 6 inches long. The flowers are large (2 to 3 inches), showy, and brownish red or purple with a pleasant, sweet, fruity odor; they appear on small brackets along the branches. The fruit is fig-shaped and contains large glossy brown seeds. Figure 77-80

Distribution: *C. fertilis* and *C. floridus* are native in the eastern United States from Pennsylvania to northern Florida and west to Alabama. *C. occidentalis* grows in California. These plants also are cultivated in parks in these areas.

Toxic Part: Seeds are poisonous.

Toxin: Calycanthin and related alkaloids

Symptoms: No human intoxications have been reported. Animals given the alkaloids experience strychnine-like convulsions, myocardial depression, and hypotension.

Capsicum species
Family: Solanaceae

C. annuum L. var. *annuum*
C. annuum var. *glabriusculum* (Dunal) Heiser &
Pickersgill
C. frutescens L.

Trivial Names:

C. annuum var. *annuum:* **Chili Pepper,** Aji de Gallina
(Puerto Rico), Ají Guaguao (Cuba), Cayenne Pepper,
Cherry Pepper, Hot Pepper, Long Pepper, NIOI or
NIOI-PEPA (Hawaii), Piment Bouc (Haiti), Red Pepper

C. annuum var. *glabriusculum*: **Bird Pepper**

C. frutescens: **Tabasco Pepper,** Ají Picante or Ají
Caballero (Puerto Rico), Piment (Haiti)

Description: There are about 20 species of *Capsicum*.
These perennial herbs are native to tropical America. The
leaves are alternate, elliptic, and smooth-edged. The
flowers appear at the point of stem branching and are
usually white with a purple tinge. The fruit is a pod
containing many seeds, which turns red, orange, or yellow
at maturity. Figure 82-84

Distribution: The bird pepper grows wild in the southern
United States and Mexico; all other forms are cultivated
as spices or ornamentals.

Toxic Part: The fruit and seeds are injurious.

Toxin: Capsaicin

Except for the grossum group of *C. annuum* var.
annuum (bell pepper, sweet pepper, green pepper),
the fruit of the pepper plant has a pungency due to the
presence of capsaicin. This material produces a burning
sensation when applied to the tongue in a concentration
of 10^{-4} mole.

Symptoms: Biting into a fruit of the more pungent
varieties by a child invariably produces a painful but

harmless irritation of the oral cavity. Skin exposure may cause erythema but not vesiculation.

Management: Severe inflammatory reactions in the eye may necessitate the application of topical anesthetics.

References:

Mensereenusorn Y, et al: Capsaicin: A literature survey. *CRC Crit Rev Toxicol* 10:321-339, 1982.

Smith JG, et al: The effects of capsaicin on human skin, liver and epidermal lysosomes. *J Invest Dermatol* 54:170-173, 1970.

Caryota species
Family: Palmae (Arecaceae)

C. mitis Lour.
C. urens L.

Trivial Names: Fishtail Palm; Cariota (Cuba); Clustered, Tufted, or Toddy Fishtail Palm; Wine Palm

Description: These palms have long compound leaves up to 20 feet in length with small fish-tail shaped leaflets. The red or black berries are about 1/2 inch in diameter and form on long clusters of strings. Figure 85

Distribution: *Caryota* are native to Asia, but are commonly planted (and have escaped from cultivation) in Florida, Guam, Hawaii, and the West Indies.

Toxic Part: The fruit pulp is injurious.

Toxin: Calcium oxalate raphides

Symptoms: The fruit pulp produces severe burning in the mouth; dermal contact results in itching and burning.

Management: The pain and edema recede slowly without therapy.

References:

Snyder D, et al: Examination of the itch response of

raphides of the fishtail palm *Caryota mitis. Toxicol Appl Pharmacol* 48:287-292, 1979.

Cassia fistula L.
Family: Leguminosae (Fabaceae)

Trivial Names: Golden Shower, Cañafístola (Cuba, Puerto Rico), Cassé (Haiti), Golden Rain, Indian Laburnum, Pudding-Pipe Tree, Purging Fistula

Description: The golden shower belongs to a genus with about 500 species of extremely showy flowering ornamental trees and shrubs. This tree grows to 30 feet and has compound leaves that are 1 foot long with four to eight pairs of leaflets, which are 2 to 6 inches in length. Huge bunches of golden flowers in pendant racemes are followed by fruit pods that are long, narrow cylinders containing up to 100 flat seeds embedded in a sticky pulp in partitioned compartments. Figure 86-88

Distribution: The golden shower is cultivated in subtropical areas, the West Indies, southern Florida, the coast of southern California, and Hawaii. Many related species of shrubs are native in the West Indies and have escaped from cultivation in Hawaii and Guam.

Toxic Part: The sticky pulp of the pods is poisonous. The leaves and bark are less toxic.

Toxin: Emodin (senna) glycosides

Symptoms: Ingestion produces catharsis, nausea, emesis, dizziness, and abdominal cramps.

Management: Catharsis is self-limiting. Fluid replacement may be desirable in young children to prevent dehydration. Emodin causes harmless discoloration of the urine (yellowish brown in acid urine, red or violet in basic urine).

References:

Mahesh VK, et al: Anthraquinones and kaempferol from *Cassia* species section fistula. *J Nat Prod* 47:733, 1984.

Sollman, T: *A Manual of Pharmacology*, ed 8. Philadelphia, WB Saunders, 1957, 211.

Cassia occidentalis L.
Family: Leguminosae (Fabaceae)

Trivial Names: Coffee Senna, Biche Prieto (Mexico), Dandelion (Jamaica), Hedionda (Puerto Rico), MIKIPALAOA or 'AUKO'I (Hawaii), Piss-a-Bed (Jamaica), Pois Puante (Haiti), Stinking or Styptic Weed, Wild Coffee, Yerba Hedionda (Cuba)

Description: This annual herb grows to a height of 3 feet. The smooth leaves are pinnately compound with an even number of leaflets. The flowers are yellow but dry to a paler shade or white. The fruit pod is about 4.5 inches long and 0.25 inches wide. The seeds are dark olive green. Figure 89

Distribution: *Cassia occidentalis* is common in waste places, particularly along highways and coastal areas. It is probably native to the southeastern United States from Virginia to Texas and the West Indies but is now pantropical, incuding Hawaii and Guam.

Toxic Part: The whole plant is toxic; human intoxications usually involve raw seeds. The roasted seed may be used with impunity as a coffee substitute.

Toxin: The irritant chrysarobin (1,8-trihydroxy-3-methyl-9-anthrone), the cathartic emodin (1,8-trihydroxy-6-methyl-9,10-anthracenedione), and a lectin (toxalbumin) have been reported.

Symptoms: Ingestion of the raw seeds exerts a pronounced cathartic action in man. Chronic ingestion of seeds or other plant parts by animals leads to myodegeneration; pathologic changes in the kidney, liver, and lung; and death.

Management: A single exposure in man is associated with self-limited intestinal involvement; intervention is required only to prevent dehydration.

References:

Bruère MP: A coffee substitute, *Cassia occidentalis*, that is toxic before roasting. *J Pharm Chim* (Paris) 2:321-324, 1942. (In French)

Graziano MJ, et al: Effects of *Cassia occidentalis* extract in the domestic chicken (*Gallus domesticus*). *Am J Vet Res* 44:1238-1244, 1983.

Hebert DC, et al: Preliminary isolation of a myodegenerative toxic principle from *Cassia occidentalis*. *Am J Vet Res* 44:1370-1374, 1983.

Suliman HB, et al: Toxicity of *Cassia occidentalis* to goats. *Vet Hum Toxicol* 24:326-330, 1982.

Watt JM, Breyer-Brandwijk MG: *Medicinal and Poisonous Plants of Southern and Eastern Africa*. Edinburgh, E & S Livingstone, 1962, 570-573.

Caulophyllum thalictroides (L.) Michaux
Family: Berberidaceae

Trivial Names: Blue Cohosh, Blueberry Root, Papoose Root, Squaw Root, Yellow or Blue Ginseng

Description: The blue cohosh is an erect herb, 1 to 3 feet tall. The flowers are yellowish green or greenish purple, about 1/2 inch across, and occur in small clusters. The seeds are globose with a thin, fleshy blue coat. Figure 90-91

Distribution: This plant is found in moist woods in Canada from southeast Manitoba to New Brunswick south to Alabama and west to Missouri.

Toxic Part: The berries and roots are cytotoxic.

Toxin: Saponins and N-methylcytisine (a nicotine-like alkaloid)

Symptoms: The extremely bitter taste usually limits the quantity ingested. The saponins act on the intestine to produce gastroenteritis; this plant also is reported to contain orally active oxytocic substances.

Management: Fluid replacement may be indicated.

References:

Ferguson HC, Edwards LD: A pharmacological study on a crystalline glycoside of *Caulophyllum thalictroides*. *J Am Pharm Assoc* 43:16-21, 1954.

Celastrus scandens L.
Family: Celastraceae

Trivial Names: Bittersweet (Note: This is also the trivial name of the toxicologically unrelated *Solanum dulcamara* L.), American Bittersweet, Bourreau des Arbres (Canada), Climbing Bittersweet, Climbing Orange Root, False Bittersweet, Fever Twig, Red Root, Roxbury Waxwork, Shrubby Bittersweet, Staff Tree or Vine

Description: The bittersweet is a climbing, vine-like shrub, which may grow to a height of 25 feet. Its ovate, toothed, alternate leaves are about 4 inches long. The flowers are inconspicuous. The fruit is a 1/2-inch, orange-yellow capsule, which opens to reveal a crimson pulp surrounding the seeds. Figure 93-94

Distribution: *Celastrus* grows in southeastern Saskatchewan to Quebec south to North Carolina and west to New Mexico. It is much employed for dried arrangements in the fall and is readily available from florists at that time (along with the oriental bittersweet, *C. orbiculatus* Thumb., Fig. 92).

Toxic Part: The fruit is reputed to be poisonous; all parts of this plant may be toxic.

Toxin: The toxin in unknown. Two alkaloids of undetermined structure were reported in *Celastrus paniculata* Willd. from India (Basu and Pabrai, 1946).

Symptoms: Ingestion is reputed to cause emesis and diarrhea. No detailed cases of human intoxication have been reported.

References:
Basu NK, Pabrai PR: Chemical investigation of *Celastrus paniculata* Willd. *J Am Pharm Assoc* 35:272-273, 1946.

Hart RC: Toxicity of traditional Christmas greens. *Indust Med Surg* 30:522-525, 1961.

Cestrum species
Family: Solanaceae

C. diurnum L.
C. nocturnum L.

Trivial Names:

C. diurnum: **Day Blooming Jessamine** (Jasmine or Cestrum), Chinese Inkberry, Dama de Día (Puerto Rico), Galán de Día (Cuba), MAKAHALA (Hawaii)

C. nocturnum: **Night Blooming Jessamine** (Jasmine or Cestrum); 'ALA-AUMOE, KUPAOA, or ONAONA-IAPANA (Hawaii); Chinese Inkberry; Dama de Noche (Puerto Rico); Galán de Noche (Cuba); Huele de Noche (Mexico); Lilas de Nuit or Jasmin de Nuit (Haiti)

Description: The day blooming jessamine is an evergreen shrub or tall bush with smooth-edged ovate leaves about 2 to 4 inches long. The tubular flowers are white and appear in small clusters. They are fragrant by day. The mature fruit is a globose, black berry. Figure 96-97

The night blooming jessamine has longer leaves (4 to 8 inches). The flowers are fragrant at night and have a cloying, sweet odor. The mature fruit is white. Figure 99

Distribution: Both species are native to the West Indies. They have escaped from cultivation in Florida, Texas, and Guam. Other species in cultivation only are: *C. parqui* L'Her., the willow-leaved jessamine from Peru, is a night bloomer with black fruit; *C. aurantiacum* Lindl. (Fig. 95), from Guatemala, has orange flowers and white fruit; and *C. elegans* (Brongn.) Schlechtend. (= *C. purpureum* (Lindl.) Standl.) (Fig. 98), from Mexico, has crimson-purple flowers and crimson fruit.

Toxic Part: The fruit and sap are poisonous.

Toxin: Saponins, traces of nicotine and allied alkaloids

Symptoms: Ingestion of the fruit results in gastroenteritis.

Management: Therapy usually is not required. Fluids should be replaced if emesis or diarrhea persists.

References:

Halim A, et al: Alkaloids produced by *Cestrum nocturnum* and *Cestrum diurnum*. *Planta Medica* 20:44-49, 1971.

Morton JF: Poisonous and injurious higher plants and fungi, in Tedeschi CG, et al (eds): *Forensic Medicine*. Philadelphia, WB Saunders, 1977, 1534.

Chelidonium majus L.
Family: Papaveraceae

Trivial Names: Celandine, Elon Wort, Felonwort, Swallow Wort, Tetterwort, Wort-Weed

Description: This herb grows 1 to 3 feet in height. The yellow flower is 0.5 to 0.75 inches in diameter with four petals. Leaves are divided into three to five lobes. The leaves, stems, and buds are whitish and hairy. The sap is reddish orange. This plant blooms from March to August. Figure 100

Distribution: Celandine grows in moist soil from Quebec south to Georgia and west to Iowa and Missouri; it also is found in southwest British Columbia, Ontario, New Brunswick, and Nova Scotia.

Toxic Part: The whole plant is poisonous.

Toxin: Isoquinoline alkaloids

Symptoms: This plant is seldom ingested because of its unpleasant smell and taste. Approximately 14 hours after ingestion, somnolence and headache develop followed in about six hours by fever, emesis and diarrhea, coma, and circulatory collapse.

Management: There is inadequate information to recommend specific therapy. The pharmacology of isolated alkaloids suggests the following regimen: Adequate hydration to replace fluids and correction of electrolyte imbalance. Some of the alkaloids are adrenergic blocking agents.

References:

Koopman H: A fatal case of celandine poisoning. *Sammlung von Vergiftungsfällen* 8(A682):93-98, 1937. (In German)

Preininger V: Pharmacology and toxicology of the Papaveraceae alkaloids, in Manske RHF (ed): *The Alkaloids*. New York, Academic Press, 1975, vol 15, 207-261.

Raffauf R: *A Handbook of Alkaloids and Alkaloid-Containing Plants*. New York, Wiley-Interscience, 1970.

Shamma M: *The Isoquinoline Alkaloids*. New York, Academic Press, 1972, 315-343.

Cicuta species
Family: Umbelliferae (Apiaceae)

C. bulbifera L.
C. douglasii (DC.) Coult. & Rose
C. maculata L.

Trivial Names: Water Hemlock, Beaver Poison, Children's Bane, Cicutaire (Canada), Death-of-Man, Musquash Poison, Musquash Root, Spotted Cowbane

Description: Most species of *Cicuta* have a similar appearance and may grow to a height of 6 feet. The leaves are multiply compound and there are small, whitish, heavily scented flowers. In the underground portion of mature plants, there is a bundle of chambered tuberous roots. A yellow, oily sap emerges from the cut stem and has a distinct odor of raw parsnip. These plants are found only in wet or swampy ground. Figure 105-107

Distribution: Species of *Cicuta* are found throughout the United States (except Hawaii) and Canada and are the most toxic plants native to Alaska.

Toxic Part: The whole plant, particularly the roots, is poisonous.

Toxin: Cicutoxin, an unsaturated, long-chain aliphatic alcohol

Symptoms: Fifteen minutes to one hour after ingestion, nausea, salivation, and sometimes emesis develop. Trismus and tonic-clonic convulsions also may occur. Death may occur before medical attention becomes available.

Management: Establish a patent airway and assist respiration; if indicated, persistent convulsions may be relieved with intravenous diazepam or another rapidly acting anticonvulsant. Acidosis should be corrected. An adequate urine flow should be assured to reduced the hazard of myoglobinuria secondary to convulsions. A prolonged postictal deficit in mental function and abnormal electroencephalograms has been reported.

References:
Anet EFLJ, et al: Oenanthotoxin and cicutoxin. Isolation and structures. *J Chem Soc* 309-322, 1953.

Carlton BE, et al: Water hemlock poisoning complicated by rhabdomyolysis and renal failure. *Clin Toxicol* 14:87-92, 1979.

Costanza DJ, Hoversten VW: Accidental ingestion of water hemlock. Report of two patients with acute and chronic effects. *Calif Med* 119:78-82, Aug 1973.

Starreveld E, Hope CHE: Cicutoxin poisoning. *Neurology* 25:730-734, 1975.

Clematis species
Family: Ranunculaceae

Trivial Names: Clematis, Blue Jessamine, Bluebell, Cabellos de Ángel (Cuba, Puerto Rico), Cabeza de Viejo (Mexico), Cascarita, Clématite or Herbe aux Geaux (Canada), Curl Flower, Curly Heads, Devils Hair, Devils Thread, Flámula (Cuba), Headache Weed, Leather Flower, Liane Bon Garçon (Haiti), Pipe-stem, Sugar-bowls, Traveler's Joy, Vase Flower or Vine, Virgin's Bower, Yerba de Pordioseros (Cuba)

Description: There are many species of this perennial flowering herb and climber. The leaves are usually compound and have a superficial resemblance to poison ivy. Figure 109-111

Distribution: Clematis are native to Canada and the north temperate United States; cultivars are available commercially throughout the United States and West Indies.

Toxic Part: The whole plant is toxic.

Toxin: Protoanemonin

Symptoms: Protoanemonin has direct irritant and vesicant actions on the skin and mucous membranes. Upon ingestion, there is intense pain and inflammation of the oral cavity, often with blistering and ulceration. Salivation is profuse. Bloody emesis and diarrhea occur in association with abdominal cramping. There is initial polyuria with painful micturition and hematuria, which may be followed by oliguria. Central nervous system involvement is manifested by dizziness, syncope, and, in severe cases, convulsions. Mental confusion also may be observed.

Management: The irritant effects usually limit ingestion. If there is any evidence that a substantial quantity has been swallowed, the stomach should be lavaged and demulcents administered. Appropriate measures to ensure hydration should be taken. Renal output should be monitored.

Clivia species
Family: Amaryllidaceae

Trivial Names: Kaffir Lily

Description: Strap-like leaves arise from a swollen leaf base and may be stacked in two opposing piles. The flowers form on a leafless stem in an umbel. They are usually orange or red. The fruit is a red, pulpy berry. Figure 112-113

Distribution: These plants are native to Africa. They are in cultivation as house plants or may be grown outdoors in subtropical climates.

Toxic Part: All parts of this plant are toxic.

Toxin: Lycorine

Symptoms: Ingestion of large quantities may produce nausea and persistent emesis with diarrhea.

Management: Human poisonings are uncommon because of the small concentration of alkaloids in these plants. Fluid replacement may be required if dehydration develops. See *Narcissus*.

References:
Jasperson-Schib R: Toxic Amaryllidaceae. *Pharm Acta Helv* 45:424-433, 1970. (In German)

Clusia rosea Jacq.
Family: Guttiferae (Clusiaceae)

Trivial Names: Balsam Apple, Copey, Cupey, Figuier

Maudit Marron (Haiti), Pitch Apple, Scotch Attorney, Wild Mamee

Description: This tree may be 20 to 50 feet high and grows on rocks or other trees. The leaves are ovate and leathery (retain scratched writing), 3 to 8 inches in diameter. The flowers are white tinged with pink and have a golden center. Globulose fruit, the size of a golf ball, turns brown and opens when mature. Figure 114-115

Distribution: *Clusia* grow in the West Indies, southern Florida, and Hawaii.

Toxic Part: The golden viscous sap and the fruit are toxic.

Toxin: Unidentified

Symptoms: Profuse diarrhea occurs after ingestion.

Management: Adequate fluid replacement is required to prevent dehydration, particularly in young children.

References:
Allen PH: Poisonous and injurious plants of Panama. *Am J Trop Med* 23(suppl):1-76, 1943.

Colchicum species
Family: Liliaceae

C. autumnale L.
C. speciosum Steven
C. vernum (L.) Ker-Gawl. (= *Bulbocodium vernum* L.)

Trivial Names: Crocus, Autumn Crocus, Fall Crocus, Meadow Saffron, Mysteria, Vellorita (Cuba), Wonder Bulb

Description: *Colchicum* are members of the lily family and are cultivated for their long, tubular, purple or white flowers, which emerge from the underground bulb. In the autumn flowering plants, eg, *C. autumnale*, the strap-like leaves appear in spring and are not present during flowering. Figure 118

Distribution: *Colchicum* are in cultivation only; they are also popular house plants.

Toxic Part: The whole plant is poisonous.

Toxin: Colchicine (*C. autumnale* is a commercial source for this drug.)

Symptoms: On ingestion, there is immediate burning pain in the mouth and throat with intense thirst followed by nausea and emesis. Abdominal colic and severe, profuse, persistent diarrhea develop. There is extensive loss of fluid that may lead to hypovolemic shock. Renal involvement with hematuria and oliguria is observed occasionally.

Management: The intoxication has a prolonged course due to the slow excretion of colchicine. Fluid replacement is required. Analgesics and atropine may be given to alleviate colic and diarrhea.

References:

Gilman AG, et al (eds): *The Pharmacological Basis of Therapeutics*, ed 6. New York, Macmillan Publishing Co, 1980, 718-720.

Gooneratne B: Massive generalized alopecia after poisoning by *Gloriosa superba*. *Br Med J* 1:1023-1024, 1966.

Murray SS, et al: Acute toxicity after excessive ingestion of colchicine. *Mayo Clin Proc* 58:528-532, 1983.

Sauder P, et al: Haemodynamic studies in eight cases of acute colchicine poisoning. *Human Toxicol* 2:169-173, 1983.

Colocasia species
Family: Araceae

C. esculenta (L.) Schott (= *C. esculenta* var. *antiquorum* Schott)
C. gigantea (Blume) Hook. f.

Trivial Names: Elephant's Ear, Caraïbe (Haiti), Dasheen, Eddo, Kalo, Malanga Isleña (Cuba), Malanga deux Palles (Haiti), Taro, Tayo Bambou (Haiti), Yautía Malanga (Puerto Rico)

Description: These large ornamentals are grown for their huge heart-shaped leaves or edible roots.
Figure 119

Distribution: Elephant's ear grows in the West Indies, south Florida, southern California, Guam, and Hawaii as landscape plants or for food. They are used elsewhere in indoor planters.

Toxic Part: The leaves are injurious.

Toxin: Insoluble crystals (raphides) of calcium oxalate

Symptoms: A painful burning sensation of the lips and oral cavity result from ingestion. There is an inflammatory reaction, often with edema and blistering. Hoarseness, dysphonia, and dysphagia may result.

Management: The pain and edema recede slowly without therapy. Cool liquids or demulcents held in the mouth may bring some relief. Analgesics may be indicated. The insoluble oxalate in these plants does not cause systemic poisoning in man.

References:

Mitchell J, Rook A: *Botanical Dermatology*. Vancouver, Greengrass, 1979.

Plowman T: Folk uses of new world aroids. *Econ Bot* 23:97-122, 1969.

Sakai WS, Hanson M: Mature raphid and raphid idioblast structure in plants of the edible Aroid genera *Colocasia*, *Alocasia*, and *Xanthosoma*. *Ann Bot* 38:739-748, 1974.

Sunell LA, Healy PL: Distribution of calcium oxalate crystal idioblasts in corms of taro (*Colocasia esculenta*). *Am J Bot* 66:1029-1032, 1979.

Conium maculatum L.
Family: Umbelliferae (Apiaceae)

Trivial Names: Poison Hemlock, Bunk, California Fern, Cashes, Cigue (Canada), Herb Bonnett, Kill Cow, Nebraska Fern, Poison Parsley, Poison Root, St. Bennet's Herb, Snake Weed, Spotted Hemlock, Spotted Parsley, Winter Fern, Wode Whistle

Description: This plant resembles a carrot with large lacy leaves, but the root is white. The leaves may extend to 4 feet and both stem and leaves may be spotted with purple. When crushed, the leaves produce an offensive "mousy" odor. The small white flowers are borne in flat clusters. Figure 124-126

Distribution: This plant is now naturalized in most of the northern and temperate zones of the United States and Canada (but not Alaska).

Toxic Part: The whole plant is poisonous, particularly the root and seeds.

Toxin: Coniine and related alkaloids

Symptoms: The symptoms of poisoning are similar to those produced by nicotine. There is usually rapid onset of irritation of the mucous membranes of the mouth and throat with salivation, nausea, and emesis. Abdominal pain is usually minimal and diarrhea is not typical. Headache, mydriasis, thirst, sweating, and dizziness may occur. Severe poisoning may result in convulsions, coma, and death due to respiratory failure.

Management: Administer a slurry of activated charcoal orally as soon as emesis ceases. Treatment is otherwise symptomatic. Despite the apparent severity of these intoxications, mortality is low.

References:

Bowman WC, Sanghvi IS: Pharmacological actions of hemlock (*Conium maculatum*) alkaloids. *J Pharm Pharmacol* 15:1-25, 1963.

Lampe K, Fagerström R: *Plant Toxicity and Dermatitis*. Baltimore, Williams & Wilkins, 1968, 113-114.

━━━━━━━━━━

Convallaria majalis L.
Family: Liliaceae

Trivial Names: Lily-of-the-Valley, Conval Lily, LILIA-O-KE-AWAWA (Hawaii), Mayflower, Muguet (Canada)

Description: These small perennials have two oblong leaves and a flower stalk bearing small, bell-shaped white flowers on one side. Occasionally, orange-red fleshy berries form. *Convallaria* spread by underground roots to form thick beds. Figure 127-128

Distribution: These Eurasian plants have escaped from cultivation throughout the north temperate United States and eastern Canada.

Toxic Part: The whole plant is poisonous, as is the water in which flowers have been kept.

Toxin: Digitalis-like glycosides, irritant saponins

Symptoms: Pain in the oral cavity, nausea, emesis, abdominal pain, cramping, and diarrhea develop after ingestion. Digitalis glycoside toxicity has a variable latent period that depends on the quantity ingested. Toxicity is usually expressed as conduction defects and sinus bradycardia. Hyperkalemia may be present. Rhythm disturbances other than escape beats may not occur.

Management: Gastric lavage or induced emesis may be performed. Activated charcoal may be given and repeated later. Saline cathartics also can be used. Repeated electrocardiographic monitoring and serum potassium determinations should be performed. Conduction defects may require the use of atropine or transvenous pacing. Phenytoin is the agent of choice for rhythm distrubances. Dialysis and forced diuresis are not useful.

References:

Ekins BR, Watanabe AS: Acute digoxin poisonings: Review of therapy. *Am J Hosp Pharm* 35:268-277, 1978.

Coriaria myrtifolia L.
Family: Coriariaceae

Trivial Names: This plant has no common name in our geographical area.

Description: Species of *Coriaria* are shrubs or small trees with opposite leaves, small greenish flowers, and a purple-black berry-like fruit. Figure 129

Distribution: *Coriaria* are in cultivation as an ornamental shrub in the southern United States and California.

Toxic Part: The fruit is poisonous.

Toxin: Coriamyrtin (convulsant)

Symptoms: Convulsions similar to those induced by picrotoxin occur.

Management: Establish a patent airway and support respiration if indicated; persistent convulsions may be treated with intravenous diazepam.

References:

Bleckwenn W, et al: A clinical comparison of picrotoxin, metrazol and coriamyrtin used as analeptics and convulsants. *J Pharmacol Exp Therap* 69:81-88, 1940.

Garcia M, et al: Poisoning caused by ingestion of *Coriaria myrtifolia*. Study of 25 cases. *An Esp Pediatr* 19:366-370, 1983. (In Spanish)

Poyen P, et al: A case of severe acute poisoning by Tanner's sumac. *Eur J Toxicol* 3:386-391, 1970. (In French)

███████

Corynocarpus laevigatus J.R. & G. Forst.
Family: Corynocarpaceae

Trivial Names: This plant has no common name in our geographical area.

Description: *Corynocarpus* is a tree with thick, dark green, glossy leaves. The greenish yellow flowers are borne in panicles. The plum-shaped fruit is green turning to orange when mature and 1 to 1.5 inches long.
Figure 131-132

Distribution: *Corynocarpus* is native to New Zealand and has been introduced in California.

Toxic Part: The fruit is poisonous.

Toxin: The prototoxin, karakin (1,4,6-tris-0-(3-nitro-propanoy1)-beta-D-glucopyranoside), on hydrolysis yields the toxin, beta-nitropropionic acid, an irreversible inhibitor of succinate dehydrogenase, a mitochondrial Krebs cycle enzyme.

Symptoms: Ingestion produces spasms and convulsions followed by paralysis.

Management: None is known.

References:

Alston TA, et al: 3-Nitropropionate, the toxic substance of *Indigofera*, is a suicide inactivator of succinate dehydrogenase. *Proc Natl Acad Sci USA* 74:3767-3771, 1977.

Carter CL, McChesney WJ: Hiptagenic acid identified as beta-nitropropionic acid. *Nature* 164:575-576, 1949.

Connor HE: *Poisonous Plants of New Zealand*, ed 2. Wellington, NZ, EC Keating, Government Printer, 1977, 61-64.

Crinum species
Family: Amaryllidaceae

Trivial Names: Spider Lily, Lirio (Spanish), Lys (Haiti)

C. asiaticum: Poison bulb

Description: These plants have onion-like bulbs. The strap-like leaves are arranged in a spiral. Lily-like flowers appear on a solid, leafless stem and are usually white but may be pink or red. Figure 135

Distribution: Some species are native to the southern United States and the West Indies. *C. bulbispermum* (Burm. f.) Milne-Redh. & Schweick., from south Africa, and *C. asiaticum* L., from tropical Asia, are most frequently encountered in cultivation.

Toxic Part: All parts of the plant are toxic, particularly the bulb.

Toxin: Lycorine

Symptoms: Ingestion of large quantities may produce nausea and persistent emesis with diarrhea.

Management: Human poisonings are uncommon because of the small concentration of alkaloids in this plant. Fluid replacement may be required if dehydration develops. See *Narcissus*.

References:
Jasperson-Schib R: Toxic Amaryllidaceae. *Pharm Acta Helv* 45:424-433, 1970. (In German)

███████████████

Crotalaria species
Family: Leguminosae (Fabaceae)

C. berteroana DC. (= *C. fulva* Roxb.)
C. incana L.
C. juncea L.
C. retusa L.
C. spectabilis Roth (= *C. retzii* A.S. Hitch.)

Trivial Names: Rattle Box, Ala de Pico (Mexico), Cascabelillo (Puerto Rico), Maromera (Cuba), Pète-Pète (Haiti), Rabbit-Bells, Rattleweed (Jamaica), Shake-Shake

Description: These coarse yellow herbs have stout branches and sweetpea-like flowers that are usually yellow. The seeds in the persistent dried pods cause a rattling noise when the pod is shaken. Figure 136-137

Distribution: *C. retusa* is cultivated in Florida. Other species of *Crotalaria* are common weeds with wide distribution in the West Indies and all of the United States except Alaska. They are not present in Canada.

Toxic Part: The whole plant is poisonous.

Toxin: Pyrrolizidine alkaloids

Symptoms: Intoxication may result from contamination of grain by *Crotalaria* seeds or use of the plant in herbal teas as a folk remedy. Drinking these teas (particularly those made with *C. berteroana* and *C. juncea*) may cause veno-occlusive disease of the liver (Budd-Chiari syndrome) with hepatic vein thrombosis leading to cirrhosis. The symptoms are abdominal pain with ascites, hepatomegaly and splenomegaly, anorexia with nausea, vomiting, and diarrhea.

The chronic consumption of the seeds of some species, eg, *C. spectabilis*, also may produce pulmonary hypertension in animals, but it is not known whether there is an analogous human response.

Management: There is no known specific therapy for toxin-induced hepatic veno-occlusive disease.

References:
Bull LB, et al: *The Pyrrolizidine Alkaloids. Their Chemistry, Pathogenicity, and Other Biological Properties*. New York, Wiley-Interscience, 1968.

Huxtable R, et al: Prevention of monocrotaline-induced right ventricular hypertrophy. *Chest* 71(S):308-310, 1977.

Huxtable RJ: Herbal teas and toxins: Novel aspects of pyrrolizidine poisoning in the United States. *Perspec Biol Med* 24:1-14, 1980.

Kay JM, Heath D: *Crotalaria spectabilis, the Pulmonary Hypertension Plant*. Springfield, Charles C Thomas, 1969.

McLean EK, Mattocks AR: Environmental liver injury: Plant toxins, in Farber E, Fisher MM (eds): *Toxic Injury of the Liver, Part B*. New York, Marcel Dekker, 1980, 517-539.

Peterson JE, Culvenor CCJ: Hepatotoxic pyrrolizidine alkaloids, in Keeler RF, Tu AT (eds): *Plant and Fungal Toxins*. New York, Marcel Dekker, 1983, 637-671.

Schoental R: Biochemical basis of liver necrosis caused by pyrrolizidine alkaloids and certain other hepatotoxins. *Biochem Soc Trans* 3:292-294, 1975.

Smith LW, Culvenor CCJ: Plant sources of hepatotoxic pyrrolizidine alkaloids. *J Nat Prod* 44:129-152, 1981.

Cryptostegia species
Family: Asclepiadaceae

C. grandiflora (Roxb.) R.Br.
C. madagascariensis Bojer ex Decne.

Trivial Names: Rubber Vine, Purple Allamanda, Alamanda Morada Falsa (Puerto Rico), Caoutchouc (Haiti), Estrella del Norte (Cuba), India Rubber Vine, Pichuco (Mexico)

Description: These are woody vines that sometimes appear shrubby. The smooth leaves are oblong, about 3 to 4 inches long, and a shiny green. When the leaves or stems are injured, they exude a milky latex. The flowers are purple; those of *C. grandiflora* are more lilac and those of *C. madagascariensis* are more red. These species may be distinguished by the length of the calyx (the green envelope holding the flower), being 0.5 inch and 1.25 inches long, respectively. Hybrids of the two species are also found. The seeds are contained in typical milkweed pods. Figure 138-140

Distribution: These plants are cultivated in south Florida and are common in the West Indies and Guam.

Toxic Part: All parts of this plant are poisonous.

Toxin: Digitalis-like glycosides

Symptoms: Human intoxications from this plant have not been reported. Poisoning would be expected to produce pain in the oral cavity, nausea, emesis, abdominal pain, cramping, and diarrhea. Digitalis glycoside toxicity has a variable latent period that depends on the quantity ingested. Toxicity is usually expressed as conduction defects and sinus bradycardia. Hyperkalemia may be present. Rhythm disturbances other than escape beats may not occur.

Management: Gastric lavage or induced emesis may be performed. Activated charcoal may be given and repeated later. Saline cathartics also can be used. Repeated electrocardiographic monitoring and serum potassium determinations should be performed. Conduction defects may require the use of atropine or transvenous pacing. Phenytoin is the agent of choice for rhythm disturbances. Dialysis and forced diuresis are not useful.

References:
Ekins BR, Watanabe AS: Acute digoxin poisonings: Review of therapy. *Am J Hosp Pharm* 35:268-277, 1978.

Sanduja R, et al: Cardenolides of *Cryptostegia madagascariensis*. *J Nat Prod* 47:260-265, 1984.

<hr>

Daphne mezereum L.
Family: Thymelaeaceae

Trivial Names: Bois Gentil or Bois Joli (Canada), Dwarf Bay, February Daphne, Flax Olive, Lady Laurel, Mezereum, Spurge Laurel, Spurge Olive

Description: *Daphne* are deciduous rounded shrubs that grow 4 to 5 feet in height. Leaves are elliptic, 3.5 by 0.75 inches. Flowers are lilac-purple or white and grow in clusters. They appear before the leaves. Fruits are scarlet or yellow with pit. Figure 143-144

Distribution: This Eurasian plant has escaped from cultivation in the northeastern United States and eastern Canada.

Toxic Part: The whole plant is poisonous, including the flower, but most intoxications have been associated with the fruit and seeds.

Toxin: Daphnetoxin and mezerein, diterpene alcohols with a daphnane skeleton

Symptoms: Ingestion of the fruit or chewing the bark produces vesication and edema of the lips, oral cavity, and oropharynx with salivation and dysphagia. This is followed by thirst, abdominal pain, emesis, and persistent bloody diarrhea. There may be renal damage. Other effects are probably secondary to hypovolemia and electrolyte disturbances.

Management: These intoxications are serious and potentially lethal. Care should be taken to restore fluids and electrolytes. Symptoms may persist for several days.

References:

Evans F, Super CJ: The tigliane, daphnane and ingenane diterpenes: Their chemistry, distribution and biological activities. *Lloydia* 41:193-237, 1978.

Nöller HG: *Daphne mezereum* poisoning in a child. *Monats Kinderheilkunde* 103:327-330, 1955. (In German)

Nyborg J, La Cour T: X-ray diffraction study of molecular structure and conformation of mezerein. *Nature* 257:824-825, 1975.

Rolán A, Wickberg B: The structure of mezerein, a major toxic principle of *Daphne mezereum* L. *Tetrahedron Letters* no 49:4261-4264, 1980.

Schwarz L, et al: *Occupational Diseases of the Skin*, ed 3. Philadelphia, Lea & Febiger, 1957.

Woods B: Irritant plants. *Trans St Johns Hosp Derm Soc (N.S.)* 48:75-82, 1962.

Datura species
Brugmansia species
Family: Solanaceae

D. inoxia Mill. (= *D. meteloides* DC.)
D. metel L. (= *D. fastuosa* L.)
D. stramonium L.
D. stramonium var. *tatula* (L.) Torr. (= *D. tatula* L.)
B. arborea (L.) Lagerh. (Most material listed as *B. arborea* or *D. arborea* is *B.* X *candida*.)
B. X *candida* (Pers.) Safford (*B. aurea* X B. *versicolor*)
B. sanguinea (Ruiz & Pav.) D. Don
B. suaveolens (Humb. & Bonpl. ex Willd.) Bercht. & Presl. (= *D. suaveolens* H. & B. ex Willd.)

Trivial Names:

D. stramonium: **Jimson weed** (originally Jamestown weed), Belladona de Pobre (Puerto Rico), Chamico (Cuba), Concombre Zombi (Haiti), Devil's Trumpet, Estramonio or Peo de Fraile (Puerto Rico), KIKANIA or LA'AU-HANO (Hawaii), Mad Apple, Pommé Epineuse or Herbe aux Sorciers (Canada), Stink Weed, Thorn Apple, Toloache (Texas, Mexico)

B. suaveolens: Florifundia (Mexico)

B. X *candida*: **Angel's Trumpet,** Belladonna (Hawaii), Campana (Cuba, Puerto Rico), Cornucopia, Floripondio (Puerto Rico), NANA-HONUA (Hawaii)

Description:

D. stramonium is an annual. The stem is stout, hollow, simple, upright, or branched and grows upright to 3 or 4 feet. The leaves have a long stem, are 6 to 8 inches long, lobed, and have an offensive smell. The white flowers are funnel-form, large and showy, and point upwards. The prickly fruits are capsules about 2 inches long, which split open along four seams to expose numerous small, kidney-shaped, brownish black seeds when mature and dry. Figure 145-146. A lavender-flowered form is named var. *tatula*. Figure 147-148

B. X *candida* may grow to 20 feet in height. The leaves are ovate, usually have smooth edges, and are pubescent. The flowers are white, yellowish white, or pinkish white; they are 10 to 12 inches long, funnel-form, have distinct teeth, and hang downward. The fruit of *Brugmansia* is

smooth and does not split open after drying. Figure
63-65

Other species of *Datura* and *Brugmansia* generally
resemble the respective descriptions above.

Distribution: *D. stramonium* is a weed throughout
the West Indies, Canada, and the United States, including
Hawaii but not Alaska. *D. inoxia* grows in the West
Indies, Texas, and New Mexico. *D. metel* is a native of
China. It is cultivated as an ornamental and has escaped
in portions of the West Indies.

Brugmansia species are native to South America. They
are cultivated as ornamentals in the West Indies, Hawaii,
and warmer regions of the United States.

Toxic Part: The whole plant is toxic, including the
nectar; however, seeds are most often implicated in
accidental poisoning. Both the seeds and dried leaves are
used to deliberately induce intoxications when a
deliriant action is sought.

Toxin: Belladonna alkaloids

Symptoms: Intoxication causes dry mouth, mydriasis,
dry warm skin sometimes with reddening of the face
and neck, tachycardia, and delirium with hallucinations.
Less frequently encountered are elevated temperature
(common in young children), decreased bowel sounds,
elevated blood pressure, and urinary retention.

Management: If the severity of the intoxication warrants
intervention (hyperthermia, delirium), a slow
intravenous administration of physostigmine should be
repeated until symptoms abate or cholinergic effects
appear. The initial pediatric dose is 0.5 mg; adolescents
and adults, 2 mg. The duration of action of the
belladonna alkaloids is longer than that of physostigmine,
and repeated administration of the latter may be
required.

References:
Klein-Schwartz W, Oderda GM: Jimsonweed intoxication
in adolescents and young adults. *Am J Dis Child*
138:737-739, 1984.

O'Grady TC, et al: Outbreak of Jimson weed abuse
among Marine Corps personnel at Camp Pendelton.
Military Med 148:732-734, 1983.

Rumack BH: Anticholinergic poisoning: Treatment with physostigmine. *Pediatrics* 52:449-451, 1973.

Dieffenbachia species
Family: Araceae

D. maculata (Lodd.) G. Don (= *D. picta* Schott)
D. sequine (Jacq.) Schott

Trivial Names: Dumbcane, Camilichigui (Mexico), Canne-à-gratter or Canne-madère (Haiti), Dicha (Cuba), Dumb Plant, Mother-in-Law's Tongue Plant, Pela Puerco (Dominican Republic), Rábano (Puerto Rico), Tuft Root

Description: These tall, erect, unbranched plants have large oblong leaves splotched with ivory markings. Figure 152-154

Distribution: Species of *Dieffenbachia* may be cultivated outdoors in southern Florida and Hawaii. The popularity of these plants is probably second only to *Philodendron* as decorative pot plants for offices, waiting rooms, and lobbies.

Toxic Part: The leaf is injurious.

Toxin: Raphides of water-insoluble calcium oxalate and unverified proteinaceous toxins

Symptoms: Chewing on the leaf produces an almost immediate intense pain, which may be followed by edematous swelling of the oral mucosa. Bullae may form. In severe cases, speech becomes unintelligible, hence the name dumbcane. Because of the immediate pain, swallowing of plant parts is uncommon but may lead to laryngeal edema. The pain and edema may persist for several days and leave superficial necrosis. These plants also produce direct contact dermatitis and keratoconjunctivitis.

Management: The pain and edema in the oral cavity recede slowly without treatment. Cool liquids or demulcents held in the mouth may bring some relief. Analgesics may be indicated. The insoluble oxalates in these plants do not produce systemic poisoning in man.

References:
Arditti J, Rodriguez E: *Dieffenbachia*: uses, abuses and

toxic constituents: a review. *J Ethnopharmacol* 5:293-302, 1982.

Barnes BA, Fox LE: Poisoning with *Dieffenbachia. J Hist Med Allied Sci* 10:173-181, 1955.

Kuballa B, et al: Study of *Dieffenbachia*-induced edema in mouse hindpaw: Respective role of oxalate needles and trypsin-like protease. *Toxicol Appl Pharmacol* 58:444-451, 1981.

Mitchell J, Rook A: *Botanical Dermatology*. Vancouver, Greengrass, 1979.

Plowman T: Folk uses of new world aroids. *Econ Bot* 23:97-122, 1969.

Pohl RW: Poisoning with *Dieffenbachia. J Am Med Assoc* 177:812-813, 1961; 187:963, 1964.

Sakai WS, Hanson M: Mature raphid and raphid idioblast structure in plants of the edible Aroid genera *Colocasia*, *Alocasia*, and *Xanthosoma*. *Ann Bot* 38:739-748, 1974.

Digitalis purpurea L.
Family: Scrophulariaceae

Trivial Names: Foxglove, Digitalis, Fairy Bells, Fairy Cap, Fairy Glove, Fairy Thimbles, Folks Glove, Ladies' Thimbles, Lion's Mouth, Pop-Dock, Rabbit Flower, Thimbles, Throatwort, Witches' Thimbles

Description: These biennial or perennial flowers form along the central stalk and droop down. They may be purple or pink (rarely white) and usually are spotted on the inside. Figure 155

Distribution: *Digitalis* is grown in cultivation and has escaped locally. Plants are hardy in the north temperate zones including Canada and Alaska.

Toxic Part: The whole plant is poisonous.

Toxin: Digitalis glycosides, irritant saponins

Symptoms: Pain in the oral cavity, nausea, emesis, abdominal pain, cramping, and diarrhea develop after ingestion. Digitalis glycoside toxicity has a variable latent period that depends on the quantity ingested and is usually expressed as conduction defects and sinus

73

bradycardia. Hyperkalemia may be present. Rhythm disturbances other than escape beats are not necessarily exhibited.

Management: Gastric lavage or induced emesis should be performed. Activated charcoal may be given repeatedly later. Saline cathartics also may be useful. Electrocardiographic monitoring and measurements of serum potassium should be done frequently.

Conduction defects may require the use of atropine or transvenous pacing. Phenytoin is the agent of choice for rhythm disturbances. Dialysis and forced diuresis are not useful.

The digitalis-specific antibodies, Fab fragments, may become the management of choice for life-threatening toxicity but are not generally available yet.

References:

Dickstein ES, Kunkel FW: Foxglove tea poisonings. *Am J Med* 69:167-169, 1980.

Ekins BR, Watanabe AS: Acute digoxin poisonings: Review of therapy. *Am J Hosp Pharm* 35:268-277, 1978.

Smith TW, et al: Treatment of life-threatening digitalis intoxication with digoxin-specific Fab antibody fragments. Experience in 26 cases. *N Engl J Med* 307:1357-1362, 1982.

Dirca palustris L.
Family: Thymelaeaceae

Trivial Names: Leatherwood, American Mezereon, Bois de Plomb (Canada), Leather Bush, Leaver Wood, Moosewood, Rope Bark, Swamp Wood, Wickerby Bush, Wickup, Wicopy

Description: This deciduous shrub grows to 6 feet. The leaves are 2 to 3 inches long and elliptical. Pale yellow flowers on short stalks appear from the branches prior to leafing. The berry is green to reddish and about 1/4 inch in diameter. Figure 156

Distribution: *Dirca* grows in woods from New Brunswick to Ontario and Minnesota south to Florida and west to Louisiana and Oklahoma.

Toxic Part: The whole plant is toxic, particularly the bark.

Toxin: Unidentified

Symptoms: No serious intoxications have been reported, probably because chewing on the plant causes immediate burning and has a nauseating taste. The bark can produce severe dermatitis, particularly during flowering and fruiting periods.

Management: No treatment is required.

References:

Fyles F: *Principal Poisonous Plants of Canada*. Otttawa, Canadian Department of Agriculture, *Exp Farms Bull* 39 (Second Series), 1920, 65.

Woods B, Calnan C: Toxic woods. *Br J Dermatol* 95 (Suppl 13):1-97, 1976.

Duranta repens L. *(= D. plumieri* Jacq.)
Family: Verbenaceae

Trivial Names: Golden Dewdrop, Azota Caballo, Bois Jambette or Maïs Bouilli (Haiti), Cuentas de Oro or Lila (Puerto Rico), Garbancillo (Cuba), Pigeon Berry, Skyflower, Velo de Novia (Mexico)

Description: A large shrub, *Duranta* is frequently cultivated as a hedge. Flowers are small and light blue or white. There are masses of persistent orange berries. Figure 157-159

Distribution: Golden dewdrop is native to Key West, Florida. It and related species are naturalized in southern Texas, are common in the West Indies, and are cultivated elsewhere, particularly in Hawaii and Guam.

Toxic Part: The berry is poisonous.

Toxin: Saponin

Symptoms: Human intoxications have been reported from Australia only. Poisoning is reputed to cause somnolence, increased body temperature, mydriasis, tachycardia, edema of lips and eyelids, and convulsions. Gastrointestinal irritation may occur.

Management: Remove plant material from the stomach. Maintain fluid and electrolyte balance. Control convulsions with diazepam.

References:

Everist S: *Poisonous Plants of Australia*. Sydney, Angus and Robertson, 1974, 519-520.

━━━━━━━━━

Echium species
Family: Boraginaceae

E. plantagineum L. (= *E. lycopsis* L.)
E. vulgare L.

Trivial Names: Viper's Bugloss, Blue Devil or Weed, Snake Flower, Vipérine (Canada)

Description: *Echium* are biennial plants. The erect stems grow to a height of about 2 feet and are speckled with red and bristly. The alternate leaves are oblong, prickly, and about 6 inches long. The bright blue flowers grow in spikes. The fruit are small nutlets. Figure 160

Distribution: These Eurasian plants are now widespread weeds in eastern North America; they are encountered infrequently west of the Mississippi but grow throughout transcontinental Canada. They are present also in Hawaii.

Toxic Part: The whole plant is poisonous.

Toxin: Pyrrolizidine alkaloids

Symptoms: Toxicity is associated with use of the plant in herbal teas for folk medicine. The chronic consumption of these teas may cause veno-occlusive disease of the liver (Budd-Chiari syndrome) with hepatic vein thrombosis leading to cirrhosis. The symptoms are abdominal pain with ascites, hepatomegaly and splenomegaly, anorexia with nausea, vomiting, and diarrhea.

Management: There is no known specific therapy for toxin-induced hepatic veno-occlusive disease.

References:

Bull LB, et al: *The Pyrrolizidine Alkaloids. Their Chemistry, Pathogenicity, and Other Biological Properties*. New York, Wiley-Interscience, 1968.

Huxtable RJ: Herbal teas and toxins: Novel aspects of pyrrolizidine poisoning in the United States. *Perspec Biol Med* 24:1-14, 1980.

McLean EK, Mattocks AR: Environmental liver injury: Plant toxins, in Farber E, Fisher MM (eds): *Toxic Injury of the Liver, Part B*. New York, Marcel Dekker, 1980, 517-539.

Peterson JE, Culvenor CCJ: Hepatotoxic pyrrolizidine alkaloids, in Keeler RF, Tu AT (eds): *Plant and Fungal Toxins*. New York, Marcel Dekker, 1983, 637-671.

Schoental R: Biochemical basis of liver necrosis caused by pyrrolizidine alkaloids and certain other hepatotoxins. *Biochem Soc Trans* 3:292-294, 1975.

Smith LW, Culvenor CCJ: Plant sources of hepatotoxic pyrrolizidine alkaloids. *J Nat Prod* 44:129-152, 1981.

Epipremnum aureum (Linden & André) Bunt.
(= *Pothos aureus* Linden & André; *Raphidophora aurea* Birdsey; *Scindapsus aureus* Engl.)
Family: Araceae

Trivial Names: Pothos, Amapalo Amarillo (Puerto Rico), Devil's Ivy, Golden Ceylon Creeper, Golden Hunter's Robe, Golden Pothos, Hunter's Robe, Ivy Arum, Malanga Trepadora (Cuba), Solomon Island Ivy, Taro Vine, Variegated Philodendron

Description: The pothos is a climbing vine with large (up to 30 inches) heart-shaped leaves that are usually streaked with yellow. Figure 161

Distribution: Pothos is an outdoor plant in the West Indies, southern Florida, Hawaii, and Guam, growing on trees for support up to a height of 40 feet. It is ubiquitous elsewhere as an indoor pot plant, either supported or in hanging baskets, where the leaves grow to only a few inches in length.

Toxic Part: The whole plant is injurious.

Toxin: Calcium oxalate raphides and, possibly, other unidentified irritants

Symptoms: Ingestion by young children is often associated with diarrhea. The plant also causes dermatitis.

Management: No specific intervention is indicated. However, care should be taken to prevent dehydration in infants and very young children.

References:
Mitchell JC, Rook AJ: *Scindapsus* dermatitis. *Contact Dermatitis* 2:125, 1976

Eriobotrya japonica (Thunb.) Lindl.
Family: Rosaceae

Trivial Names: Loquat, Japanese Medlar, Japanese Plum, Níspero del Japón (Cuba, Puerto Rico)

Description: This small evergreen tree grows to about 20 feet. The large stiff leaves are rough to the touch and 8 to 12 inches in length. The fragrant, dingy white flowers grow in clusters. The fruit is pear-shaped, yellow, and about 3 inches long. Figure 163-164

Distribution: The loquat is cultivated in California, Florida, the West Indies, the Gulf coast states, and Hawaii.

Toxic Part: The pit kernel is toxic; the unbroken seed is harmless.

Toxin: Cyanogenetic glycoside that releases hydrocyanic acid on hydrolysis

Symptoms: Since the cyanogenetic glycosides must be hydrolyzed in the gastroenteric tract before cyanide ion is released, some hours may elapse before symptoms appear. Abdominal pain, vomiting, lethargy, and sweating then develop. Cyanosis is not inevitable. In severe intoxications, coma develops and may be accompanied by tetanic convulsions, muscle flaccidity, and incontinence.

Management: Conscious patients may require only gastric lavage. Activated charcoal adsorbs cyanide but releases it slowly during passage through the intestine. A 25% solution of sodium thiosulfate (300 ml for adults) instead may be instilled into the stomach following lavage. In unconscious patients or those who are losing consciousness, acidosis should be corrected, volume expanders given if shock is present or developing, respiratory assistance with oxygen should be instituted, and cyanide antidote should be administered.

References:
Polson CJ, et al: *Clinical Toxicology*, ed 3. Philadelphia, JB Lippincott, 1983, 162-166.

___

Euonymus species
Family: Celastraceae

E. americanus L.
E. atropurpureus Jacq.
E. europaeus L.
E. occidentalis Nutt. ex Torr.

Trivial Names:

E. americanus: **Strawberry Bush,** Bursting Heart, Hearts-Bursting-with-Love

E. atropurpureus: **Burning Bush,** Wahoo

E. europaeus: **European Spindle Tree**

E. occidentalis: **Western Burning Bush**

Description:

E. americanus: This small shrub has almost stemless leaves that are bright green and ovate, coming to a sharp point. The flowers are green-purple. The fruit is a warty capsule that is red when mature; it splits open to reveal a conspicuous, scarlet, fleshy aril to which the seed is attached. Figure 166

E. atropurpureus: This small tree branches close to the ground and has thin gray bark. The leaves are opposite and finely toothed along the margin. Flowers and mature fruit are purple. The fruit is a four-lobed capsule

79

with scarlet arils and a small brown seed. The fruit persists through winter.

E. europaeus: The European spindle tree resembles *E. atropurpureus*, but the flowers are yellow-green, the mature capsule is pink, and the aril is bright orange. Figure 167-168

E. occidentalis: This small tree grows to 20 feet. The leaves are opposite, broadest at the base (0.5 to 2 inches), and 1.2 to 3.5 inches long; they are finely toothed on the margin. Flowers are brownish purple. The fruit capsule has three lobes and is reddish purple when mature. The aril is red.

Distribution:

E. americanus: Strawberry bush grows from southeastern New York to Florida west to southern Illinois, Missouri, Oklahoma, and Texas.

E. atropurpureus: This species grows in Ontario and New York south to Georgia and west to North Dakota and Texas (excluding South Carolina and Louisiana).

E. europaeus: The European spindle tree was introduced from Europe. It spread from cultivation in Massachusetts to Wisconsin and southward.

E. occidentalis: The western burning bush grows on the Pacific coast from British Columbia to southern California.

Toxic Part: Intoxications have been reported only from the fruit of *E. europaeus*. The bark from *E. atropurpureus* once was used medicinally (Euonymus N.F. VII).

Toxin: *E. europaeus* contains evomonoside, a digitalis-like cardioactive glycoside; a number of alkaloids, principally evonine, which have not been evaluated; and a protein, which has been shown to inhibit protein synthesis in intact cells *in vitro*.

Symptoms: Ingestion of the fruit of *E. europaeus* is followed in 10 to 12 hours by watery diarrhea and persistent emesis. Fever, hallucinations, somnolence, coma, and convulsions have been reported. The bark of *E. atropurpureus* is cathartic and may produce emesis.

Management: Recommendation of therapy is difficult because the underlying toxic mechanism is unknown. Symptoms are consistent with poisoning by a plant

lectin acting on the intestinal wall. Treatment should
include aggressive replacement of fluids and electrolytes.

References:

Bishay DW, et al: Peptide and tetrahydroisoquinoline
alkaloids from *Euonymus europaeus*. *Phytochemistry*
12:693-698, 1973.

Frohne D, Pfänder HJ: *A Colour Atlas of Poisonous
Plants. A Handbook for Pharmacists, Physicians,
Toxicologists and Biologists*. London, Wolfe House,
1983, 87-88.

Gasperi-Campani A, et al: Seed extracts inhibiting
protein synthesis *in vitro*. *Biochem J* 186:439-441, 1980.

Hermkes L: An unusual poisoning from the fruit of the
spindle tree (Pfaffenhütchen). *Munch Med Wochenschr*
88:1011-1012, 1941. (In German)

Smith RM: The Celastraceae alkaloids, in Manske RHF
(ed): *The Alkaloids*. New York, Academic Press, 1977,
vol 16, 213-248.

Urban G: Pfaffenhütchen poisoning. *Sammlung
Vergiftungsfällen* 13:27-32, 1943/44. (In German)

von Oettingen WF: *Poisoning. A Guide to Clinical
Diagnosis and Treatment*, ed 2. Philadelphia, WB
Saunders, 1958, 361.

Zorbach WW, et al: Partial synthesis of evomonoside.
J Org Chem 27:1766-1769, 1962.

Euphorbia species
Family: Euphorbiaceae

E. cotinifolia L.
E. cyathophora J. Murr. (= *Poinsettia cyathophora*
Klotzch & Garcke; *E. heterophylla* of cultivation)
E. lactea Haw.
E. lathyris L.
E. marginata Pursh
E. milii Des Moulins
E. myrsinites L.
E. tirucalli L.

Trivial Names:

E. cotinifolia: Carrasco (Puerto Rico), Mala Mujer (Mexico), Red Spurge, Yerba Lechera (Cuba)

E. cyathophora: Corazón de María, Fiddlers Spurge, Fire-on-the-Mountain, Maravilla (Puerto Rico), Mexican Fire Plant, Painted Leaf

E. lactea: **Candelabra Cactus,** Candelero (Puerto Rico), Cardón (Cuba), Dragon Bones, False Cactus, Hatrack Cactus, Mottled Spurge

E. lathyris: Caper Spurge, Mole Plant, Myrtle Spurge

E. marginata: **Snow-on-the-Mountain,** Ghostweed, Mountain Snow

E. milii: **Crown of Thorns,** Christ Plant, Christ Thorn, Corona de Cristo (Puerto Rico), Couronne du Christ (Haiti), Gracia de Dios (Cuba)

E. myrsinites: Creeping Spurge, Donkey Tail, Spurge

E. pulcherrima: **Poinsettia,** Christmas Flower, Christmas Star, Easter Flower, Feuilles St-Jean (Haiti), Flor de Noche Buena (Mexico), Flor de Pascua (Cuba, Puerto Rico), Lobster Plant, Mexican Flame Leaf, Painted Leaf

E. tirucalli: **Pencil Tree,** Disciplinilla (Cuba), Esqueleto (Puerto Rico), Finger Tree, Indian Spurge Tree, Milkbush, Rubber Euphorbia

Description: The genus *Euphorbia* contains about 1,600 species of extremely variable form; plants may appear as herbs, shrubs, or trees. Many are cactus-like with thorns. Some species contain a milky latex. Figure 169-179

Distribution: *Euphorbia* are found throughout the United States, except Alaska. There are approximately 20 species in Canada. The genus is widespread in the West Indies and Guam.

Toxic Part: The latex of some species is poisonous.

Toxin: Complex terpenes (eg, euphorbol)

Symptoms: Primary irritant dermatitis occurs and may be severely corrosive, depending on the species of *Euphorbia*. Keratoconjunctivitis also can develop. Ingestion may produce gastritis.

Most inquiries on poisoning concern the poinsettia (*E. pulcherrima*), which has been found to produce either no effect (orally or topically) or occasional cases of vomiting. This plant does not contain irritant diterpenes.

Management: All patients experiencing protracted emesis after ingestion should receive fluids to prevent dehydration. This is particularly important in children.

References:

Crowder JI, Sexton RR: Keratoconjunctivitis resulting from the sap of candelabra cactus and the pencil tree. *Arch Ophthalmol* 72:476-484, 1964.

Dorsey C: Plant dermatitis in California. *Calif Med* 96:412-413, 1962.

Edwards N: Local toxicity from a poinsettia plant: A case report. *J Pediatr* 102:404-405, 1983.

Evans FJ, Soper CJ: The tiglane, daphnane, and ingenane diterpenes: Their chemistry, distribution and biological activities. *Lloydia* 41:193-233, 1978.

Hickey TA, et al: Irritant contact dermatitis in humans from phorbol and related esters. *Toxicon* 19:841-850, 1981.

Kingsbury J: *Poison Ivy, Poison Sumac, and Other Rash Producing Plants*. Cornell Ext Bull 1154, NY State College Agr, 1966.

Galanthus nivalis L.
Family: Amaryllidaceae

Trivial Names: Snowdrop

Description: The snowdrop blooms in early spring. There are two grass-like leaves about 4 inches long that appear with the flower. The single drooping flower is about 1 inch across and white marked with green. The fruit is a berry. Figure 182

Distribution: This plant is native to Europe and is cultivated in the northern United States.

Toxic Part: The bulb is poisonous.

Toxin: Lycorine

Symptoms: Ingestion of large quantities may produce nausea and persistent emesis with diarrhea.

Management: Human poisonings are uncommon because of the small concentration of alkaloids in this plant. Fluid replacement may be required if dehydration develops. See *Narcissus*.

References:
Jasperson-Schib R: Toxic Amaryllidaceae. *Pharm Acta Helv* 45:424-433, 1970. (In German)

Gelsemium sempervirens (L.) St. Hil.
Family: Loganiaceae

Trivial Names: Yellow Jessamine, Carolina Jasmine, Carolina Yellow Jasmine, Carolina Wild Woodbine, Evening Trumpet Flower, Madreselva (Mexico), Wood Vine, Yellow False Jessamine

Description: This perennial evergreen shrubby climber has lance-shaped, paired leaves that are about 4 inches long. The flowers are funnel-form, fragrant, and bright yellow; they are occasionally solitary but usually grow in clusters of up to six. The fruit is a small capsule with winged seeds. Figure 183

Distribution: *Gelsemium* is found in woodlands from eastern Virginia to Tennessee and Arkansas south to Florida and west to Texas. It is also in cultivation in these regions and in southern California.

Toxic Part: Most intoxications are associated with galenical preparations of this plant; however, there are cases of children who were poisoned after sucking on the flowers.

Toxin: Gelsemine, gelsemicine, and related alkaloids

Symptoms: Headache, dizziness, visual disturbances, and dry mouth with dysphagia and dysphonia result from poisoning. In severe cases, muscular weakness occurs and may be manifested by falling of the jaw and marked ptosis. There may be signs of a weak strychnine-like action, eg, tetanic contractions and extensor spasms of the extremities following tendon taps, general rigidity, trismus, rarely convulsions.

Management: Treatment consists of immediate evacuation of the gastric contents, instillation of a slurry of activated charcoal, administration of intravenous fluids, and respiratory support and airway management if indicated.

References:
Blaw ME, et al: Poisoning with Carolina jessamine. *J Pediatr* 94:998-1001, 1979.

Lampe K, Fagerström R: *Plant Toxicity and Dermatitis*. Baltimore, Williams & Wilkins, 1968, 177.

Gloriosa species
Family: Liliaceae

G. rothschildiana O'Brien
G. superba L.

Trivial Names: Glory Lily, Climbing Lily, Gloriosa Lily, Pipa de Turco (Cuba)

Description: These climbing lilies have tuberous roots and lance-shaped leaves tipped with tendrils. The flowers are striking, bright crimson and yellow with separated, finger-like petals. Figure 185

Distribution: *Gloriosa* are primarily cultivated and rarely have escaped in the extreme southern United States, the West Indies, and Hawaii.

Toxic Part: The whole plant is poisonous, particularly the tubers.

Toxin: Colchicine

Symptoms: Burning pain in the mouth and throat with intense thirst occurs immediately, followed by nausea and emesis. Abdominal pain and severe diarrhea develop after a two or more hour delay. Extensive fluid and electrolyte loss may lead to hypovolemic shock. Renal involvement is evidenced by hematuria and oliguria.

Management: Fluid replacement is required to prevent dehydration. The blood pressure and renal function should be monitored for an extended period. The intoxication has a prolonged course due to the slow excretion of colchicine. Analgesics and atropine may be required for severe colic and diarrhea. Muscular depression occasionally requires respiratory assistance.

References:

Angunawela RM, Fernando HA: Acute ascending polyneuropathy and dermatitis following poisoning by tubers of *Gloriosa superba*. *Ceylon Med J* 16:233-235, 1971.

Gilman AG, et al (eds): *The Pharmacological Basis of Therapeutics*, ed 6. New York, MacMillan, 1980, 718-720.

Gooneratne BWM: Massive generalized alopecia after poisoning by *Gloriosa Superba*. *Br Med J* 1:1023-1024, 1966.

Murray SS, et al: Acute toxicity after excessive ingestion of colchicine. *Mayo Clin Proc* 58:528-532, 1983.

Sauder P, et al: Haemodynamic studies in eight cases of acute colchicine poisoning. *Human Toxicol* 2:169-173, 1983.

Gymnocladus dioicus (L.) K. Koch
Family: Leguminosae (Fabaceae)

Trivial Names: Kentucky Coffee Bean or Tree, American Coffee Berry, Chicot or Gros Févier (Canada), Coffee Bean, Kentucky Mahogany, Nicker Tree, Stump Tree

Description: *Gymnocladus* is a large tree that grows up to 100 feet. Leaves are twice-compound and feather-like. The greenish white flowers grow in bunches. The distinctive flat bulging pods are 3 to 6 inches long and 1 to 2 inches wide; thick black seeds are embedded in a green sticky pulp. The pods persist through winter. Figure 188

Distribution: *Gymnocladus* grow in southern Ontario south to New York and Virginia and west to eastern Nebraska; they are most common in western Ohio to Missouri.

Toxic Part: Seeds are toxic. The cytisine content of the seeds is quite low, and chewing one or two would not be expected to produce toxic effects. The roasted seeds have been employed as a coffee substitute.

Toxin: Cytisine (a nicotine-like alkaloid)

Symptoms and Management: If symptoms occur (eg, nausea, sweating), management should be as for *Laburnum anagyroides*.

Hedera species
Family: Araliaceae

H. canariensis Willd.
H. helix L.

Trivial Names:

H. canariensis: **Algerian Ivy,** Canary Ivy, Madeira Ivy

H. helix: **English Ivy,** Ivy, Yedra (Cuba)

Description: *Hedera* are climbing vines commonly cultivated as wall covers. The leaves usually have five lobes on juvenile shoots and on root-bearing stems. Mature sections usually have nonlobed leaves on root-free stems. Berries are black and globular. Figure 189-191

Distribution: Ivy is commonly employed in the northeastern United States, but is cultivated everywhere. These plants have escaped in some areas, particularly in Virginia. They are common house plants.

Toxic Part: The berry and leaf are poisonous.

Toxin: Hederin, a saponin

Symptoms: Usually there is only a burning sensation in the throat. Sometimes gastroenteritis occurs with emesis and diarrhea.

Management: Conservative therapy is sufficient for gastroenteritis. Fluid replacement may be indicated, particularly in young children.

References:
Frohne D, Pfänder HJ: *A Colour Atlas of Poisonous Plants. A Handbook for Pharmacists, Physicians,*

Toxicologists and Biologists, London, Wolfe House, 1983, 61-62.

Kingsbury JM: *Poisonous Plants of the United States and Canada*. Englewood Cliffs, NJ, Prentice Hall, 1964, 371-372.

Heliotropium species
Family: Boraginaceae

H. angiospermum Murr. (= *H. parviflorum* L.)
H. curassavicum L.
H. indicum L.

Trivial Names:

H. angiospermum: Alacrancillo (Cuba), Crête Coq (Haiti), Cotorrilla (Puerto Rico), Dog's Tail (Jamaica), Mocos de Pavo (Dominican Republic), Rabo de Alacrán (Puerto Rico), Scorpion's Tail, White or Wild Clary (Barbados)

H. curassavicum: Alacrancillo de Playa (Cuba), Cotorrera de Playa (Puerto Rico), KIPUKAI or NENA (Hawaii), Seaside Heliotrope, Wild or Small Seaside Lavender (Barbados)

H. indicum: Alacrancillo (Cuba); Cotorrera, Yerba Cotorra, or Pico de Cotorra (Puerto Rico); Indian Heliotrope; Moco de Pavo (Puerto Rico); Scorpion Weed; Wild Clary (Barbados, Jamaica)

Description: *Heliotropium* are fleshy herbs, mostly annuals, that grow to 2 to 4 feet. The flowers are white, blue, purple, or pink and appear in scorpoid clusters (cymes). The fruit is a nutlet that separates into two parts, each with two nuts. Figure 192

Distribution: *H. curassavicum* may be found throughout the United States (except Alaska), in southwestern Canada, Mexico, and the West Indies. *H. angiospermum* and *H. indicum*, an Old World plant, are pantropical species in Florida and the West Indies.

Toxic Part: The whole plant is poisonous.

Toxin: Pyrrolizidine alkaloids

Symptoms: Toxicity is associated with use of the plant in herbal teas for folk medicine. The chronic consumption of these teas may cause veno-occlusive disease of the liver (Budd-Chiari syndrome) with hepatic vein thrombosis leading to cirrhosis. The symptoms are abdominal pain with ascites, hepatomegaly and splenomegaly, anorexia with nausea, vomiting, and diarrhea.

Management: There is no known specific therapy for toxin-induced hepatic veno-occlusive disease.

References:

Bull LB, et al: *The Pyrrolizidine Alkaloids. Their Chemistry, Pathogenicity, and Other Biological Properties*. New York, Wiley-Interscience, 1968.

Huxtable RJ: Herbal teas and toxins: Novel aspects of pyrrolizidine poisoning in the United States. *Perspec Biol Med* 24:1-14, 1980.

McLean EK, Mattocks AR: Environmental liver injury: Plant toxins, in Farber E, Fisher MM (eds): *Toxic Injury of the Liver, Part B*. New York, Marcel Dekker, 1980, 517-539.

Peterson JE, Culvenor CCJ: Hepatotoxic pyrrolizidine alkaloids, in Keeler RF, Tu AT (eds): *Plant and Fungal Toxins*. New York, Marcel Dekker, 1983, 637-671.

Schoental R: Biochemical basis of liver necrosis caused by pyrrolizidine alkaloids and certain other hepatotoxins. *Biochem Soc Trans* 3:292-294, 1975.

Smith LW, Culvenor CCJ: Plant sources of hepatotoxic pyrrolizidine alkaloids. *J Nat Prod* 44:129-152, 1981.

Helleborus niger L.
Family: Ranunculaceae

Trivial Names: Christmas Rose, Hellebore

Description: This evergreen perennial herb grows to 2 feet with stout rootstocks and ovate leaves that are slightly toothed at the apex. The flower is 2 to 3 inches across with five white or pinkish white petals. The fruit is a small capsule with many glossy black seeds. Figure 195

Distribution: Hellebores are of European origin and have escaped from cultivation in the northern United States and across Canada. Other *Helleborus* species, eg, *H. foetidus* L. (Fig. 193-194), *H. viridis* L., also have escaped in the northeastern United States.

Toxic Part: The whole plant is poisonous.

Toxin: Hellebrin, helleborin, and helleborein (digitalis-like glycosides); saponins and protoanemonin (direct irritants)

Symptoms: Pain occurs in the mouth and abdomen with nausea, emesis, cramping, and diarrhea. Digitalis glycoside toxicity has a variable latent period depending on the quantity ingested. Toxicity is usually expressed as conduction defects and sinus bradycardia. Hyperkalemia may be present. Rhythm disturbances other than escape beats usually do not occur.

Management: Gastric lavage or induced emesis should be performed. Activated charcoal may be given repeatedly. Saline cathartics also may be useful. Electrocardiographic monitoring and serum potassium determinations also should be done. Conduction defects may require the use of atropine or transvenous pacing. Phenytoin is the agent of choice for rhythm disturbances. Dialysis and forced diuresis are not useful.

References:

Ekins BR, Watanabe AS: Acute digoxin poisoning: Review of therapy. *Am J Hosp Pharm* 35:268-277, 1978.

Frohne D, Pfänder HJ: *A Colour Atlas of Poisonous Plants. A Handbook for Pharmacists, Doctors, Toxicologists, and Biologists.* London, Wolfe House, 1983, 176-177.

Morton J: Poisonous and injurious higher plants and fungi, in Tedeschi C, et al (eds): *Forensic Medicine.* Philadelphia, WB Saunders Co, 1977, 1526-1527.

Hippobroma longiflora **(L.) G. Don**
(= *Isotoma longiflora* (L.) Presl.; *Laurentia longiflora* (L.) Peterm.)
Family: Campanulaceae

Trivial Names: Cipril (Puerto Rico), Feuilles Crabe (Haiti), Ginbey (Dominican Republic), Horse Poison or

Madame Fate (Jamaica), PUA-HOKU (Hawaii), Revienta Caballos (Cuba), Star-of-Bethlehem, Tibey (Puerto Rico)

Description: *Hippobroma* are mostly unbranched perennial herbs with a milky latex. The simple alternate leaves are about 8 inches long. The funnel-form flower is long (2 to 3 inches), narrow (1/4 inch), and white. Figure 201

Distribution: This plant is a weed in the tropics, throughout the West Indies, Hawaii, and Guam.

Toxic Part: All parts of this plant are poisonous.

Toxin: Diphenyl lobelidiol (similar to the central nervous system stimulant lobeline)

Symptoms: Convulsions result from *Hippobroma* poisoning.

Management: Secure a patent airway and support respiration if indicated. Persistent convulsions may respond to intravenous diazepam.

References:

Arthur HR, Chan RPK: A new alkaloid from *Isotoma longiflora. J Chem Soc* 750-751, 1963.

Sánchez GC: Pharmacology of *Isotoma longiflora. Revista Med Exp* (Peru) 4:284-318, 1945. (In Spanish) *Chem Abs* 42:1350G, 1948.

Hippomane mancinella **L.**
Family: Euphorbiaceae

Trivial Names: Manchineel, Beach Apple, Mancenillier (Haiti), Manzanillo (Cuba, Puerto Rico, Dominican Republic)

Description: This deciduous tree grows to about 30 feet and has thick gray bark. The leaves are elliptical and glossy. The fruit resembles a small crabapple and has a pleasant odor. The white latex blackens on exposure to air. Figure 202-203

Distribution: This plant grows in the Florida everglades and is common in the West Indies.

Toxic Part: The latex is toxic.

Toxin: Hippomane A and B, diterpenes with a daphnane skeleton; hippomane A (or M), identical to huratoxin (from *Hura crepitans*)

Symptoms: Chewing on the fruit without swallowing may produce severe oral pain, profound salivation, and dysphagia after one or two hours. The lips become blistered and swollen and the mouth can be opened only with difficulty. The tongue, gums, buccal mucosa, and palate desquamate in large patches. Ingestion usually produces emesis, extremely painful gastritis, and bloody diarrrhea. Fluid loss may lead to hypovolemic shock.

The latex produces both direct and allergic contact dermatitis and keratoconjunctivitis. Inhalation of the sawdust causes cough, rhinitis, laryngitis, and bronchitis.

Management: Fluid replacement is required after ingestion to prevent dehydration. Demulcents may be given and analgesics can be considered for pain.

References:

Adolf W, Hecker E: On the active principles of the spurge family, X. Skin irritants, cocarcinogens, and cryptic cocarcinogens from the latex of the manchineel tree. *J Nat Prod* 47:482-496, 1984.

Earle KV: Toxic effects of *Hippomane mancinella*. *Trans Roy Soc Trop Med Hyg* 32:363-370, 1938.

Grant W: *Toxicology of the Eye*, ed 2. Springfield, Charles C Thomas, 1974, 641-642.

Rao KV: Toxic principles of *Hippomane mancinella*. *Planta Medica* 25:166-177, 1974.

Rao KV: Toxic principles of *Hippomane mancinella* . II. Structure of hippomane A. *Lloydia* 40:169-172, 1977.

Woods B, Calnan CD: Toxic woods. *Br J Dermatol* 95(suppl 13):1-97, 1976.

Hura crepitans L.
Family: Euphorbiaceae

Trivial Names: Javillo (Dominican Republic, Puerto Rico), Molinillo (Puerto Rico), Monkey's Dinner Bell,

Monkey Pistol, Possum Wood, Sablier (Haiti), Salvadera (Cuba), Sandbox Tree

Description: This tree grows to a height of 60 feet or more with a trunk diameter of over 3 feet at the base. The trunk and exposed roots are covered by short woody thorns. The leaves are oval, slightly serrate, and approximately 7 to 8 inches long. The green, inverted, cone-shaped male flowers are 1.5 to 2 inches long; female flowers are bright red. The woody fruits resemble a small pumpkin and are about 3 inches wide and 1.5 inches thick. The fruit pod explodes with considerable force on drying and makes a popping noise that is used in several of its common names. The seeds are round and flat. Figure 205-207

Distribution: *H. crepitans* has limited distribution in southern Florida and Hawaii; it is common in the West Indies.

Toxic Part: The seeds are poisonous.

Toxin: Hurin (crepitin), a plant lectin (toxalbumin), inhibits protein synthesis in the intestinal wall. Huratoxin, an ester of the diterpene daphnane, also is present and is presumed to be nontoxic in man; however, it may cause irritant dermatitis.

Symptoms: After a latent period of several hours, nausea, emesis, and diarrhea occur. Other effects are due to extensive fluid and electrolyte loss. The sap may produce keratoconjunctivitis and direct irritant dermatitis.

Management: Correction of dehydration and electrolyte losses and parenteral alimentation may be required. The ingestion of more than two or three seeds should be considered life-threatening.

References:

Blohm H: *Poisonous Plants of Venezuela*. Cambridge, Harvard University Press, 1962, 51-53.

Jaffé WG, Seidl D: Crepitin, a phytohemagglutinin from *Hura crepitans*. *Experientia* 25:891-892, 1969.

McPherson A, Hoover S: Purification of mitogenic proteins from *Hura crepitans* and *Robinia pseudoacacia*. *Biochem Biophys Res Com* 89:713-720, 1979.

Sakata K, et al: Structure and stereochemistry of huratoxin, a piscicidal constituent of *Hura crepitans*. *Tetrahedron Lett* No. 16:1141-1144, 1971.

Woods B, Calnan CD: Toxic woods. *Br J Dermatol* 95(suppl 13):1-97, 1976.

Hydrangea macrophylla (Thunb.) Ser.
Family: Saxifragaceae

Trivial Names: Hydrangea, Hills-of-Snow, Hortensia (Cuba), POPO-HAU (Hawaii), Seven Bark

Description: Hydrangea is a large bush of up to 15 feet. The stems and twigs are usually reddish brown. The leaves are 6 inches or longer, dark green above, grayish and fuzzy beneath, and scalloped around the margin. The tiny white flowers are borne in huge clusters. Horticultural varieties may have rose, deep blue, or greenish white blossoms. The flowers are persistent, turning brown as they dry. Figure 209

Distribution: Hydrangea is cultivated in all parts of the United States and Canada.

Toxic Part: The flower bud is poisonous.

Toxin: Human toxicity is assumed to be due to a cyanogenetic glycoside (hydrangin), which releases hydrocyanic acid on hydrolysis.

Symptoms: Ingestion of significant quantities of the buds may produce cyanide poisoning. Since the cyanogenetic glycosides must be hydrolyzed in the gastroenteric tract before cyanide ion is released, some hours may elapse before symptoms appear. Abdominal pain, vomiting, lethargy, and sweating then develop. Cyanosis is not inevitable. In severe intoxications, coma develops and may be accompanied by tetanic convulsions, muscle flaccidity, and sphincter incontinence.

Management: Conscious patients may require only gastric lavage. Activated charcoal adsorbs cyanide but releases it slowly during passage through the intestine. A 25% solution of sodium thiosulfate (300 ml for adults) instead may be instilled into the stomach following lavage. In unconscious patients or those who are losing consciousness, acidosis should be corrected, volume expanders should be given if shock is present or

developing, respiratory assistance with oxygen should
be instituted, and cyanide antidote should be administered.

References:

Polson CJ, et al: *Clinical Toxicology*, ed 3. Philadelphia,
JB Lippincott, 1983, 162-196.

West E: *Poisonous Plants Around the Home*. Gainesville,
Florida, Agr Ext Serv Bull 175, 1960, 16-17.

Hymenocallis species
Family: Amaryllidaceae

Trivial Names: Spider Lily, Alligator Lily, Basket Flower,
Crown Beauty, Lirio (Spanish), Tararaco Blanco (Cuba),
Sea Daffodil

Description: The spider lilies are bulb plants with
strap-like leaves that emerge from the ground. The white
or yellow flowers form in an umbel at the end of a
solid, leafless stem. The fruit is a capsule. Figure 210-212

Distribution: These plants are native to the southeastern
United States and tropical America. They are popular for
cultivation.

Toxic Part: The bulbs are poisonous.

Toxin: Lycorine (emetic) and small amounts of related
alkaloids

Symptoms: Ingestion of large quantities may produce
nausea and persistent emesis with diarrhea.

Management: Human poisonings are uncommon
because of the small concentration of alkaloids in this
plant. Fluid replacement may be required if dehydration
develops. See *Narcissus*.

References:

Jasperson-Schib R: Toxic Amaryllidaceae. *Pharm Acta
Helv* 45:424-433, 1970. (In German)

Hyoscyamus niger L.
Family: Solanaceae

Trivial Names: Henbane, Beleño (Mexico),
Fetid Nightshade, Insane Root, Jusquiame (Canada), Poison
Tobacco, Stinking Nightshade

Description: These are hairy, erect, annual or biennial
weeds about 2 feet high with spindle-shaped roots.
The large leaves (8 inches) are coarsely and somewhat
irregularly toothed. The flowers emerge singly from
the main stem just above the leaves. They are greenish
yellow to yellowish white with a purple throat and
veins. The seeds are contained in a pod. Figure 213

Distribution: Henbane was introduced from Europe
and is found mostly in waste areas of the northeastern
United States. It also can be found sporadically, generally
in sandy prairie, across the United States to the Pacific
coast. It has been reported in all southern Canadian
provinces. Henbane has not been reported in Hawaii and
Alaska.

Toxic Part: The seed is poisonous.

Toxin: Belladonna alkaloids

Symptoms: Intoxication results in dry mouth with
dysphagia and dysphonia, tachycardia, and dry skin.
Elevation of body temperature may be accompanied by
rash. Mydriasis, blurred vision, excitement and delirium,
headache, and confusion may be observed. Hallucinations
are more common in children.

Management: If the severity of the intoxication warrants
intervention (hyperthermia, delirium), a slow
intravenous administration of physostigmine is repeated
until symptoms abate or cholinergic effects appear.
The initial pediatric dose is 0.5 mg; for adolescents and
adults, 2 mg. The duration of action of the belladonna
alkaloids is longer than that of physostigmine, and repeated
administration of the latter may be required.

References:

Kürkçüoğlu M: Henbane (*Hyoscyamus niger*) poisonings
in the vicinity of Erzurum. *Turkish J Pediatr* 12:48-56,
1970. (In English)

Ilex species
Family: Aquifoliaceae

I. aquifolium L.
I. opaca Ait.
I. vomitoria Ait.

Trivial Names:

I. aquifolium: **Holly, English Holly,** European Holly,
Oregon Holly

I. opaca: **American Holly**

I. vomitoria: **Yaupon,** Appalachian or Carolina Tea,
Cassena, Deer Berry, Emetic Holly, Evergreen Cassena,
Indian Black Drink

Description: *Ilex* are evergreen trees with stiff leathery
leaves. Fruit are usually bright red but may be yellow, as
in *I. vomitoria*. Figure 214-216

Distribution: *I. opaca* is native from Massachusetts to
Florida west to Missouri and Texas. *I. aquifolium* is
cultivated from Virginia to Texas, the Pacific coast states,
and British Columbia. *I. vomitoria* is native to the
Atlantic and Gulf coast states and North Carolina to Texas
and Arkansas.

Toxic Part: The fruit is poisonous.

The leaves are nontoxic and, in many species, are
brewed for their content of caffeine (or other xanthines).

Toxin: Saponins

Symptoms: Poisoning causes nausea and multiple episodes
of vomiting with occasional diarrhea.

Management: Conservative management is adequate for
gastroenteritis and includes administration of fluids to
prevent dehydration in young children.

References:

Rodriguez TD, et al: Holly berry ingestion: Case report.
Vet Human Toxicol 26:157-158, 1984.

West LG, et al: Saponins and triterpenes from *Ilex opaca*.
Phytochemistry 16:1846-1847, 1977.

Iris species
Family: Iridaceae

I. X *germanica* L.
I. X *germanica* var. *florentina* (L.) Dykes
I. pseudoacorus L.

Trivial Names: Flag, Iris, Fleur-de-Lis (Canada), Lirio Cárdeno (Cuba), Orris

Description: *I.* X *germanica* is a blue-purple bearded iris; var. *florentina* is white and *I. pseudoacorus* has a bright yellow flower with purple-veined leaves. Figure 217-218

Distribution: Irises are popular garden flowers. *I. pseudoacorus*, which is native to western Europe and northern Arica, has become naturalized in eastern North America.

Toxic Part: The rootstock is toxic.

Toxin: Unidentified (may be an irritant resin)

Symptoms: Poisoning has been reported only for these species of iris. Gastroenteric pain, nausea, vomiting, and diarrhea may occur.

Management: Fluid replacement is required to prevent dehydration, particularly in children.

References:
Fyles F: *Principal Poisonous Plants of Canada*. Ottawa, Canadian Dept Agr, Exp Farm Bull 39 (2nd Series), 1920,26.

Jatropha species
Family: Euphorbiaceae

J. cathartica Terán & Berland.
J. curcas L.
J. gossypiifolia L.
J. integerrima Jacq. (includes var. *integerrima* Jacq. and var. *hastata* (Jacq.) Fosb.)
J. macrorhiza Benth.

J. multifida L.
J. podagrica Hook.

Trivial Names:

J. cathartica: **Jicamilla** (Mexico/Texas)

J. curcas: **Barbados Nut, Physic Nut,** Cuipu (Mexico), Médecinier Béni (Haiti), Piñón (Puerto Rico, Dominican Republic), Piñón Botija (Cuba), Tártago (Puerto Rico)

J. gossypiifolia: **Bellyache Bush;** Frailecillo (Cuba); Higuereta Cimarrona, Tautuba, or Túatúa (Puerto Rico); Mala Mujer (Mexico); Médecinier Barachin (Haiti)

J. integerrima: **Peregrina** (Puerto Rico, Cuba, United States), Rose-Flowered Jatropha, Spicy Jatropha

J. macrorhiza: **Jicamilla** (Mexico/Texas)

J. multifida: **Coral Plant,** Don Tomás or Tártago Emético (Puerto Rico), Juca Cimarrona (Dominican Republic), Médecinier Espagnol or Papayc Sauvage (Haiti), Piñón Purgante (Mexico)

J. podagrica: **Gout Stalk,** Coral Vegetal (Cuba), Tinaja (Puerto Rico)

Description: This is a large genus of shrubs or small trees with variously formed leaves and flowers. The flowers are usually red and some resemble coral. Except in some Mexican species not included here, the fruit is a three-sided capsule, each section containing one seed. *J. gossypiifolia* usually is an annual, regardless of growing conditions; the stems of *J. macrorhiza* die above ground in winter; all other species are perennials of pantropical origin. Figure 219-225

Distribution: *J. cathartica* grows in Texas; *J. macrorhiza* is found in Texas, New Mexico, and Arizona. All other species are of New World origin but are now pantropical in distribution. *Jatropha* are popularly in cultivation.

Toxic Part: Seeds are poisonous.

Toxin: Jatrophin (curcin), a plant lectin (toxalbumin), and cathartic oils are toxic. The plant lectin inhibits protein synthesis in cells of the intestinal wall and may cause serious or fatal intoxication.

Symptoms: Unlike poisoning with other plants containing toxic lectins, the onset of symptoms (nausea, vomiting, and diarrhea) is usually rapid. Other symptoms are probably secondary to fluid and electrolyte loss and suppression of intestinal function. Severe poisoning may follow ingestion of a single seed.

Management: Dehydration should be corrected and parenteral alimentation should be instituted, if required.

References:

Consroe RF, Glow DE: Clinical toxicology of the "desert potato": Two case reports of acute *Jatropha macrorhiza* ingestion. *Ariz Med* 32:475-477, 1975.

Ho RKB: Acute poisoning from the ingestion of seeds of *Jatropha curcas*. Report of five cases. *Hawaii Med J* 19:421-423, 1960.

Joubert PH, et al: Acute poisoning with *Jatropha curcas* (purging nut tree) in children. *S Afr Med J* 65:729-730, 1984.

Morton JF: Poisonous and injurious plants and fungi, in Tedeschi CG, et al (eds): *Forensic Medicine*. Philadelphia, WB Saunders, 1977, 1497-1500.

Kalmia species
Family: Ericaceae

K. angustifolia L.
K. latifolia L.
K. microphylla (Hook.) Heller

Trivial Names: Mountain Laurel; American or Dwarf or Sheep or Wood Laurel; Big Leaf Ivy; Calf-, Kid-, or Lamb-Kill; Calico Bush; Ivy Bush; Spoonwood; Spoonwood Ivy; Wicky

Description: These evergreen shrubs have leathery leaves and white, pink, or purple flowers. Figure 226

Distribution: *K. angustifolia* grows in eastern North America from Ontario to Labrador east to Nova Scotia and south to Michigan, Virginia, and Georgia. *K. latifolia* grows in the northeastern United States but not in Canada. *K. microphylla* occurs from Alaska to central California.

Toxic Part: The leaves and nectar (in honey) are poisonous.

Toxin: Grayanotoxins (andromedotoxins)

Symptoms: Transient burning in the mouth develops after ingestion. After several hours, increased salivation, emesis, diarrhea, and a prickling sensation of the skin occur. The patient may complain of headache, muscular weakness, and dimness of vision. Bradycardia is followed by severe hypotension. Coma may develop and convulsions are the terminal event.

Management: Fluid replacement is required and respiratory support if indicated. Atropine is administered as required for bradycardia. Ephedrine should be given if hypotension does not respond to replacement of fluids and positioning. Monitor the electrocardiogram. Recovery is complete within 24 hours.

References:

Carey FM, et al: Pharmacological and chemical observations on some toxic nectars. *J Pharm Pharmacol* 11:269T-274T, 1959.

Catterall WA: Neurotoxins that act on voltage-sensitive sodium channels in excitable membranes. *Ann Rev Pharmacol Toxicol* 20:15-43, 1980.

Honerjäger P: Ceveratrum alkaloids: Progress in understanding their membrane and inotropic actions. *Trends Pharmacol Sci* 4:258-262, 1983.

Kakisawa H, et al: Stereochemistry of grayanotoxins. *Tetrahedron* 21:3091-3104. 1965.

Kumazawa A, Iriye R: Stereochemistry of grayanotoxin II. *Tetrahedron Lett* 12:927-930, 1970.

Moran NC, et al: Pharmacological actions of andromedotoxin, an active principle from *Rhododendron maximum*. *J Pharmacol Exp Therap* 110:415-432, 1954.

Scott PM, et al: Grayanotoxins. Occurrence and analysis in honey and a comparison of toxicities in mice. *Fd Cosmet Toxicol* 9:179-184, 1971.

White JW Jr, Riethof ML: Composition of honey. III. Detection of acetylandromedol in toxic honeys. *Arch Biochem Biophys* 79:165-167, 1959.

Karwinskia humboldtiana (Roemer & Schultes) Zucc.
Family: Rhamnaceae

Trivial Names: Buckthorn, Coyotillo, Tullidora

Description: This shrubby tree grows to about 6 feet. Leaves are opposite and elliptical, 1 to 2 inches long. The berry-shaped fruit turns black when mature and contains a pit. Figure 227

Distribution: *Karwinskia* grows in western Texas and New Mexico.

Toxic Part: The fruit is poisonous.

Toxin: Anthracenones

Symptoms: Progressive bilateral ascending paralytic neuropathy (demyelination) may terminate in respiratory paralysis. Weakness occurs only after a latent period of several weeks and paralysis may progress for a month or more.

Management: Treatment is only supportive. In patients who survive, improvement progresses slowly to almost complete functional recovery.

References:

Arai I, et al: Neurotoxins of *Karwinskia humboldtiana*. Atropisomerism and diastereomeric oxidation products. *J Org Chem* 43:1253-1254, 1978.

Calderon-Gonzalez R, Rizzi-Hernandez H: Buckthorn polyneuropathy. *N Engl J Med* 277:69-71, 1967.

Carrada-Bravo T, et al: Outbreak of polyradiculoneuritis from tullidora *Karwinskia humboldtiana*. *Bol Med Hosp Infantil Mex* 40:139-147, 1983. (In Spanish)

Dreyer DL, et al: Toxins causing noninflammatory paralytic neuronopathy. Isolation and structure elucidation. *J Am Chem Soc* 97:4985-4990, 1975.

Gonzalez GH: Polyneuropathy secondary to *Karwinskia humboldtiana* induced demyelination. Thesis, University of Miami, Coral Gables, FL, 1971.

Mitchell J, et al: Buckthorn neuropathy: Effects of

intraneural injection of *Karwinskia humboldtiana* toxins. *Neuropathol Appl Neurobiol* 4:85-97, 1978.

_____

Laburnum anagyroides Medic (= *Cytisus laburnum* Bercht. & J. Presl.)
Family: Leguminosae (Fabaceae)

Trivial Names: Golden Chain, Bean Tree, Laburnum

Description: This small tree grows to 30 feet and bears golden-yellow, sweetpea-shaped flowers in masses. The seeds are contained in flattened pods. Figure 228-230

Distribution: *Laburnum* is widely cultivated in the southern United States.

Toxic Part: All parts of the plant, particularly the seeds, are poisonous.

Toxin: Cytisine, an alkaloid pharmacologically related to nicotine

Symptoms: Ingestion is followed rapidly by emesis, drowsiness, weakness, incoordination, sweating, pallor, headache, mydriasis, and tachycardia.

Management: An oral slurry of activated charcoal should be administered when vomiting subsides. If emesis has not occurred spontaneously, the stomach should be evacuated first. Treatment is otherwise supportive. Ingestion of massive amounts may require controlled respiration as in nicotine poisoning. Severe constipation and urinary retention are occasional late complications and respond to bethanechol.

References:

Bramley A, Goulding R: Laburnum "poisoning." *Br Med J* 283:1220-1221, 1981.

Mitchell RG: Laburnum poisoning in children. *Lancet* 2:57-58, 1951.

Richards HGH, Stephens A: A fatal case of laburnum seed poisoning. *Med Sci Law* 10:260-266, 1970.

Lantana camara L.
Family: Verbenaceae

Trivial Names: Lantana, Bonbonnier or Herbe à Plomb
(Haiti), Cariaquillo (Puerto Rico), Cinco Negritos
(Mexico), Filigrana (Cuba), LAKANA, MIKINOLIA-HIHIU
(Hawaii), Shrub Verbena, Yellow Sage

Description: Lantanas are sprawling shrubs with squarish
prickly stems. The opposite leaves are coarse and have
a pronounced odor when crushed. Flowers grow in flat
clusters. The individual flowers in a cluster change
color gradually over 24 hours after opening from yellow
to orange then red. The outer flowers open first, and
the flower assumes the appearance of concentric circles
with a bull's eye effect: yellow in the center, a
surrounding circle of orange, and an outermost circle of
red. Horticultural varieties may exhibit other color
combinations. Figure 231-232

Distribution: Lantanas are weeds in southern Florida,
Texas, California, Hawaii, Guam, and the West Indies.
These plants are cultivated as ornamentals in more
temperate areas.

Toxic Part: The immature berries are poisonous. No
intoxications have been reported following ingestion of
mature fruit.

Toxin: Unknown (not the phototoxin, lantadene A, as
stated in some publications)

Symptoms: Weakness, lethargy, emesis, diarrhea, mydriasis,
and bradypnea result from poisoning.

Management: Gastric lavage, fluids, and respiratory
support should be given if indicated. The onset of
poisoning may be delayed for two to six hours after
ingestion.

References:

Wolfson SL, Solomons TWG: Poisoning by fruit of
Lantana camara. Am J Dis Child 107:173-176, 1964.

104

Leucaena leucocephala (L.) de Wit
(= *L. glauca* Britt. & Millsp. non Benth.)
Family: Leguminosae (Fabaceae)

Trivial Names: Lead Tree, Acacia or Acacia Pálida
(Puerto Rico), Aroma Blanca (Cuba, Hawaii), Campeche
(Puerto Rico), Cowbush (Bahamas), EKOA or False
KOA (Hawaii), Grains de Lin Pays (Haiti), Granalino
(Dominican Republic), Guacis (Mexico), Hediondilla
(Puerto Rico), Jimbay or Jumbie Bean (Bahamas),
Jump-and-Go (Bahamas), KOA-HAOLE (Hawaii), Tantan
(Puerto Rico), White popinac, Wild Tamarind (Hawaii,
Puerto Rico), Zarcilla (Puerto Rico)

Description: These shrubs or small trees have feathery,
twice-compound leaves. The flowers are creamy white
and grow clustered in heads. There are numerous flat
pods that turn reddish when mature; each contains 18
to 25 brown seeds. Figure 235

Distribution: *L. leucocephala* grows in Florida, Texas,
Hawaii, Guam, the Bahamas, and throughout the West
Indies to Barbados. The seeds are in common use for
novelty jewelry.

Toxic Part: All parts of this plant are toxic, but it is
commonly eaten cooked in the West Indies and Indonesia.

Toxin: Mimosine, a toxic amino acid, inhibits DNA
synthesis. The toxin does not appear to be present in
significant quantity in the immature pod. It is destroyed
by roasting or cooking in an iron or aluminum vessel.

Symptoms: Ingestion causes loss of hair within 48
hours. In animals, consumption also results in cataract
formation and growth retardation.

Management: No treatment is available.

References:

Montagna W, Yun JS: The effects of seeds of *Leucaena
glauca* on the hair follicles of the mouse. *Invest
Dermatol* 40:325-332, 1963.

Tsai WC, Ling KH: Toxic action of mimosine. I.
Inhibition of mitosis and DNA synthesis of H.Ep-2 cell by
mimosine and 3,4-dihydroxypyridine. *Toxicon*
9:241-247, 1971.

Van Veen AG: Toxic properties of some unusual foods,
in *Toxicants Occurring Naturally in Foods*. Pub 1354,

National Academy of Sciences/ National Research
Council, Washington, DC, 1966, 174-182.

Leucothoe species
Family: Ericaceae

Trivial Names: Dog Hobble, Dog Laurel, Fetter Bush,
Pepper Bush, Switch Ivy, Sweet Bells, White Osier

Description: These deciduous or evergreen shrubs
have simple alternate leaves and white or pink flowers
that grow in clusters. Figure 236

Distribution: *Leucothoe* grow from Virginia to Florida,
Tennessee, Louisiana, and California.

Toxic Part: The leaves and nectar (in honey) are toxic.

Toxin: Grayanotoxins (andromedotoxins)

Symptoms: There is transient burning in the mouth after
ingestion followed after several hours by increased
salivation, emesis, diarrhea, and a prickling sensation in
the skin. The patient may complain of headache,
muscular weakness, and dimness of vision. Bradycardia is
followed by severe hypotension. Coma may develop
and convulsions are the terminal event.

Management: Fluid replacement should be instituted
with respiratory support if indicated. Atropine should be
administered as required for bradycardia. Ephedrine
should be used if hypotension does not respond to
replacement of fluids and positioning. Monitor the
electrocardiogram. Recovery is complete within 24 hours.

References:
Carey FM, et al: Pharmacological and chemical observations
on some toxic nectars. *J Pharm Pharmacol*
11:269T-274T, 1959.

Catterall WA: Neurotoxins that act on voltage-sensitive
sodium channels in excitable membranes. *Ann Rev
Pharmacol Toxicol* 20:15-43, 1980.

Honerjäger P: Ceveratrum alkaloids: Progress in
understanding their membrane and inotropic actions.
Trends Pharmacol Sci 4:258-262, 1983.

Kakisawa H, et al: Stereochemistry of grayanotoxins.
Tetrahedron 21:3091-3104, 1965.

Kumazawa A, Iriye R: Stereochemistry of grayanotoxin II.
Tetrahedron Lett 12:927-930, 1970.

Moran NC, et al: Pharmacological actions of
andromedotoxin, an active principle from *Rhododendron
maximum. J Pharmacol Exp Therap* 110:415-432,
1954.

Scott PM, et al: Grayanotoxins. Occurrence and analysis
in honey and a comparison of toxicities in mice.
Fd Cosmet Toxicol 9:179-184, 1971.

White JW Jr, Riethof ML: Composition of honey. III.
Detection of acetylandromedol in toxic honeys.
Arch Biochem Biophys 79:165-167, 1959.

Ligustrum vulgare L.
Family: Oleaceae

Trivial Names: Privet, Hedge Plant, Lovage, Prim

Description: This deciduous shrub has opposite elliptical
leaves with smooth margins that are 1 to 2.5 inches
long, dark green above, and lighter green beneath. Small
white flowers form in clusters followed by large numbers
of blue or black wax-coated berries, which persist through
winter. Figure 237-238

Distribution: The privet is native to the Mediterranean
region. It is cultivated as a hedge plant throughout
most of the United States and Canada, and it is naturalized
in eastern North America. It also is cultivated in Hawaii.
A number of other species having generally similar
appearance also are in cultivation.

Toxic Part: The whole plant, including the berries, is
toxic.

Toxin: Syringin (ligustrin), an irritant glycoside;
nuzhenids, secoiridoid glucosides

Symptoms: Ingestion of a large quantity of berries
causes colic, emesis, and diarrhea. Gastroenteritis may

persist for 48 to 72 hours. Fatalities in children have been recorded.

Management: In systemic poisoning, fluids should be replaced to prevent dehydration.

References:
Frohne D, Pfänder HJ: *A Colour Atlas of Poisonous Plants. A Handbook for Pharmacists, Physicians, Toxicologists and Biologists*, London, Wolfe House, 1983, 157-158.

Inouye H, Nishioka T: Concerning the structure of the nuzhenids, bitter tasting glucosides from *Ligustrum lucidum* as well as *Ligustrum japonicum*. *Tetrahedron* 28:4231-4237, 1972 (In German).

Kozlov VA, Gulyaeva TN: Poisoning by the fruit of the common privet. *Subdebno Meditsinskaya Ekspertiza* 26(3):56-57, 1983. (In Russian)

Lobelia species
Family: Campanulaceae

L. cardinalis L.
L. inflata L.
L. siphilitica L.

Trivial Names:
L. cardinalis: **Cardinal Flower,** Cardenal de Maceta (Mexico), Hog Physic, Indian Pink, Red Lobelia, Scarlet Lobelia

L. inflata: **Indian Tobacco,** Asthma Weed, Bladderpod Lobelia, Emetic Weed, Eye Bright, Gag Root, Kinnikinnik, Low Belia, Puke Weed, Wild Tobacco

L. siphilitica: **Blue Cardinal Flower,** Great Blue Lobelia, Great Lobelia, High Belia, Louisiana Lobelia

Description: *Lobelia* flowers are distinctive in having two small petals opposed by three large petals. The flowers may be blue, pink, red, yellow, or white.
Figure 239-241

Distribution: The lobelias are annual weeds in most of the United States and some (eg, *L. cardinalis*) are widely cultivated. *L. inflata* is cultivated as a drug plant. *L. cardinalis* grows on damp shores, meadows, and swamps in Minnesota east to Michigan north to Ontario east to New Brunswick south to eastern Texas and east to

Florida. *L. inflata* grows by road sides and in open woods in New Brunswick and Nova Scotia west to Ontario and south to Kansas, Arkansas, and Georgia. *L. siphilitica* occurs in rich moist woods and swamps in southwest Manitoba east to Ontario south to Texas and Louisiana and from Maine south to North Carolina.

Toxic Part: The whole plant is poisonous.

Toxin: Lobeline and related alkaloids (similar to nicotine)

Symptoms: Poisoning is uncommon except when plant extracts are employed in home medicine. *Lobelia* leaves are sold in the form of tea or tobacco as a psychoactive "herbal." The dry plant material has little activity. Poisoning resembles that produced by nicotine (see *Nicotiana* species) but is usually more transient. Lobeline was once used as a central nervous system stimulant in the treatment of respiratory depression and as an emetic.

References:
Sollman T: *A Manual of Pharmacology*, ed 8. Philadelphia, WB Saunders Co, 1957, 466-467.

Lonicera species
Family: Caprifoliaceae

L. periclymenum L.
L. tatarica L.
L. xylosteum L.

Trivial Names: Honeysuckle Bush, Fly Tataria, Woodbine Honeysuckle; Chèvrefeuille (Canada); Madreselva; Medaddy Bush

Description: *Lonicera* are shrubs or climbing woody vines. The flowers are two-lipped and yellow, pink, white, or rose. The fruit is a red berry. Figure 240-241

Distribution: Honeysuckles are extensively cultivated in the northeastern United States and Canada (Ontario, Quebec) and have escaped cultivation in these areas.

Remarks: Honeysuckle berries are eaten with impunity in the United States, but ingestion of berries from the same species has been associated with severe and even fatal poisoning in Europe. Severe and persistent emesis, colic, and diarrhea resulted. In severe intoxications, hypovolemic shock, cardiac arrhythmias, muscular twitching and convulsions, and respiratory failure also were reported. Some nonfatal poisonings were associated with the later development of blood dyscrasias. A more recent European review casts doubt on these earlier reports.

References:

Brugsch H: *Vergiftungen in Kindesalter*. Stuttgart, Ferdinand Enke, 1956, 177. (In German)

Frohne D, Pfänder HJ: *A Colour Atlas of Poisonous Plants. A Handbook for Pharmacists, Physicians, Toxicologists and Biologists*, London, Wolfe House, 1983, 76-78.

Gessner O: *Die Gift- Und Arzneipflanzen von Mittel Europa*. Heidelberg, Carl Winter, 1953, 636-637. (In German)

Schurno A: Observation on an intoxication from the berries of the tatarian honeysuckle. *Kinder-Arztliche Praxis* 26:357-360, 1958. (In German)

Lycium species
Family: Solanaceae

L. carolinianum Walter
L. halimifolium Miller

Trivial Names: Matrimony Vine, Box Thorn, False Jessamine

Description: These upright or spreading shrubs grow to 10 feet tall. The numerous branches sometimes have woody thorns. The flowers appear in clusters and are a dull lilac to pinkish color. The fruit is an elliptical scarlet berry about 3/4 inch in length. Figure 244

Distribution: *L. carolinianum* is native to the southeastern United States from Texas to Florida and north to South Carolina.

L. halimifolium, a Eurasian plant, is cultivated in all north temperate zones. It has escaped in the northeastern United States as far south as South Carolina and west to

Tennessee and Kentucky, across southern Canada, and in California.

Toxic Part: The leaves are poisonous.

Toxin: Unknown, possibly solanine glycoalkaloids or belladonna alkaloids

Symptoms: This plant is listed only because it has caused occasional fatalities in animals that have eaten the foliage. No cases of human poisoning have been recorded.

Lycoris species
Family: Amaryllidaceae

L. africana (Lam.) M.J. Roem (= *L. aurea* (L'Her.) Herb.; *Amaryllis aurea* L'Her.)
L. radiata (L'Her.) Herb. (= *Amaryllis radiata* L'Her.)
L. squamigera Maxim. (= *Amaryllis ballii* Hovey ex Bak.)

Trivial Names:

L. africana: Golden Hurricane Lily, Golden Spider Lily

L. radiata: Red Spider Lily, Spider Lily

L. squamigera: Magic Lily, Resurrection Lily

Description: *Lycoris* grow from bulbs. The linear leaves emerge from the ground and die back before the flowers emerge. Flowers are borne on a long, leafless stalk. The fruit is a capsule with a few smooth, black seeds. Figure 245-246

Distribution: These plants are native to the Far East. All are cultivated extensively. *L. radiata* has become naturalized in the southern United States.

Toxic Part: The bulbs are poisonous.

Toxin: Lycorine

Symptoms: Ingestion of large quantities may produce nausea and persistent emesis with diarrhea.

Management: Human poisonings are uncommon because of the small concentration of alkaloids in this plant. Fluid replacement may be required if dehydration develops. See *Narcissus*.

References:

Jasperson-Schib R: Toxic Amaryllidaceae. *Pharm Acta Helv* 45:424-433, 1970. (In German)

Lyonia species
Family: Ericaceae

Trivial Names: Fetter Bush, Cereza or Clavellina (Cuba), He Huckleberry, Male Berry, Male Blueberry, Pepper Bush, Pipe Stem, Privet Andromeda, Seedy Buckberry, Stagger Bush, Swamp Andromeda, Tetter Bush, Wicopy, Wicks

Description: These small evergreen or deciduous shrubs have white or pink flowers. Figure 247

Distribution: *Lyonia* grow along the Atlantic coastal plain from Rhode Island to Florida west to Arkansas and Louisiana. It is common in the West Indies.

Toxic Part: The leaves and nectar (in honey) are toxic.

Toxin: Lyoniol A (lyoniatoxin), which is chemically related to the grayanotoxins (andromedotoxins) of *Rhododendron* species

Symptoms: There is transient burning in the mouth after ingestion. After several hours, increased salivation, emesis, diarrhea, and a prickling sensation in the skin develop. The patient may complain of headache, muscular weakness, and dimness of vision. Bradycardia is followed by severe hypotension. Coma may develop and convulsions are the terminal event.

Management: Fluid replacement should be instituted and respiratory support if indicated. Atropine should be given as required for bradycardia. Ephedrine may be given if hypotension does not respond to replacement of

fluids and positioning. Monitor the electrocardiogram.
Recovery is complete within 24 hours.

References:

Carey FM, et al: Pharmacological and chemical observations
on some toxic nectars. *J Pharm Pharmacol*
11:269T-274T, 1959.

Catterall WA: Neurotoxins that act on voltage-sensitive
sodium channels in excitable membranes. *Ann Rev
Pharmacol Toxicol* 20:15-43, 1980.

Honerjäger P: Ceveratrum alkaloids: Progress in
understanding their membrane and inotropic actions.
Trends Pharmacol Sci 4:258-262, 1983.

Kakisawa H, et al: Stereochemistry of grayanotoxins.
Tetrahedron 21:3091-3104, 1965.

Kumazawa A, Iriye R: Stereochemistry of grayanotoxin II.
Tetrahedron Lett 12:927-930, 1970.

Moran NC, et al: Pharmacological actions of
andromedotoxin, an active principle from *Rhododendron
maximum*. *J Pharmacol Exp Therap* 110:415-432,
1954.

Scott PM, et al: Grayanotoxins. Occurrence and analysis
in honey and a comparison of toxicities in mice.
Fd Cosmet Toxicol 9:179-184, 1971.

White JW Jr, Riethof ML: Composition of honey. III.
Detection of acetylandromedol in toxic honeys.
Arch Biochem Biophys 79:165-167, 1959.

Malus species
Family: Rosaceae

Trivial Names: Apple, Manzana (Spanish), Pommier
(French)

Description: The apple is a deciduous tree with
flowers that form in simple clusters.
The fruit is a pome with seeds.

Distribution: Apple trees are widely cultivated in
temperate climates. The fruit is available commercially.

Toxic Part: Seeds are poisonous.

Toxin: Cyanogenetic glycoside

Symptoms: Apple seeds that are swallowed whole or chewed and eaten in small quantities are harmless. A single case of fatal cyanide poisoning has been reported in an adult who chewed and swallowed a cup of apple seeds.

Since the cyanogenetic glycosides must be hydrolyzed in the gastroenteric tract before cyanide ion is released, some hours may elapse before symptoms appear. Abdominal pain, vomiting, lethargy, and sweating then develop. Cyanosis is not inevitable. In severe intoxications, coma develops and may be accompanied by tetanic convulsions, muscle flaccidity, and incontinence.

Management: Conscious patients may require only gastric lavage. Activated charcoal adsorbs cyanide but releases it slowly during passage through the intestine. A 25% solution of sodium thiosulfate (300 ml for adults) instead may be instilled into the stomach following lavage. In unconscious patients or those who are losing consciousness, acidosis should be corrected, volume expanders given if shock is present or developing, respiratory assistance with oxygen should be instituted, and cyanide antidote should be administered.

References:

Kingsbury J: *Poisonous Plants of the United States and Canada*. Englewood Cliffs, NJ, Prentice-Hall, 1964, 385.

Polson CJ, et al: *Clinical Toxicology*, ed 3. Philadelphia, JB Lippincott, 1983, 162-196.

Manihot esculenta **Crantz** (= *M. utilissima* Pohl; *M. manihot* (L.) Cockerell; *Jatropha manihot* L.)
Family: Euphorbiaceae

Trivial Names: Cassava, Juca, Manioc, Manioka, Sweet Potato Plant, Tapioca, Yuca or Yuca Brava

Description: This bushy shrub grows to 9 feet. It has milky juice and alternate leaves that are deeply parted into three to seven lobes. The roots are long and tuberous. Figure 255

Distribution: Cassava is cultivated in Guam, Hawaii, West Indies, Florida, and the Gulf coast states.

Toxic Part: Primarily the roots are poisonous; the leaves contain variable concentrations of toxin.

Toxin: Cyanogenetic glycosides (linamarin and lotaustralin) undergo enzymatic or acid hydrolysis to liberate hydrocyanic acid.

Symptoms: Since the cyanogenetic glycosides must be hydrolyzed in the gastroenteric tract before cyanide ion is released, some hours may elapse before symptoms appear. Abdominal pain, vomiting, lethargy, and sweating then develop. Cyanosis is not inevitable. In severe intoxications, coma develops and may be accompanied by tetanic convulsions, muscle flaccidity, and incontinence.

Management: Conscious patients may require only gastric lavage. Activated charcoal adsorbs cyanide but releases it slowly during passage through the intestine. A 25% solution of sodium thiosulfate (300 ml for adults) instead may be instilled into the stomach following lavage. In unconsious patients or those who are losing consciousness, acidosis should be corrected, volume expanders given if shock is present or developing, respiratory assistance with oxygen should be instituted, and cyanide antidote should be administered.

References:
Lancaster PA, Brooks JE: Cassava leaves as human food. *Econ Bot* 37:331-348, 1983.

Nestel BL, MacIntyre R (eds): *Chronic Cassava Toxicity*. Ottawa, International Development Research Centre, IDRC-010e, 1973.

Polson CJ, et al: *Clinical Toxicology*, ed 3. Philadelphia, JB Lippincott, 1983, 162-196.

Melia azedarach L.
Family: Meliaceae

Trivial Names: Chinaberry; African Lilac Tree; Arbol del Quitasol (Cuba); Bead Tree; China Tree; False

Sycamore; Hog Bush; Indian Lilac; 'INIA (Hawaii); Lilas (Haiti, Dominican Republic); Lilaila, Alelaila, or Pasilla (Puerto Rico); Paradise Tree; Paraîso (Mexico); Persian Lilac; Pride of China; Pride of India; Syrian or Japanese Bead Tree; Texas Umbrella Tree; West Indian Lilac; White Cedar

Description: The chinaberry is a tree that grows to 50 feet. The compound leaves are composed of leaflets that are 2 inches long and serrated. The delicate purplish flowers are fragrant and grow in clusters. The fruit is a yellow globose berry, which persists after the leaves have been shed. It contains three to five smooth, black, ellipsoidal seeds. Figure 256-257

Distribution: The trees are commonly planted and have escaped widely in the south from Virginia to Florida west to Texas, in Hawaii, and in the West Indies and Guam.

Toxic Part: The fruit and bark are poisonous.

Toxin: Tetranortriterpene neurotoxins and unidentified gastroenteric toxins

There are genetic variations in toxin content. The fruit may be eaten with impunity in some areas.

Symptoms: There may be a prolonged latent period following ingestion. Faintness, ataxia, mental confusion, and stupor develop. Some patients experience intense gastritis, emesis, and diarrhea, which may lead to hypovolemic shock. Labored respiration, convulsions, and partial to complete paralysis also have been observed. Autopsies show gastrointestinal irritation, fatty degeneration of the liver, and hyperemia of the kidneys.

Management: Intoxications are extremely variable in severity and nature, depending on the toxin concentration. Fluid and electrolyte replacement are given as indicated. Otherwise, there should be individualized symptomatic care. Monitoring of renal and hepatic function is probably desirable.

References:

Carratala R: Fatal intoxication by the fruit of *Melia azedarach* L. (paraíso vegetal). *Revista Asoc Med Argentina* 53:338-340, 1939. (In Spanish)

Kiat TK: *Melia azedarach* poisoning. *Singapore Med J*
10:24-28, 1969. (In English).

Oelrichs PB, et al: Toxic tetranortriterpenes of the fruit of
Melia azedarach. *Phytochemistry* 22:531-534, 1983.

Menispermum canadense L.
Family: Menispermaceae

Trivial Names: Moonseed, Canada Moonseed, Raisin de
Couleuvre (Canada), Texas Sarsaparilla, Yellow Parilla
(Canada), Yellow Sarsaparilla

Description: This woody twining vine grows to 12
feet. The large broad leaves are 8 inches long and slightly
lobed, resembling grape leaves but with smoother
edges. The grape-like fruit forms in clusters and is bluish
black with a crescent-shaped pit. The plant may be
confused with wild grape. Figure 258-260

Distribution: Moonseed grows in moist wooded areas
from western Quebec to Manitoba and south to Georgia
and Oklahoma. Occasionally it is seen in cultivation
on arbors or fences.

Toxic Part: The fruit is poisonous.

Toxin: Alkaloids with picrotoxin-like activity

Symptoms: Convulsions result from poisoning with
Menispermum.

Management: Secure a patent airway and support
respiration if indicated. Persistent seizures may be
terminated with intravenous diazepam.

References:

Doskotch R, Knapp J: Alkaloids from *Menispermum
canadense*. *Lloydia* 34:292-300, 1971.

Sharma M: *The Isoquinoline Alkaloids*. New York,
Academic Press, 1972.

Momordica species
Family: Cucurbitaceae

M. balsamina L.
M. charantia L.

Trivial Names:

M. charantia: Balsam Pear, Bitter Cucumber, Bitter Gourd, Cundeamor (Cuba, Puerto Rico), Fuqua, Momordique à Feuilles de Vigne, Sorci, Sorrosie or Yesquin (Haiti), Wild Balsam Apple

M. balsamina: Balsam Apple

Description: *Momordica* are creeping vines with deeply cut leaves, trailing tendrils, and tubular yellow flowers. The warty yellow-orange pear-shaped or oval fruit contains bright red pulp. The fruit splits open at maturity to reveal the pulp and seeds. Figure 263-264

Distribution: These plants are common weeds in the Gulf Coast states, Florida, the West Indies, Hawaii, and Guam.

Toxic Part: The seeds and outer rind of ripe fruit are poisonous. The red aril surrounding the seeds is edible. Boiled leaves drained of the cooking water are eaten as vegetables in the Philippines.

Toxin: Momordin, a plant lectin (toxalbumin), interferes with protein synthesis in the intestinal wall. An unidentified hypoglycemic agent also may be present.

Symptoms: Delayed nausea, emesis, and diarrhea result from ingestion. Hypoglycemia occurs when large amounts have been consumed.

Management: The taste of *Momordica* fruit is disagreeable and the plant lectin is relatively weak; therefore, serious intoxications are unlikely but potentially serious. Care should be taken to replace fluid and electrolyte losses; parenteral alimentation may be required if intestinal function is severely compromised.

References:

Lin JY, et al: Isolation of toxic and non-toxic lectins from the bitter pear melon *Momordica charantia* Linn. *Toxicon* 16:653-660, 1978.

Morton JF: *Plants Poisonous to People in Florida and Other Warm Areas*, ed 2. Miami, published by the author, 1982, 73-74.

Monstera deliciosa Liebm.
Family: Araceae

Trivial Names: Monstera, Breadfruit Vine, Cerimán, Cerimán de Méjico (Cuba), Cut Leaf Philodendron, Fruit Salad Plant, Hurricane Plant, Mexican Breadfruit, Piñanona or Casiman (Mexico, Puerto Rico), Shingle Plant, Split Leaf Philodendron, Swiss Cheese Plant, Window Plant, Windowleaf

Description: *Monstera* are woody stemmed climbers similar to *Alocasia* except that the thick leaves are perforated with iregularly shaped and placed holes. Figure 265

Distribution: *Monstera* is native to Mexico. It is cultivated in the West Indies, Hawaii, and Guam and grown as a greenhouse plant elsewhere.

Toxic Part: The leaves are injurious. The spadix of some *Monstera* species is edible.

Symptoms: Painful burning of the lips and oral cavity occurs on ingestion. An acute inflammatory reaction develops, sometimes with blistering and edema of the tissues. Hoarseness, dysphonia, and dysphagia result. Due to the rapid onset of pain, plant material is rarely swallowed.

Management: The pain and edema recede slowly without therapy. Cool liquids or demulcents held in the mouth may bring some relief. Analgesics may be considered. The insoluble oxalates in these plants do not cause systemic poisoning in man.

References:

Mitchell J, Rook A: *Botanical Dermatology*. Vancouver, Greengrass, 1979.

Plowman T: Folk uses of new world aroids. *Econ Bot* 23:97-122, 1969.

Myoporum laetum Forst. f.
Family: Myoporaceae

Trivial Names: There are no common names in our geographical area.

Description: *Myoporum* is a large tree with a thick trunk that often has buttresses. The bark is pale grayish white. The leaves are elliptic, coarsely toothed, and about 3 inches long. A leaf held up to the light shows numerous distinctive small dark spots (glands) that make this tree easy to identify. Many small flowers form along the terminal branches. The fruit is a small ball, less than 0.25 inches in diameter, containing a single seed. Figure 270-271

Distribution: This tree is native to New Zealand but is planted extensively along streets in northern California.

Toxic Part: The greatest amount of toxin is contained in the leaves; however, reported intoxications in humans have involved only the fruit.

Toxin: (-)-Ngaione, an essential oil, is a furanoid sesquiterpene ketone.

Symptoms: Ingestion of the fruit produces persistent emesis, convulsions, and coma. Death was reported in a 1-year-old child.

Management: A patent airway should be assured and respiratory support provided if necessary. Fluid replacement should be given to prevent dehydration.

References:

Connor HE: *Poisonous Plants of New Zealand*, ed 2. Wellington, NZ, EC Keating, Government Printer, 1977, 128-131.

Hegarty BF, et al: Triterpenoid chemistry. XVII. (-)-Ngaione, a toxic component of *Myoporum deserti*. The absolute configuration of (-)-ngaione. *Australian J Chem* 23:107-117, 1970.

Pronczuk de Garbino L, Laborde A: Plants that are poisonous in Uruguay. *Clin Toxicol* 22:95-102, 1984.

Narcissus species
Family: Amaryllidaceae

N. poeticus L.
N. pseudonarcissus L.

Trivial Names: Daffodil, Jonquil, Narciso (Cuba, Mexico), Narcissus, Paciencia

Description: The *Narcissus* is native to Europe and North Africa; plants grown in the New World are mostly horticultural hybrids. The plant is grown from a bulb that is similar in structure and appearance to an onion. The leaves arise from the ground. The flowering stalk (scape) may have one or more blooms, which are usually white or yellow with a flat corona having a flaring trumpet emerging from the center. Figure 272

Toxic Part: Human poisoning has been associated only with ingestion of the bulbs, which were mistaken for onions.

Toxin: Lycorine and related alkaloids

Symptoms: Ingestion of large quantities can result in nausea, persistent emesis, and sometimes diarrhea.

Management: Systemic poisoning is infrequent. Fluid replacement may be indicated to prevent dehydration, particularly in children.

References:

Lampe K, Fagerström R: *Plant Toxicity and Dermatitis*. Baltimore, Williams & Wilkins, 1968, 20.

Litovitz TL, Fahey BA: Please don't eat the daffodils. *N Engl J Med* 306:547, 1982.

Wilson T: The common daffodil (*Narcissus pseudonarcissus*) as a poison. *Pharmaceutical J Pharmacist* (London) 112:141-142, 1924.

Nerium oleander L. (= *N. indicum* Mill.)
Family: Apocynaceae

Trivial Names: Oleander; Adelfa (Puerto Rico); Alheli Extranjero (Puerto Rico); Laurier Rose (Haiti); 'OLIWA,

'OLEANA, or 'OLINANA (Hawaii); Rosa Laurel (Mexico); Rose Bay or Rosa Francesa (Cuba)

Description: The oleander is a shrub that grows to 20 feet. The long narrow leaves are up to 10 inches long and usually occur in groups of three about the stem. Flowers form in small clusters and are red, pink, or white. The fluffy winged seeds develop in long narrow capsules, which are 3/8 inch in diameter by 5 inches long, and are dispersed by the wind. Fruiting is uncommon in cultivated plants. Figure 273-275

Distribution: The oleander is native to the Mediterranean. It is widely cultivated outdoors in warm climates and as a tub plant elsewhere.

Toxic Part: The whole plant is toxic, including smoke from burning, and water in which the flowers have been placed.

Toxin: Cardioactive glycosides similar to digitalis

Symptoms: Pain in the oral cavity, nausea, emesis, abdominal pain, cramping, and diarrhea develop after ingestion. Digitalis glycoside toxicity has a variable latent period, which depends on the quantity ingested and is usually expressed as conduction defects and sinus bradycardia. Hyperkalemia may be present. Rhythm disturbances other than escape beats are not necessarily exhibited.

Management: Gastric lavage or induced emesis should be performed. Activated charcoal may be given repeatedly later. Saline cathartics also may be useful. Electrocardiographic monitoring and measurement of serum potassium should be done frequently.

Conduction defects may require the use of atropine or transvenous pacing. Phenytoin is the agent of choice for rhythm disturbances. Dialysis and forced diuresis are not useful.

References:

Dickstein ES, Kunkel FW: Foxglove tea poisoning. *Am J Med* 69:167-169, 1980.

Ekins BR, Watanabe AS: Acute digoxin poisonings: Review of therapy. *Am J Hosp Pharm* 35:268-277, 1978.

Osterloh H, et al: Oleander interference in the digoxin

radioimmunoassay in a fatal ingestion. *JAMA* 247:1596-1597, 1982.

Shaw D, Pearn J: Oleander poisoning. *Med J Australia* 2:267-269, 1979.

Nicotiana species
Family: Solanaceae

N. attenuata Torr. ex S. Wats.
N. glauca Graham
N. longiflora Cav.
N. rustica L.
N. tabacum L.

Trivial Names: Tobacco, PAKA (Hawaii), Tabac (French), Tabaco (Spanish)

Description: *Nicotiana* may be annuals or perennials; the latter generally are large shrubs or small trees. The five-lobed flowers are distinctively tubular, flare at the mouth, and may be white, yellow, greenish yellow, or red. The fruit is a capsule with many minute seeds. The leaves are simple and opposite, usually have smooth edges, and often are broad, hairy, and sticky. Figure 276-278

Distribution:

N. attenuata grows from Idaho to Baja California east to Texas.

N. glauca is naturalized from South America in the southwestern United States, Hawaii, Mexico, and the West Indies.

N. longiflora is commonly cultivated as a garden ornamental. It has been naturalized in the United States along the Gulf of Mexico from Texas to Florida and north to the Great Lakes.

N. rustica is from South America and has been sporadically naturalized in eastern North America in southern Ontario, Minnesota to New Mexico in the western range, and Massachusetts to Florida in the east.

N. tabacum is the principal cultivated smoking tobacco.

Toxic Part: The whole plant is poisonous. Most acute intoxications result from ingestion of the leaves as a salad (particularly *N. glauca*), from the use of *N. tabacum* infusions for enemas as home remedy vermifuges, or from the cutaneous absorption of alkaloid during commercial tobacco harvesting.

Toxin: The specific toxin depends on the species but involves chemically related alkaloids, eg, nicotine in *N. tabacum*, anabasine in *N. glauca*.

Symptoms: Salivation, nausea, emesis, a sensation of sweating, dizziness, sensory disturbances, and clonic convulsions result from poisoning. Vasomotor collapse and failure of the muscles of respiration (curare-like action) can appear suddenly and early in the intoxication.

Management: Controlled ventilation and vascular support should be performed as indicated. The stomach should be evacuated and activated charcoal given. Recovery from the acute phase is fairly rapid, but there may be residual constipation and urinary retention.

References:

Gehlbach SH, et al: Nicotine absorption by workers harvesting green tobacco. *Lancet* 1:478-480, 1975.

Manoguerra AS, Freeman D: Acute poisoning from the ingestion of *Nicotiana glauca*. *J Toxicol, Clin Toxicol* 19:861-864, 1983.

Oberst BB, McIntyre RA: Acute nicotine poisoning. *Pediatrics* 11:338-340, 1953.

Oenanthe crocata L.
Family: Umbelliferae (Apiaceae)

Trivial Names: Water Dropwort, Dead Men's Fingers, Hemlock Water Dropwort

Description: This perennial grows to 5 feet. Its bundle of spindle-shaped roots (dead men's fingers) contain white latex, which turns orange on exposure to air. The stem is hollow and much branched. The leaves are compound. The white flowers form clustered balls (umbels). Figure 279

Distribution: *O. crocata* is a European plant and has been introduced accidently into marshy areas surrounding Washington, DC.

Oenanthe sarmentosa K. Presl ex DC (Fig. 280), which is common on the west coast from southwest Alaska and western British Columbia to central California, is not known to be toxic.

Toxic Part: The whole plant is poisonous, but most intoxications have involved ingestion of the roots.

Toxin: Oenanthotoxin, an unsaturated aliphatic compound, is closely related chemically to the toxin in *Cicuta* species.

Symptoms: Usually there is salivation and emesis initially, followed within minutes by convulsions.

Management: Establish a patent airway and assist respiration if indicated. Persistent convulsions respond to intravenous diazepam.

References:

Anet EFLJ, et al: Oenanthotoxin and cicutoxin. Isolation and structures. *J Chem Soc* 309-322, 1953.

Mitchell MI, Routledge PA: Hemlock water dropwort poisoning: A review. *Clin Toxicol* 12:417-426, 1978.

Ornithogalum species
Family: Liliaceae

O. thyrsoides Jacq.
O. umbellatum L.

Trivial Names:

O. thyrsoides: **Wonder Flower,** African Wonderflower, Chincherinchee (sometimes sold as "Star-of-Bethlehem" during Christmas)

O. umbellatum: **Star-of-Bethlehem,** Dove's Dung, Nap-at-Noon, Summer Snowflake

Description: These plants have onion-like bulbs and grass-like leaves. The flowers are borne in a cluster on an upright spike. Flowers of *O. thyrsoides* are white and

those of *O. umbellatum* are green and white. Seeds
are contained in a capsule. Figure 284-285

Distribution: These lilies are of Old World origin. *O.
umbellatum* has escaped and become naturalized in the
southeastern United States, in the prairies of Mississippi,
Missouri, Kansas, and eastward. Both species are common
garden plants.

Toxic Part: All parts of the plant are poisonous, particularly
the bulb.

Toxin: Convallatoxin and convalloside, digitalis-like
glycosides identical to those of lily-of-the-valley
(*Convallaria majalis*)

Symptoms: Pain in the oral cavity, nausea, emesis,
abdominal pain, cramping, and diarrhea develop after
ingestion. Digitalis glycoside toxicity has a variable
latent period that depends on the quantity ingested and is
usually expressed as conduction defects and sinus
bradycardia. Hyperkalemia may be present. Rhythm
disturbances other than escape beats are not necessarily
exhibited.

Management: Gastric lavage or induced emesis should
be performed. Activated charcoal may be given repeatedly
later. Saline cathartics also may be useful. Electrocardiographic monitoring and measurements of serum
potassium should be done frequently.

Conduction defects may require the use of atropine or
transvenous pacing. Phenytoin is the agent of choice
for rhythm disturbances. Dialysis and forced diuresis are
not useful.

The digitalis-specific antibodies, Fab fragments, may
become the management of choice for life-threatening
toxicity but are not generally available yet.

References:

Dickstein ES, Kunkel FW: Foxglove tea poisonings. *Am J
Med* 69:167-169, 1980.

Ekins BR, Watanabe AS: Acute digoxin poisonings: Review
of therapy. *Am J Hosp Pharm* 35:268-277, 1978.

Smith TW, et al: Treatment of life-threatening digitalis
intoxication with digoxin-specific Fab antibody fragments.

Experience in 26 cases. *N Engl J Med* 307:1357-1362, 1982.

Pachyrhizus erosus (L.) Urban
(= *Cacara erosa* (L.) Kuntze)
Family: Leguminosae (Fabaceae)

Trivial Names: Yam Bean, Chopsui Potato, Habilla (Puerto Rico), Jícama de Agua (Cuba), Jícamo (Mexico), Pois Cochon (Haiti), Pois Manioc (Haiti), Sargott, Wild Yam Bean

Description: Yam bean is a twining vine with large tuberous roots. The violet, sweetpea-like flowers grow in racemes and produce pods 4 to 6 inches long. Seeds are square or rounded, flat, and yellow, brown, or red. Figure 286

Distribution: This plant is cultivated in the southern Gulf coast states and has become naturalized in Florida, Hawaii, the West Indies, and Guam.

Toxic Part: The seeds and mature pods are toxic. The fleshy roots and the immature pods are edible.

Toxin: Saponin. Two other components, rotenone and pachyrrhizin, are insecticidal compounds that are not toxic to man.

Symptoms: Approximately one-half of a seed produces pronounced catharsis. The seeds have been employed as a vermifuge in folk medicine.

Management: Therapy may not be required. Care should be taken to prevent dehydration, particularly in young children.

References:

Quisumbing E: *Medicinal Plants of the Philippines*. Manila, Dept Agr Nat Resources Tech Bull 16, 1951, 416-418.

Pedilanthus tithymaloides (L.) Poit.
Family: Euphorbiaceae

Trivial Names: Slipper Flower, Slipper Plant, Candelilla (Mexico), Christmas Candle, Devil's Backbone, Fiddle Flower, Itamo Real (Puerto Rico), Japanese Pointsettia, Jew Bush, Redbird Flower or Cactus, Ribbon Cactus

Description: Slipper flower is a shrubby, succulent plant characterized by numerous zigzag stems. The leaves are alternate and ovate, 2 to 4 inches long, and pointed at the tip; they fall shortly after developing. Red shoe-shaped flowers appear on the ends of the stems. Milky white latex appears if the stem is cut. Figure 291-292

Distribution: This common house plant is cultivated in warm areas and grows in the West Indies, Florida, California, Hawaii, and Guam.

Toxic Part: The latex is poisonous.

Toxin: Euphorbol and other terpenes

Symptoms: Ingestion causes gastritis.

Management: Fluid replacement should be given as required if protracted emesis and diarrhea occur.

References:

Blohm H: *Poisonous Plants of Venezuela*. Cambridge, Harvard University Press, 1962, 60.

Oakes AJ, Butcher JO: *Poisonous and Injurious Plants of the U.S. Virgin Islands*. Washington, DC, Agricultural Research Service, US Department of Agriculture, miscellaneous publication No. 882, April 1962, 80-82.

Pernettya species
Family: Ericaceae

Trivial Names: There are no common names for this species in our geographic area.

Description: *Pernettya* are small evergreen shrubs with simple, alternate, leathery leaves. The white flowers usually appear singly. The fruit is a persistent white or brightly colored berry that lasts all winter. Figure 293

Distribution: *Pernettya* are native to Central and South America, New Zealand, and Tasmania. They only are in cultivation in the United States.

Toxic Part: The leaves and nectar (in honey) are poisonous.

Toxin: Grayanotoxins (andromedotoxins)

Symptoms: Poisoning can result from eating the leaves or honey made from plant nectar. A transitory burning in the mouth occurs on ingestion followed several hours later by salivation, emesis, diarrhea, and a prickling sensation in the skin. The patient may complain of headache, muscular weakness, and dimness of vision. Bradycardia is followed by severe hypotension. Coma and convulsions are terminal events.

Management: Fluid replacement and respiratory support are administered. Atropine is given for bradycardia. Ephedrine may be used for hypotension if replacement of fluids and positioning are inadequate. The electro-cardiogram should be monitored. Recovery is complete in 24 hours.

References:

Carey FM, et al: Pharmacological and chemical observations on some toxic nectars. *J Pharm Pharmacol* 11:269T-274T, 1959.

Catterall WA: Neurotoxins that act on voltage-sensitive sodium channels in excitable membranes. *Ann Rev Pharmacol Toxicol* 20:15-43, 1980.

Honerjäger P: Ceveratrum alkaloids: Progress in understanding their membrane and inotropic actons. *Trends Pharmacol Sci* 4:258-262, 1983.

Moran NC, et al: Pharmacological actions of andro-medotoxin, an active principle from *Rhododendron maximum*. *J Pharmacol Exp Therap* 110:415-432, 1954.

Scott PM, et al: Grayanotoxins. Occurrence and analysis in honey and a comparison of toxicities in mice. *Fd Cosmet Toxicol* 9:179-184, 1971.

White JW Jr, Riethof ML: Composition of honey. III.
Detection of acetylandromedol in toxic honeys. *Arch
Biochem Biophys* 79:165-167, 1959.

Philodendron species
Family: Araceae

Trivial Names: Philodendron, Bejuco de Lombriz
(Cuba), Paisaje (Puerto Rico)

Description: Philodendrons are mostly climbing vines
with aerial roots. The leaves are often large and variable
and two types are encountered: The first resembles
Alocasia but has more pronounced irregular notching
about the entire leaf margin. The other form (*P.
scandens* C. Koch & H. Sello subsp. *oxycardium* (Schott)
Bunt.), which is widely available in variety stores, has
heart-shaped or oblong leaves with smooth margins,
sometimes with variegated patterns. Figure 296-299

Distribution: Philodendron grows outdoors in warm
climates. It is probably the most popular house plant
in the United States.

Toxic Part: The leaves are injurious.

Toxin: Raphides of calcium oxalate and questionable
unidentified proteins

Symptoms: Painful burning of the lips, mouth, tongue,
and throat develop. Due to the rapid onset of pain,
plant material is rarely swallowed. Contact dermatitis is
common.

Management: The pain and edema recede slowly without
therapy. Holding cool liquids or demulcents in the
mouth may give some relief. The insoluble oxalate does
not produce systemic poisoning in man.

References:

Ayres S Jr, Ayres S III: Philodendron as a cause of
contact dermatitis. *Arch Dermatol* 78:330-333, 1958.

Dorsey C: Philodendron dermatitis. *Calif Med*
88:329-330, 1958.

Harris J: Dermatitis of the eyelids due to philodendron
(Scandens Cardatum) plants. *Arch Dermatol Syph*
45:1066-1068, 1942

Mitchell J, Rook A: *Botanical Dermatology*. Vancouver, Greengrass, 1979.

Plowman T: Folk uses of new world aroids. *Econ Bot* 23:97-122, 1969.

Phoradendron species
Family: Loranthaceae

P. rubrum (L.) Griseb. (= *P. quadrangulare* (H.B.K.) Kr. & Urb.)

P. serotinum (Raf.) M.C. Johnston (= *P. flavescens* (Pursh) Nutt.)

P. tomentosum (DC.) Gray

Trivial Names:

P. rubrum: Cepa Caballero (Cuba)

P. serotinum: (American) **Mistletoe,** False Mistletoe

P. tomentosum: Injerto (Texas, Mexico)

Description: Mistletoes are parasitic plants that grow on the trunks and branches of trees. These species have thick, leathery, smooth-edged, opposite leaves. The berries are globose, white and translucent in *P. serotinum* and *P. tomentosum* and pinkish in *P. rubrum*. Figure 300-302

Distribution:

P. rubrum is parasitic only on the mahogany (*Swietenia mahogani*) throughout its entire range: southernmost Florida, the Bahamas, Cuba, Jamaica, Haiti, Dominican Republic, and Puerto Rico.

P. serotinum is the mistletoe plant sold at Christmas. It is parasitic on deciduous trees in the southeast from New Jersey to Florida west to southern Illinois and Texas.

P. tomentosum grows from Kansas to Louisiana west to Texas and into Mexico.

Toxic Part: The leaves and stems are toxic. The berries may be toxic if consumed in large amounts.

Toxin: Phoratoxin, a toxic lectin (toxalbumin), inhibits protein synthesis in the intestinal wall.

Symptoms: Serious or fatal poisoning is rare. In the fatal cases reported, berries were the source of toxin. (Berries from the European mistletoe (*Viscum album*) are essentially innocuous.) After a delay of two or more hours, there are multiple episodes of emesis, abdominal cramping, and diarrhea.

Management: Treatment is similar to that for severe gastroenteritis. Fluids and electrolyte replacement should be given as indicated.

References:

Buster OC: Poisoning by mistletoe (*Viscum flavescens*). *Texas Courier-Record Med* 5:218-219, 1887-88.

Moore HW: Mistletoe poisoning: A review of the available literature, and the report of a case of probable fatal poisoning. *J South Carolina Med Assoc* 59:269-271, 1963.

Samuelsson G, Ekblad M: Isolation and properties of phoratoxin, a toxic protein from *Phoradendron serotinum* (Loranthaceae). *Acta Chem Scand* 21:849-856, 1967.

Physalis species
Family: Solanaceae

Trivial Names: Chinese or Japanese Lantern Plant, Ground Cherry, Husk Tomato, Alquequenje (Puerto Rico), Barbados Gooseberry, Battre Autour (Haiti), Cape Gooseberry, Coque Molle (Haiti), Coqueret (Canada), Farolito (Cuba), Gooseberry Tomato, Huevo de Gato (Cuba), Jamberry, Maman Laman (Haiti), Mexican Husk Tomato, PA'INA or POHA (Hawaii), Sacabuche (Puerto Rico), Strawberry Tomato, Tomates (Mexico), Tope-Topes (Dominican Republic), Vejiga de Perro (Cuba), Winter Cherry, Yellow Henbane

Description: There are about 17 species of *Physalis* growing in the United States. A large number are cultivated for their attractive Chinese lantern-like fruit pods. Inside the paper-like pod is a globose berry with minute seeds. When mature, the berries of some species are edible when raw or cooked. Figure 303-306

Distribution: *Physalis* plants are both native and cultivated throughout the United States (including Hawaii), central and eastern Canada, the West Indies, and Guam.

Toxic Part: The unripe berries are poisonous.

Toxin: Solanine glycoalkaloids

Symptoms: Solanine has little toxicity in adults, but fatal poisonings have occurred in children. Symptoms generally are restricted to gastroenteric irritation, which may be confused with bacterial gastroenteritis. A harsh, scratchy feeling may develop in the throat hours after ingestion. Diarrhea and elevated temperature may be present.

Management: Fluid replacement may be required to prevent dehydration and general supportive care as for gastroenteritis can be administered.

Phytolacca americana L. (= *P. decandra* L.)
Family: Phytolaccaceae

Trivial Names: Pokeweed (Polkweed); American Nightshade; Bledo Carbonero (Cuba); Cancer Jalap; Chongrass; Cocum, Cokan, or Coakum; Crow Berry; Garget; Indian Polk; Ink Berry; Pigeon-Berry; Pocan Bush; Poke; Pokeberry; Red Ink Plant; Red Weed; Scoke

Description: The pokeweed has a large perennial rootstock (up to 6 inches in diameter) from which stout, purplish, branching, leaf stalks emerge up to 12 feet in height. The plant has a strong, unpleasant odor. The single leaves are 4 to 12 inches long. Flowers are greenish white to purplish, small, and appear on the vertical stalk. The dark berries are purplish to black and are attached to the stalk by a short stem. Figure 307-308

Distribution: Pokeweed grows in damp fields and woods from Maine to Minnesota, southern Ontario to southwest Quebec, south to the Gulf of Mexico, Florida, and Texas and in Hawaii. It has been introduced in California where it is an occasional weed.

Toxic Part: The leaves and roots are poisonous. In some regions, the young sprouts and stems are boiled and eaten after discarding the cooking water or the cooked product may be purchased commercially in cans. The mature berries are relatively nontoxic. Intoxications generally arise from eating uncooked leaves in salads or mistaking the roots for parsnips or horseradish.

Toxin: Phytolaccatoxin and related triterpenes

Symptoms: After a delay of two to three hours, nausea and gastroenteric cramps, profuse sweating, and persistent vomiting develop, which are later accompanied by diarrhea. The intoxication may continue for up to 48 hours.

Management: Symptomatic treatment for pain and replacement of fluid to prevent dehydration, particularly in children, are required.

References:
Johnson A, Shimizu Y: Phytolaccinic acid, a new triterpene from *Phytolacca americana*. *Tetrahedron* 30:2033-2036, 1974.

Kang SS, Woo WS: Triterpenes from the berries of *Phytolacca americana. J Nat Prod* 43:510-513, 1980.

Lampe KF, Fagerström R: *Plant Toxicity and Dermatitis.* Baltimore, Williams & Wilkins, 1968, 31-34.

Morton J: Poisonous and injurious higher plants and fungi, in Tedeschi C, et al (eds): *Forensic Medicine.* Philadelphia, WB Saunders Co, vol III, 1977, 1523-1524.

Stout GH, et al: Phytolaccagenin: A light atom x-ray structure proof using chemical information. *J Am Chem Soc* 86:957-958, 1964.

Pieris **species**
Family: Ericaceae

P. floribunda (Pursh ex Sims) Benth. & Hook.
P. japonica (Thunb.) D. Don ex G. Don

Trivial Names: Fetterbush, Lily-of-the-Valley Bush

Description: *Pieris* are evergreen shrubs or small trees. The leaves are simple, usually alternate, and leathery. The flowers are usually white and grow in clusters. Figure 309-310

Distribution: *Pieris floribunda* is a bush that grows from Virginia to Georgia. *P. japonica*, a small tree from Japan, is widely cultivated in temperate climates, particularly the Pacific coast. Numerous horticultural varieties exist.

Toxic Part: The leaves and nectar (in honey) are poisonous.

Toxin: Grayanotoxins (andromedotoxins)

Symptoms: A transient burning sensation occurs in the mouth after ingestion, followed by salivation, emesis, diarrhea, and a prickling sensation in the skin after several hours. The patient may complain of headache, muscular weakness, and dimness of vision. Bradycardia followed by severe hypotension can develop. Coma may occur and convulsions develop. Ingestion of leaves has produced fatal poisoning in children.

Management: Fluid replacement should be initiated with respiratory support if indicated. Atropine can be given as required to treat bradycardia. If hypotension does not respond to fluids and positioning, ephedrine should be administered. The electrocardiogram should be monitored. Recovery is complete within 24 hours.

References:

Carey FM, et al: Pharmacological and chemical observations on some toxic nectars. *J Pharm Pharmacol* 11:269T-274T, 1959.

Catterall WA: Neurotoxins that act on voltage-sensitive sodium channels in excitable membranes. *Ann Rev Pharmacol Toxicol* 20:15-43, 1980.

Honerjäger P: Ceveratrum alkaloids: Progress in understanding their membrane and inotropic actions. *Trends Pharmacol Sci* 4:258-262, 1983.

Kakisawa H, et al: Stereochemistry of grayanotoxins. *Tetrahedron* 21:3091-3104, 1965.

Kumazawa Z, Iriye R: Stereochemistry of grayanotoxin II. *Tetrahedron Lett* 12:927-930, 1970.

Moran NC, et al: Pharmacological actions of andromedotoxin, an active principle from *Rhododendron maximum*. *J Pharmacol Exp Therap* 110:415-432, 1954.

Scott PM, et al: Grayantoxins. Occurrence and analysis in honey and a comparison of toxicities in mice. *Fd Cosmet Toxicol* 9:179-184, 1971.

White JW Jr, Riethof ML: Composition of honey. III.
Detection of acetylandromedol in toxic honeys.
Arch Biochem Biophys 79:165-167, 1959.

Podophyllum peltatum L.
Family: Berberidaceae

Trivial Names: May Apple, American Mandrake,
Behen, Devil's Apple, Hog Apple, Indian Apple, Raccoon
Berry, Umbrella Leaf, Wild Jalap, Wild Lemon

Description: This herb grows to 1.5 feet and has two
large umbrella-like leaves with five to nine lobes that
grow up to 1 foot across. Between the leaf stem emerges a
single, white, nodding flower with a 2-inch diameter.
This is followed by a yellowish green fruit about the size
and shape of an egg. Sterile (nonflowering) plants have
a single leaf. Figure 313-314

Distribution: May apples grow in moist woodlands
from Quebec to Florida west to southern Ontario,
Minnesota, and Texas.

Toxic Part: The whole plant, except the fruit (which
causes, at most, only slight catharsis), is poisonous.

Toxin: Podophylloresin (purgative), the glucoside of
podophyllotoxin, and alpha- and beta-peltatin (antimitotic)

Symptoms: Ingestion of plant parts or extracts (other
than of the fruit) produces emesis and catharsis.
Ingestion of large quantities or repeated topical application
of the resin has produced fatalities characterized by
coma; depression of deep tendon reflexes; ileus; renal
failure; elevation of SGOT, LDH, alkaline phosphatase,
and uric acid; and hematologic abnormalities. Industrial
processing of rhizomes causes dermatitis and keratitis
in workers.

Management: Fluids and antiemetics are indicated.
Blood transfusion may be necessary. There is no other
specific therapy.

References:
Balucani M, Zellers DD: Podophyllin resin poisoning.
JAMA 189:639-640, 1964.

Cassidy DE, et al: Podophyllum toxicity: A report of a fatal case and a review of the literature. *Clin Toxicol* 19:35-44, 1982.

Filley CM, et al: Neurologic manifestations of podophyllin toxicity. *Neurology* 32:308-311, 1982.

Leslie KO, Shitamato B: The bone marrow in systemic podophyllin toxicity. *Am J Clin Path* 77:478-480, 1982

Slater G, et al: Podophyllin poisoning. *Obstet Gynecol* 52:94-96, 1978.

Poncirus trifoliata (L.) Raf.
Family: Rutaceae

Trivial Names: Trifoliate Orange, Hardy Orange, Mock Orange (Do not confuse *Poncirus* with the southern mock orange, *Prunus caroliniana*, which has cyanogenetic toxins, or with a number of harmless ornamentals, eg, *Murraya, Pittosporum, Philadelphus, Styrax.*)

Description: This small deciduous tree has stiff thorns that may be 2.5 inches long. The white flowers are 2 inches across and form at the base of the thorns before leafing. Leaves are shiny, thick, and leathery. The fruit resembles a small orange and has a pronounced aroma. It is filled with an acrid pulp. Figure 315

Distribution: *Poncirus* is used in the southern United States and along both coasts as a hedge plant. It also is cultivated extensively to obtain root stock for citrus grafts.

Toxic Part: The fruit is toxic.

Toxin: Unidentified (reputed to be a saponin)

Symptoms and Management: Although serious intoxications are unlikely because of the bitter taste of the fruit, gastroenteritis may occur and require fluid replacement.

References:

Martin FM Jr: Poisonous cultivated plants. *Bull Tulane Med Fac* 12:159-172, 1953.

Prunus species
Family: Rosaceae

Trivial Names: Apricot (Spanish: Albaricoque), **Cherry** (Spanish: Cereza), **Choke Cherry, Peach** (Spanish: Melocoton), **Plum, Sloe**

Description: Species of *Prunus* are trees and shrubs, usually with deciduous leaves that are alternate and mostly serrate. The flowers are white or pink with five sepals and five petals. The fruit is a drupe with a fleshy outer layer over a stone or pit. Figure 318-321

Distribution: *Prunus* species are widely cultivated in the north temperate zone, and there are a number of native species. A large number of fruit varieties is available commercially.

Toxic Part: The kernel in the pit is poisonous. Most fatal intoxications involve ingestion of apricot pits or products made from them.

Toxin: Cyanogentic glycosides (amygdalin) liberate hydrocyanic acid on hydrolysis.

Symptoms: Since the cyanogenetic glycosides must be hydrolyzed in the gastroenteric tract before cyanide ion is released, some hours may elapse before symptoms appear. Abdominal pain, vomiting, lethargy, and sweating then develop. Cyanosis is not inevitable. In severe intoxications, coma develops and may be accompanied by tetanic convulsions, muscle flaccidity, and incontinence.

Management: Conscious patients may require only gastric lavage. Activated charcoal adsorbs cyanide but releases it slowly during passage through the intestine. A 25% solution of sodium thiosulfate (300 ml for adults) instead may be instilled into the stomach following lavage. In unconscious patients or those who are losing consciousness, acidosis should be corrected, volume expanders given if shock is present or developing, respiratory assistance with oxygen should be instituted, and cyanide antidote should be administered.

References:

Braico KT, et al: Laetrile intoxication. *N Engl J Med* 300:238-240, 1979.

Pijoan M: Cyanide poisoning from a choke cherry seed. *Am J Med Sci* 204:550-553, 1942.

Polson CJ, et al: *Clinical Toxicology*, ed 3. Philadelphia JB Lippincott, 1983, 162-196.

Sayre JW, Kaymakcalan S: Hazards to health. Cyanide poisoning from apricot seeds among children in central Turkey. *N Engl J Med* 270:1113-1115, 1964.

Timbrook J: Use of wild cherry pits as food by the California Indians. *J Ethnobiol* 2:162-176, 1982.

Ranunculus species
Family: Ranunculaceae

R. acris L.
R. bulbosus L.
R. sceleratus L.

Trivial Names: Buttercup; Crowfoot; Bassinet (Canada); Blister Flower or Wort; Bouton d'Or (Canada); Butter-Cress, -Daisy, or -Flower; Crain; Devil's Claws; Figwort; Goldballs; Goldweed; Horse Gold; Hunger Weed; Lesser Celandine; Pilewort; Ram's Claws; Renoncule (Canada); St. Anthony's Turnip; Sitfast; Spearwort; Starve-Acre; Water Crowfoot; Yellow Gowan

Description: These annual or perennial herbs have yellow, white, or rarely red flowers. They are a few inches to under 3 feet in height. Figure 322-325

Distribution: Buttercups grow mainly in wet, swampy areas throughout the United States, including Hawaii and Alaska, and Canada.

Toxic Part: The sap is toxic. Poisoning has occurred in children who ate the bulbous roots of *R. bulbosus*.

Toxin: Protoanemonin has a direct irritant and vesicant action on the skin and mucous membranes.

Symptoms: Intense pain and inflammation of the mouth with blistering and ulceration and profuse salivation occur. Bloody emesis and diarrhea develop in association with severe abdominal cramps. Renal irritation is associated with polyuria and painful micturition initially and hematuria, which may be followed by oliguria. Central nervous system involvement is manifested by dizziness, syncope, and, in severe cases, convulsions.

Management: The immediate irritant effects usually limit the quantity ingested. If substantial amounts have been swallowed, gastric lavage should be performed followed by instillation of demulcents. Appropriate measures should be instituted to prevent dehydration, and renal output should be measured.

References:

Forsyth AA: *British Poisonous Plants*. London, Ministry of Agriculture, Fisheries, and Food Bull 161, 1968, 33-36.

Rhamnus species
Family: Rhamnaceae

R. californica Eschsch.
R. cathartica L.
R. frangula L.

Trivial Names: Buckthorn, Alder Buckthorn, Arrow Wood, Berry Alder, Black Dogwood, Cascara, Hart's Horn, May Thorn, Nerprun (Canada), Persian Berry, Purging Buckthorn, Rhine Berry

R. californica: Coffeeberry

Description: Buckthorn shrubs are small (12 foot) trees.

R. californica is an evergreen with finely toothed leaves. The two-seeded fruit may be green, black, or red when mature. Figure 326

R. cathartica has spine-tipped branchlets; opposite, toothed leaves; scaly buds; and greenish white flowers that grow in clusters. The fruit turns from red to black and contains four stones. Figure 327

R. frangula has no spines and smooth leaves and buds. The flowers grow in a flat cluster and the fruit contains three stones. Figure 328

Distribution: *R. cathartica* and *R. frangula* grow in the northeastern United States and Canada; *R. californica*

grows in California. Related species are found throughout the north temperate zone.

Toxic Part: Fruit and bark are poisonous.

Toxin: Hydroxymethylanthraquinones

Symptoms: Nausea, emesis, and catharsis result from intoxication.

Management: Poisoning is self-limited. Replacement of fluids may be indicated, particularly in children, to prevent dehydration.

References:

Frohne D, Pfänder JH: *A Colour Atlas of Poisonous Plants. A Handbook for Pharmacists, Physicians, Toxicologists and Biologists*. London, Wolfe House, 1983, 183-185.

Rheum rhabarbarum L. (incorrectly called *R. rhaponticum* L. in older U.S. literature)
Family: Polygonaceae

Trivial Names: Pie Plant, Rhubarb, Rhubarbe (Canada), Wine Plant

Description: This perennial has stalks that grow several feet long and become red-faced at maturity. The large ovate leaves are wrinkled with wavy margins. Figure 329

Distribution: Rhubarb is widely cultivated for its edible stalk.

Toxic Part: Raw or canned leaves are toxic in large quantity.

Toxin: Anthraquinone glycosides, soluble oxalates

Symptoms: Symptoms probably are caused entirely by anthraquinone cathartics. A few reports of renal damage have been ascribed to oxaluria.

Management: Adequate fluid replacement is required to prevent dehydration or renal shutdown.

References:

Fassett D: Oxalates, in *Intoxicants Occurring Naturally in Foods*, ed 2. Washington, DC, National Academy of Sciences, 1973, 346-362.

Rhododendron species
Family: Ericaceae

Trivial Names: Azalea, Rhododendron, Rhodora (Canada), Rosa Laurel (Mexico), Rosebay

Description: There are about 800 species of *Rhododendron* divided into eight subgenera. The genus includes the former genus, *Azalea*. They are evergreen, semievergreen, or deciduous shrubs with simple alternate leaves. The flowers are of various colors and bell-shaped or funnel-form. Figure 330-332

Distribution: Rhododendrons are cultivated in Canada and most of the United States with the exception of the north central states and subtropical Florida. A number of native species exist in the same geographic range.

Toxic Part: The leaves are toxic as is honey made from flower nectar.

Toxin: Grayanotoxins (andromedotoxins)

Symptoms: Rhododendrons have caused serious intoxications in children who chewed on the leaves. Poisoning also may result from eating honey made from rhododendron nectar. There is a transitory burning in the mouth on ingestion. Several hours later, salivation, emesis, and diarrhea occur, and there is a prickling sensation in the skin. The patient may complain of headache, muscular weakness, and dimness of vision. Bradycardia is followed by severe hypotension. Coma and convulsions are terminal events.

Management: Fluid replacement and respiratory support are administered. If indicated, atropine is given for bradycardia. Ephedrine may be required for hypotension if administration of fluid and positioning are

142

inadequate. The electrocardiogram should be monitored. Recovery is complete in 24 hours.

References:

Rhododendron ingestion. *Hosp Formulary Management* 9:41, May 1974.

Carey FM, et al: Pharmacological and chemical observations on some toxic nectars. *J Pharm Pharmacol* 11:269T-274T, 1959.

Catterall WA: Neurotoxins that act on voltage-sensitive sodium channels in excitable membranes. *Ann Rev Pharmacol Toxicol* 20:15-43, 1980.

Honerjäger P: Ceveratrum alkaloids: Progress in understanding their membrane and inotropic actions. *Trends Pharmacol Sci* 4:258-262, 1983.

Kakisawa H, et al: Stereochemistry of grayanotoxins. *Tetrahedron* 21:3091-3104, 1965.

Kumazawa Z, Iriye R: Stereochemistry of grayanotoxin II. *Tetrahedron Lett* 12:927-930, 1970.

Leach DG: History of rhododendron poisoning. *Garden J* 16:215-237, 239, 1966; 17:15-18, 33, 1977.

Moran NC, et al: Pharmacological actions of andromedotoxin, an active principle from *Rhododendron maximum*. *J Pharmacol Exp Therap* 110:415-432, 1954.

Scott PM, et al: Grayanotoxins. Occurrence and analysis in honey and a comparison of toxicities in mice. *Fd Cosmet Toxicol* 9:179-184, 1971.

White JW Jr, Riethof ML: Composition of honey. III. Detection of acetylandromedol in toxic honeys. *Arch Biochem Biophys* 79:165-167, 1959.

Rhodotypos scandens (Thunb.) Makino

(= R. kerrioides Siebold & Zucc.; *R. tetrapetala* Makino)

Family: Rosaceae

Trivial Names: Jetbead, White Kerria

Description: This shrub-like rose grows 3 to 6 feet high. It is the only rose cultivated in the United States with opposite leaves. The flowers are white and about

2 inches in diameter. The fruit is a shining black berry about 1/4 inch in diameter. Figure 333-334

Distribution: Jetbead is hardy in the northern United States and is a popular ornamental.

Toxic Part: Berries are toxic.

Toxin: Not identified (reputed to also contain a cyanogenetic glycoside)

Symptoms: In the only recorded case of human poisoning attributed to this plant, the patient exhibited severe hypoglycemia, ketosis, hyperthermia, and convulsions.

Management: The patient was given antipyretics and anticonvulsants. Recovery was complete by day five.

References:

Rascoff H, Wasser S: Poisoning in a child simulating diabetic coma. *JAMA* 152:1134-1135, 1953.

███████████

Ricinus communis L.
Family: Euphorbiaceae

Trivial Names: Castor Bean; African Coffee Tree; Castor Oil Plant; Higuereta (Cuba, Puerto Rico); Higuerilla (Mexico); KOLI, PA'AILA, or LA'AU-'AILA (Hawaii); Man's Motherwort; Mexico Weed; Palma Christi (Haiti); Ricin (Haiti); Ricino (Puerto Rico); Steadfast; Wonder Tree

Description: This annual grows to 15 feet or higher in the tropics. The large lobed leaves are up to 3 feet across. Spiny seed pods form clusters along spikes. The pods contain plump seeds resembling fat ticks in shape and size, usually mottled black or brown on white. The seeds have a pleasant taste. Figure 336-337

Distribution: The castor bean grows throughout the West Indies and is a naturalized weed in Florida, along the Gulf coast in Texas, along the Atlantic coast to New Jersey, in southern California, and in Hawaii. It is widely planted elsewhere for its foliage and is grown commercially in some of the Gulf coast states and Guam.

Toxic Part: The seeds are poisonous.

Toxin: Ricin, a plant lectin (toxalbumin), inhibits protein synthesis in the intestinal wall. Small quantities of the harmless cathartic, castor oil, also are present.

Symptoms: Poisoning is apparent only after a latent period of several hours and is characterized by nausea, emesis, and diarrhea. Other effects are secondary to massive fluid and electrolyte loss and intestinal dysfunction.

Management: Correction of hypovolemia and electrolyte derangements and parenteral alimentation may be required. Ingestion of two to six seeds of this extremely toxic plant may be fatal.

References:

Balint GA, et al: Ricin: The toxic protein of castor oil seeds. *Toxicology* 2:77-102, 1974.

Kopferschmidt J, et al: Acute voluntary intoxication by ricin. *Human Toxicol* 2:239-242, 1983.

Malizia E, et al: Ricinus poisoning: a familiar epidemy. *Acta Pharmacol Toxicol* 41 suppl II: 351-361, 1977. (In English)

Olsnes S: Abrin and ricin: Two toxic lectins inactivating eukaryotic ribosomes, in Bernheimer AW (ed): *Perspectives in Toxinology*. New York, John Wiley & Son, 1977, 121-144.

Olsnes S, Pihl A: Toxic lectins and related proteins, in Cohen P, Van Heyninger S (eds): *Molecular Action of Toxins and Viruses*. Amsterdam, Elsevier, 1982, 51-105.

Rivina humilis L.
Family: Phytolaccaceae

Trivial Names: Rouge Plant, Baby Pepper, Bloodberry, Caïmonicillo (Dominican Republic), Carmín (Puerto Rico), Cat's Blood, Coral Berry, Coralitos (Cuba), Pigeon Berry

Description: This small shrub is under 3 feet. The leaves are ovate and about 4 inches long. The hanging sprays of flowers are pinkish white. The fruit is a shining bright crimson or orange berry. Figure 338

Distribution: Rouge plant grows in Hawaii, the southern United States from New Mexico to Florida, and the West Indies; it is a popular house plant elsewhere.

Toxic Part: The leaves and roots are poisonous. The absence of reports of poisoning from the attractive berries suggests that they do not contain clinically significant concentrations of toxin.

Toxin: Presumed to be identical to that in *Phytolacca americana*

Symptoms: Slight gastric distress, nausea, emesis, and diarrhea may occur.

Management: No specific therapy is indicated except for fluid replacement to prevent dehydration, particularly in children.

References:

Lampe KF, Fagerström R: *Plant Toxicity and Dermatitis*. Baltimore, Williams & Wilkins, 1968, 27, 31-34.

Robinia pseudoacacia L.
Family: Leguminosae (Fabaceae)

Trivial Names: Black Locust, Bastard Acacia, Black Acacia, False Acacia, Green Locust, Pea Flower Locust, Post Locust, Silver Chain, Treesail, White Honey Flower, White Locust, Whyo Tree, Yellow Locust

Description: The locust tree grows to 80 feet. The compound leaves have 7 to 19 elliptical leaflets, 1 inch in length. There is a pair of woody thorns on the branch where the leaf stem emerges. The white, fragrant flowers are borne in clusters (racemes). The fruit is a flat, reddish brown pod, about 4 inches long, which persists over winter. Figure 339-340

Distribution: The locust is native to the Smoky Mountains and the Ozarks. It is widely planted in the north temperate zones, particularly in the east and in Ontario east to Nova Scotia and southern British Columbia.

Toxic Part: The bark, seeds, and leaves are toxic.

Toxin: Robin, a plant lectin (toxalbumin), interferes with protein synthesis in the small intestine.

Symptoms: After a latent period of several hours, nausea, emesis, and diarrhea develop. Other effects are probably secondary to hypovolemia from fluid loss. Poisoning from this tree is potentially serious, but exceedingly uncommon.

Management: Correction of hypovolemia and electrolyte disturbances is required. Parenteral alimentation may be needed. See *Abrus precatorius* and *Ricinus communis*.

References:

Emery AT: Report of thirty-two cases of poisoning by locust bark. *NY Med J* 45:92, 1887.

McPherson A, Hoover S: Purification of mitogenic proteins from *Hura crepitans* and *Robinia pseudoacacia*. *Biochem Biophys Res Com* 89:713-720, 1979.

Sambucus species
Family: Caprifoliaceae

S. caerulea Raf. (= *S. glauca* Nutt.)
S. canadensis L.
S. melanocarpa A. Gray
S. mexicana Presl ex A. DC. (= *S. simpsonii* Rehder)
S. racemosa L.

Trivial Names: Elderberry, American Elder, Saúco (Mexico, Puerto Rico), Saúco Blanco (Cuba), Sureau or Fleur Sureau (Canada, Haiti)

Description: The common elderberry (*S. canadensis*) in the eastern half of the United States and Canada is a 6- to 12-foot shrub with much branched stems. The compound leaves usually have seven serrated oval leaflets. The small, white flowers are borne in clusters. The purplish black fruits are about 1/8 inch in diameter.

Flowers and fruit may be borne simultaneously.
Figure 342-345

Distribution: Species of elderberry may be found in all
states including Hawaii and Alaska, across Canada, and
in the Greater Antilles.

Toxic Part: The whole plant is poisonous. The ripe
fruit is harmless when cooked and is generally considered
to have no adverse effect if limited amounts are eaten
raw. The flowers are probably nontoxic.

Toxin: Cyanogenetic glycosides, primarily in the roots,
stems, and leaves; unidentified cathartic, primarily in the
bark and roots of some species

Symptoms: Injudicious consumption of uncooked
berries usually has a laxative effect that does not require
medical attention. Consumption of the leaves, root, bark,
or immature berries may cause protracted, severe
diarrhea.

Juice made from pressing the berries and stems of *S.
mexicana* caused nausea, vomiting, and abdominal cramps
within 15 minutes followed by dizziness, numbness,
and, in one patient, stupor. All patients recovered without
intervention.

There are no documented cases of cyanide poisoning in
man from this genus.

Management: Fluid replacement should be given as
indicated.

References:

Kunitz S, et al: Poisoning from elderberry juice,
California. *MMWR* 33:173-174, 1984.

Pammel LH: *A Manual of Poisonous Plants*. Cedar
Rapids, Torch Press, 1910, 745-747.

Sapindus species
Family: Sapindaceae

S. saponaria L. (= *S. marginatus* Willd.)
S. drummondii Hook. & Arn.

Trivial Names:

S. saponaria: **Soapberry,** A'E (Hawaii), Bois Savonette or Savonette Pays (Haiti), False Dogwood, Indian Soap Plant, Jaboncillo (Mexico, Cuba, Puerto Rico), Wild China Tree, Wingleaf Soapberry

S. drummondii: Western Soapberry

Description: These tropical evergreen trees grow to about 30 feet. Each leaflet of the compound leaves is 4 inches long. White flowers grow in racemes. The fruit is a shiny orange-brown berry that has been employed as a soap. Figure 346-347

Distribution: *S. saponaria* grows in Florida, the West Indies, Mexico, and Hawaii.

S. drummondii grows from Arizona to Louisiana north to Kansas.

Toxic Part: The fruit is poisonous.

Toxin: Saponin

Symptoms: Intoxications are very rare. Decoctions have been used in folk medicine. It is presumed that ingestion of a large quantity may produce gastroenteritis. The plant also produces contact dermatitis.

Management: Ingestion of small amounts probably is harmless. If emesis and diarrhea occur, fluids should be given to avoid dehydration, particularly in children.

Schinus species
Family: Anacardiaceae

S. molle L.
S. terebinthifolius Raddi

Trivial Names:

S. molle: **Pepper Tree,** Arbol de Perú (Mexico), California Pepper Tree, Peruvian Mastic Tree, Pimiento de América (Cuba)

S. terebinthifolius: **Christmas Berry Tree,** Brazilian Pepper Tree, Copal (Cuba), Florida Holly, NANI-O-HILO or WILELAIKI (Hawaii), Pimienta del Brazil (Puerto Rico)

Description:

S. molle: This tree grows to a height of about 35 feet and often has a twisted trunk. When viewed from a distance, the compound leaves and hanging branches are markedly similar to the willow. *Schinus* bears small red fruits. The crushed leaves emit a distinct odor of black pepper. Figure 349

S. terebinthifolius: This fast-growing tree usually attains a height of about 20 feet. The leaves are compound; individual leaflets are about 2.5 inches long. The leaves emit a pepper-like odor when crushed, but it is not as pronounced as with *S. molle*. The fruit forms in clusters of persistent berries. Figure 350

Distribution: *S. molle* is cultivated in California, Hawaii, and the West Indies.

S. terebinthifolius, an introduced weed tree, is becoming common in south Florida, Hawaii, Guam, and the West Indies.

Toxic Part: Berries are poisonous.

Toxin: Triterpenes

Symptoms: Ingestion of the berries produces irritation of the throat, gastroenteritis, diarrhea, and emesis. In sensitized patients, perianal contact dermatitis may occur.

Management: Therapy is not required except to prevent dehydration or to provide relief from itching of perianal dermatitis.

References:

Campello JdP, Marsaioli AJ: Triterpenes of *Schinus terebinthifolius*. *Phytochemistry* 13:659-660, 1974.

Campello JdP, Marsaioli AJ: Terebinthifolic acid and bauerone: New triterpenoid ketones from *Schinus terebinthifolius*. *Phytochemistry* 14:2300-2302, 1975.

Kier LB, et al: Nuclear magnetic resonance spectroscopy of natural products. IV. Structure and stereochemistry of terebinthone in schinol. *Bull Soc Chim Fr*, 911-912, 1963. (In French)

Lloyd HA, et al: Terpenes of *Schinus terebinthifolius*. *Phytochemistry* 16:1301-1302, 1977.

Morton JF: *Plants Poisonous to People in Florida and Other Warm Areas*, ed 2. Miami, published by the author, 1982, 125-126.

Stahl E, et al: Cardanol, a skin irritant in pink pepper. *Planta Medica* 48:5-9, 1983.

Woods B, Calnan CD: Toxic woods. *Br J Dermatol* 95(suppl 13):1-97, 1976.

Schoenocaulon species
Family: Liliaceae

S. drummondii Gray
S. texanum Scheele

Trivial Names:

S. drummondii: Green Lily

Description: These two species are similar and their botanical names once were considered to be synonyms. They are perennial herbs growing from bulbs. The leaves are grass-like, emerging only at the base. The flowering stalk is leafless. Flowers grow in a dense raceme and are pale green to yellowish white. *S. drummondii* usually flowers in the fall, *S. texanum* during spring and summer. The fruit is a persistent, three-lobed capsule; each capsule contains four or more seeds.

Distribution: *Schoenocaulon* is a New World genus of about ten species distributed mostly in Mexico south to Peru. *S. drummondii* and *S. texanum* occur in western Texas; *S. texanum* extends into southern New Mexico.

Toxic Part: It is presumed that the whole plant, particularly the seeds, is toxic.

Toxin: Presumed to be veratridine alkaloids

Symptoms: The Mexican plant, *Schoenocaulon officinalis* (Schlect. & Cham.) Gray ex Benth. (= *Sabadilla officinalis* Standl.), known in Mexico as cebolleja, has been a commercial source for a topical parasiticide. Ingestion of the seeds of this plant results in profound emesis and catharsis. Fatalities have been reported. Other members of this genus probably contain the veratridine alkaloids and would produce a similar response. Serious

151

intoxications would be expected to produce severe bradycardia and hypotension.

Management: Therapy may not be required despite the apparent severity of discomfort. Hypotension that does not respond to positioning or replacement of fluids should be managed with ephedrine. Bradycardia responds to atropine. Even severe intoxications may be expected to resolve within 24 hours.

References:

Benforado J: Veratrum alkaloids, in Root W, Hoffmann F (eds): *Physiological Pharmacology*. New York, Academic Press, vol 4, 1967, 331-398.

Catterall WA: Neurotoxins that act on voltage-sensitive sodium channels in excitable membranes. *Ann Rev Pharmacol Toxicol* 20:15-43, 1980.

Williams LO: Useful plants in Central America. *Ceiba* 24:1-381, 1981.

Scilla species
Family: Liliaceae

Trivial Names: Squill, Cuban Lilly, Hyacinth-of-Peru, Jacinto de Perú (Cuba), Peruvian Jacinth, Sea Onion, Star Hyacinth

Description: The flowers of this hyacinth-like plant are usually blue, purple, or white. Figure 351

Distribution: These European or Asian plants are hardy perennials in the north temperate zones to British Columbia and Quebec to Newfoundland. They are often cultivated.

Toxic Part: The whole plant is poisonous.

Toxin: Digitalis-like glycosides

Symptoms: Pain in the oral cavity, nausea, emesis, abdominal pain, cramping, and diarrhea may develop. Digitalis glycoside toxicity has a variable latent period that depends on the quantity ingested. It is usually expressed as conduction defects and sinus bradycardia.

Hyperkalemia may be present. Rhythm disturbances other than escape beats are not necessarily exhibited.

Management: Gastric lavage or induced emesis should be performed. Activated charcoal may be given repeatedly later. Saline cathartics may be useful. Electrocardiographic monitoring and measurement of serum potassium should be performed frequently.

Conduction defects may require the use of atropine or transvenous pacing. Phenytoin is the agent of choice for rhythm disturbances. Dialysis and forced diuresis are not useful. The digitalis-specific antibodies, Fab fragments, may become the management of choice for life-threatening digitalis toxicity but are not generally available.

References:

Dickstein ES, Kunkel FW: Foxglove tea poisonings. *Am J Med* 69:167-169, 1980.

Ekins BR, Watanabe AS: Acute digoxin poisonings: Review of therapy. *Am J Hosp Pharm* 35:268-277, 1978.

Smith TW, et al: Treatment of life-threatening digitalis intoxication with digoxin-specific Fab antibody fragments. Experience in 26 cases. *N Engl J Med* 307:1357-1362, 1982.

Senecio species
Family: Compositae (Asteraceae)

S. *jacobaea* L.
S. *longilobus* Benth. (— S. *douglasii* DC. var. *jamesii* (T. & G.) Ediger)
S. *vulgaris* L.

Trivial Names:

S. *jacobaea*: **Ragwort,** Hierba de Santiago (Mexico), Stinking Willie, Tansy Ragwort

S. *longilobus*: **Threadleaf Groundsel** (Gordolobo Yerba is the Mexican name used in the southwestern United States for herbal medications prepared from this plant.)

S. *vulgaris*: **Groundsel** or Common Groundsel

Groundsel, Ragwort, and Butterweed are common names applied to many species of *Senecio* in the

United States; in Canada, Squaw Weed and Sénéçon are used.

Description: There are 2,000 to 3,000 species of *Senecio*, many of which contain a toxic concentration of pyrrolizidine alkaloids.

S. jacobaea: This biennial or perennial herb grows to 4 feet. The yellow flowers form a showy cluster (corymb) at the end of the stem. The branches are variably "cottony."

S. longilobus: This very showy perennial has white flowers and a shrubby form with many stems arising from the base that branch above. The new stems and leaves have a cottony covering.

S. vulgaris: This annual grows to about 1 foot high. Young stems are cottony but become smooth with aging. The leaves are soft, fleshy, and somewhat lobed. The flowers are golden yellow. Figure 352

Distribution: *S. jacobaea* is of Old World origin and has become naturalized as a weed in Newfoundland, Quebec, and Ontario south to Massachusetts and, on the west coast, in British Columbia, Washington, and Oregon west of the Cascade Mountain range.

S. longilobus grows in Colorado and Utah south to western Texas and northern Mexico.

S. vulgaris is a European plant that has become naturalized as a weed in Alaska, all of the Canadian provinces, and New England south to North Carolina and west to Wisconsin; in the southwest, it grows in California, New Mexico, and Texas.

Toxic Part: The whole plant is poisonous. Milk from animals who have grazed on these plants and honey made from nectar of *Senecio* contain the toxic alkaloids.

Toxin: Pyrrolizidine alkaloids

Symptoms: Toxicity is associated primarily with use of these plants in herbal teas for folk medicine. The chronic consumption of these teas may cause veno-occlusive disease of the liver (Budd-Chiari syndrome) with formation of hepatic vein thrombosis leading to cirrhosis. Deaths have been reported recently in the United States from such use. The symptoms are abdominal pain with ascites, hepatomegaly and splenomegaly, anorexia with nausea, vomiting, and diarrhea.

Management: There is no known specific therapy for toxin-induced hepatic veno-occlusive disease.

References:
Bull LB, et al: *The Pyrrolizidine Alkaloids. Their Chemistry, Pathogenicity, and Other Biological Properties*. New York, Wiley-Interscience, 1968.

Deinzer ML, et al: Pyrrolizidine alkaloids: Their occurrence in honey from tansy ragwort (*Senecio jacobaea* L.). *Science* 195:497-499, 1977.

Huxtable RJ: Herbal teas and toxins: Novel aspects of pyrrolizidine poisoning in the United States. *Perspec Biol Med* 24:1-14, 1980.

McLean EK, Mattocks AR: Environmental liver injury: Plant toxins, in Farber E, Fisher MM (eds): *Toxic Injury of the Liver, Part B*. New York, Marcel Dekker, 1980, 517-539.

Peterson JE, Culvenor CCJ: Hepatotoxic pyrrolizidine alkaloids, in Keeler RF, Tu AT (eds): *Plant and Fungal Toxins*. New York, Marcel Dekker, 1983, 637-671.

Schoental R: Biochemical basis of liver necrosis caused by pyrrolizidine alkaloids and certain other hepatotoxins. *Biochem Soc Trans* 3:292-294, 1975.

Smith LW, Culvenor CCJ: Plant sources of hepatotoxic pyrrolizidine alkaloids. *J Nat Prod* 44:129-152, 1981.

Stillman AE, et al: Hepatic veno-occlusive disease due to pyrrolizidine (*Senecio*) poisoning in Arizona. *Gastroenterology* 73:349-352, 1977.

Sesbania species
Family: Leguminosae (Fabaceae)

Trivial Names: Báculo (Puerto Rico); Colorado River Hemp; Egyptian Rattlepod; Gallito (Cuba); 'OHAI-KE'OKE'O, 'OHAI-'ULA'ULA, or 'OHAI (Hawaii); Pois Vallière (Haiti); Scarlet Wistaria Tree; Vegetable-Humming-Bird

Description: These annuals have green stems 3 to 8 feet tall that become woody. The compound leaves have numerous linear leaflets. The small sweetpea-shaped flowers are yellow dotted with purple. Seed pods are curved. Figure 353-355

Distribution: *Sesbania* grow in southern California, the south Atlantic and Gulf coast states, Hawaii, Guam, and the West Indies.

Toxic Part: All parts of this plant are poisonous.

Toxin: Pyrrolizidine alkaloids

Symptoms: Toxicity is associated with use of this plant in herbal teas for folk medicine. Chronic consumption of these teas may cause veno-occlusive disease of the liver (Budd-Chiari syndrome) with hepatic vein thrombosis leading to cirrhosis. The symptoms are abdominal pain with ascites, hepatomegaly and splenomegaly, anorexia with nausea, vomiting, and diarrhea.

Management: There is no known specific therapy for toxin-induced hepatic veno-occlusive disease.

References:

Bull LB, et al: *The Pyrrolizidine Alkaloids. Their Chemistry, Pathogenicity, and Other Biological Properties.* New York, Wiley-Interscience, 1968.

Huxtable RJ: Herbal teas and toxins: Novel aspects of pyrrolizidine poisoning in the United States. *Perspec Biol Med* 24:1-14, 1980.

McLean EK, Mattocks AR: Environmental liver injury: Plant toxins, in Farber E, Fisher MM (eds): *Toxic Injury of the Liver, Part B.* New York, Marcel Dekker, 1980, 517-539.

Peterson JE, Culvenor CCJ: Hepatotoxic pyrrolizidine alkaloids, in Keeler RF, Tu AT (eds): *Plant and Fungal Toxins.* New York, Marcel Dekker, 1983, 637-671.

Schoental R: Biochemical basis of liver necrosis cause by pyrrolizidine alkaloids and certain other hepatotoxins. *Biochem Soc Trans* 3:292-294, 1975.

Smith LW, Culvenor CCJ: Plant sources of hepatotoxic pyrrolizidine alkaloids. *J Nat Prod* 44:129-152, 1981.

Stillman AE, et al: Hepatic veno-occlusive disease due to pyrrolizidine (*Senecio*) poisoning in Arizona. *Gastroenterology* 73:349-352, 1977.

Solandra species
Family: Solanaceae

Trivial Names: Chalice Vine, Bejuco do Peo (Puerto Rico), Chamico Bejuco (Cuba), Cup-of-Gold, Palo Guaco (Cuba), Silver Cup, Trumpet Plant

Description: These climbing or erect woody vines have large, showy, trumpet-shaped flowers of yellow or creamy yellow. The fruit is a fleshy, elongated berry. Figure 357-359

Distribution: These plants are native to tropical America and Mexico. They are cultivated outdoors in Florida, the West indies, and Hawaii.

Toxic Part: All parts of this plant are toxic, including the flower nectar.

Toxin: Atropine alkaloids

Symptoms: Dry mouth; dysphagia and dysphonia; tachycardia; hot, dry, flushed skin sometimes with a rash; elevated body temperature; blurred vision; and sometimes mydriasis result from poisoning. Excitement, headache, delirium, and hallucinations are particularly likely in young children.

Management: If the severity of the intoxication warrants intervention (hyperthermia, delirium), a slow intravenous administration of physostigmine should be repeated until symptoms abate or cholinergic effects appear. The duration of action of the belladonna alkaloids is longer than that of physostigmine; therefore, repeated administration of the latter may be required. The initial pediatric dose of physostigmine is 0.5 mg; adolescents and adults should receive 2 mg.

References:
Rumack BH: Anticholinergic poisoning: Treatment with physostigmine. *Pediatrics* 52:449-451, 1973.

Solanum species
Family: Solanaceae

S. americanum P. Mill, *S. nigrum* L., and the *S. nigrum*-complex

S. capsicastrum Link ex Schauer
S. capsicoides All. (= *S. aculeatissimum* Britt. & Millsp.
non Jacq.; *S. ciliatum* Lam.)
S. carolinense L.
S. dulcamara L.
S. mammosum L.
S. pseudocapsicum L.
S. seaforthianum Andr.
S. sodomeum L.
S. tuberosum L.

Trivial Names:

S. americanum, *S. nigrum*, and the *S. nigrum*-
complex: **Nightshade,** Black or Deadly Nightshade, Hierba
Mora (Mexico), Lanment (Haiti), Mata Gallina (Puerto
Rico), Poisonberry, Pop-Bush, Tue-Chien (Canada), Yerba
Mora (Cuba, Puerto Rico)

S. capsicastrum: **False Jerusalem Cherry,** Christmas Orange

S. capsicoides: **Love Apple,** Berenjena de Jardín (Puerto
Rico), Cockroach Berry, KIKANIA-LEI (Hawaii), Pantomina
(Cuba), Soda-Apple Nightshade, Thorny Popolo

S. carolinense: **Carolina Horse Nettle,** Ball or Bull Nettle,
Ball Nightshade, Sandbriar, Tread Softly

S. dulcamara: **Bittersweet,** Agridulce (Mexico), Dog-Wood,
Fellen or Felonwort, Morelle Douce-Amère (Canada),
Poison Berry or Flower, Poisonous or Deadly Nightshade,
Scarlet Berry, Snake Berry, Woody or Climbing Nightshade

S. mammosum: **Nipplefruit,** Berenjena de Cucarachas or
Berenjena de Marimbo (Puerto Rico), Berengena de
Gallina (Dominican Republic), Güirito (Cuba), Love
Apple (Puerto Rico), Pomme d'Amour or Tété Jeune
Fille (Haiti)

S. pseudocapsicum: **Jerusalem Cherry,** Coral (Mexico)

S. seaforthianum: **Star-Potato Vine,** Brazilian Nightshade,
Falsa Belladona (Puerto Rico), Jazmín de Italia (Cuba,
Puerto Rico), Lilas (Haiti)

S. sodomeum: **Apple of Sodom,** Dead Sea Apple,
POPOLO-KIKANIA (Hawaii), Yellow or Thorny Popolo

S. tuberosum: **Potato,** Papa (Spanish), Patate (Canada),
'UALA-KAHIKI (Hawaii)

Description: *Solanum* is a very large genus with
1,700 species, most of which have not been evaluated
toxicologically. These plants are mostly herbs (sometimes
climbing) or shrubs. They are often spiny, hairy, or have
stinging hairs. The flowers usually are five-toothed,

often showy, and usually white or blue. The berries are black, orange, yellow, or red. Figure 360-367

Distribution: *S. americanum* is ubiquitous but grows primarily in the eastern United States, Nova Scotia to Florida west to North Dakota and Texas. *S. nigrum* is native to Europe and has been introduced on both coasts of the United States, across Canada, Alaska, Hawaii, and Guam.

S. capsicastrum is a decorative pot plant that is occasionally cultivated and now has escaped in southern Texas.

S. capsicoides grows in Hawaii, on the coastal plain from Texas to North Carolina, and in the West Indies.

S. carolinense grows from Nebraska to Texas east to the Atlantic, in extreme northern Ohio, southern Ontario, and southern California.

S. dulcamara is a naturalized weed from Eurasia that is now common in the northern United States and Canada.

S. mammosum grows in the West Indies and tropical America.

S. pseudocapsicum, a decorative pot plant, has escaped from cultivation in Hawaii and the Gulf coast states.

S. seaforthianum is a South American plant cultivated in warmer areas, including Hawaii; it has become naturalized in Florida.

S. sodomeum is a common weed in Hawaii.

S. tuberosum, the white potato of commerce, is a widely cultivated vegetable. An occasional plant escapes from cultivation or from dumps.

Toxic Part: In *S. tuberosum*, the uncooked sprout and sun-greened skin are toxic. In the remaining species, human poisoning is generally attributed to immature fruit. Several species produce dermatitis.

Toxin: Solanine glycoalkaloids

Symptoms: Solanine has relatively little toxicity in adults, but fatal intoxications have occurred in children. Gastric irritation, a scratchy feeling in the throat, fever, and diarrhea develop after ingestion. Solanine poisoning is often confused with bacterial gastroenteritis. Symptoms usually appear only after a latent period of several hours after ingestion and they may persist for several days.

Management: Fluid replacement may be required to prevent dehydration. General supportive care as for gastroenteritis also may be given.

References:

Solanine poisoning. *Br Med J* 2:1458-1459, 1979.

Alexander RF, et al: A fatal case of solanine poisoning. *Br Med J* 2:518, 1948.

Dalvi RR, Borvic WC: Toxicity of solanine: An overview. *Vet Human Toxicol* 23:13-15, 1983.

Jadhav SJ, et al: Naturally occurring toxic alkaloids in foods. *Crit Rev Toxicol* 9:21-104, 1981.

Lampe K, Fagerström R: *Plant Toxicity and Dermatitis*. Baltimore, Williams & Wilkins, 1968, 71-78.

McMillan M, Thompson JC: An outbreak of suspected solanine poisoning in schoolboys. Examination of criteria of solanine poisoning. *Quart J Med* 48:227-243, 1979.

Morton J; Poisoning and injurious higher plants and fungi, in Tedeschi C, et al (eds): *Forensic Medicine*. Philadelphia, WB Saunders Co, vol II, 1977, 1541-1544.

Sophora species
Family: Leguminosae (Fabaceae)

S. secundiflora (Ortega) Lag. ex DC.
S. tomentosa L.

Trivial Names:

S. secundiflora: Burn Bean, Coral Bean, Colorines (Mexico), Frijolillo (Mexico), Mescal Bean, Pagoda Tree, Red Bean, Red Hots, Texas Mountain Laurel

S. tomentosa: **Necklacepod Sophora,** Silver Bush, Tambalisa (Cuba)

Description: *S. secundiflora* is a shrub or small tree with compound leaves. The purple flowers grow in showy racemes. Seeds are bright red and are contained in woody pods. Figure 368-369

S. tomentosa is a shrub with numerous branches and compound leaves. Bright yellow flowers grow in racemes. The yellow seeds are pea-like and contained in pods.

Distribution: *S. secundiflora* grows in Texas, New Mexico, Mexico, the coastal dunes of Baja California, Hawaii, and Guam.

S. tomentosa grows in Florida, Bermuda, and the West Indies from the Bahamas to Barbados.

Toxic Part: The seeds are poisonous.

Toxin: Cytisine and related alkaloids similar to nicotine

Symptoms: The effects of poisoning usually occur within one hour after ingestion. Nausea, emesis, headache, vertigo, salivation and perspiration, and diarrhea develop. Serious intoxications are rare, but convulsions and paralysis of the respiratory muscles may occur.

Management: Conservative management as for gastroenteritis and fluid replacement usually are adequate. Severe intoxications require airway management and respiratory support.

References:

Hatfield GM, et al: An investigation of *Sophora secundiflora* seeds (mescalbeans). *J Nat Prod* 40:374-383, 1977.

Izaddoost M, et al: Structure and toxicity of alkaloids and amino acids of *Sophora secundiflora. J Pharm Sci* 65:352-354, 1976.

Sullivan G, Chavez PI: Mexican good-luck charm potentially dangerous. *Vet Hum Toxicol* 23:259-260, 1980.

Spathiphyllum **species**
Family: Araceae

Trivial Names: Spathe Flower, White Anthurium

Description: *Spathiphyllum* are tropical perennial herbs that grow to about 2 feet. The elliptical leaves grow on short stems and emerge in clusters. The flower has a

161

white or greenish spathe with a short, usually white, spadix resembling a miniature ear of corn. Figure 370

Distribution: This plant is primarily of South American origin and may be grown outdoors in subtropical climates. They are commonly cultivated as indoor plants elsewhere.

Toxic Part: All parts of this plant are injurious.

Toxin: Water-insoluble needles (raphides) of calcium oxalate

Symptoms: Burning and irritation with edema of the lips, mouth, tongue, and pharynx occur. Plant material is seldom ingested but can cause gastroenteritis. Contact dermatitis may be caused by the root juices.

Management: No treatment is required unless swelling of the oropharynx produces mechanical obstruction. Cool liquids or demulcents held in the mouth may provide some relief.

References:

Mitchell J, Rook A: *Botanical Dermatology*. Vancouver, Greengrass, 1979.

Plowman T: Folk uses of new world aroids. *Econ Bot* 23:97-122, 1969.

Spigelia species
Family: Loganiaceae

S. anthelmia L.
S. marilandica L.

Trivial Names:

S. anthelmia: **West Indian Pinkroot** (Florida), Espigelia (Cuba), Herbe-à-Brinvilliers (Haiti), Loggerhead Weed (Barbados), Lombricera (Puerto Rico), Pink or Pink Weed, Waterweed, Worm Grass

S. marilandica: **Pinkroot,** Carolina Pink, Indian Pink, Worm Grass

Description: *S. anthelmia* is an annual herb that grows to about 1.5 feet. The opposite leaves have very short stems and are about 6 inches long and 3 inches wide. The tubular flowers grow in a terminal spike and flare into five petals. Petals are pink; the tube is white with magenta stripes. Fruits are globose and two-lobed.

S. marilandica is a perennial herb growing to 2 feet. The ovate opposite leaves are about 4 inches long. The tubular flowers are about 2 inches long, red on the outside, and yellow on the inside. Figure 371

Distribution: *S. anthelmia* grows in southern Florida, the Bahamas, and the West Indies to Barbados.

S. marilandica grows in Florida to Texas north to southern Indiana and South Carolina.

Toxic Part: The whole plant is poisonous.

Toxin: Spigeline

Symptoms: Most cases of poisoning have resulted from the folk use of decoctions of the plant as a vermifuge, although serious intoxications have resulted from chewing the leaf. Vomiting may occur early; vertigo, muscle spasm, mydriasis, and strychnine-like convulsions also may develop.

Management: Persistent convulsions should be controlled with intravenous diazepam. Systemic acidosis should be corrected. Fluid replacement and alkalization may be indicated to avoid the renal complications of rhabdomyolysis.

References:

Blohm H: *Poisonous Plants of Venezuela*. Cambridge, Harvard University Press, 1962, 75.

Strychnos nux-vomica L.
Family: Loganiaceae

Trivial Names: Nux-Vomica Tree, Strychnine

Description: This small tree has ovate leaves about 2 by 3.5 inches. The yellowish white tubular flowers grow in terminal clusters. The fruit is 1.5 inches across, hard-shelled, and varies in color from yellow to orange, resembling a small grapefruit. It contains several grey

velvety seeds that resemble nickel-sized buttons.
Figure 373

Distribution: *Strychnos* is grown in Hawaii.

Toxic Part: The whole plant, including the seeds, is poisonous.

Toxin: Strychnine

Symptoms: The patient may feel restless or anxious and experience fasciculations and hyperreflexia. In severe poisoning, generalized symmetrical tonic spasms with opisthotonic posturing develop, during which consciousness is maintained; the spasms last a few seconds to several minutes. They are induced by external sensory stimuli and are not associated with postictal confusion. Hyperthermia, anoxia, and metabolic acidosis also may develop.

Management: Establish a patent airway and support respiration if required. Persistent convulsions may require use of a general anesthetic and a muscle relaxant, such as pancuronium. Adequate urine flow should be maintained to avoid the renal complications of rhabdomyolysis. Hyperthermia should be managed with external cooling measures. Intravenous sodium bicarbonate should be given to correct metabolic acidosis.

References:
Dittrich K, et al: A case of fatal strychnine poisoning. *J Emerg Med* 1:327-330, 1984.

McGuigan MA: Strychnine. *Clin Toxicol Rev* 6(2):1-2, (Nov) 1983.

Swietenia mahagoni (L.) Jacq.
Family: Meliaceae

Trivial Names: Mahogany, Acajou (Haiti), Caoba (Cuba, Dominican Republic, Puerto Rico)

Description: This large tree has dark brown, rough bark and pinnately compound leaves with an even number of leaflets. The tree is semideciduous; older leaves are discarded in the spring during the period of new growth. The flowers occur in inconspicuous clusters. Usually a single flower in each cluster develops into an erect, five-lobed, woody pod, which splits from the base

to release winged seeds about 1 inch long.
Figure 374-375

Distribution: The mahogany is native to south Florida, the Bahamas, Cuba, Jamaica, Haiti, the Dominican Republic, and Puerto Rico. It is cultivated in Hawaii.

Toxic Part: Seeds are poisonous.

Toxin: Unknown

Symptoms: The following discussion is from a single case report. Two well-chewed seeds were ingested by an adult with an empty stomach. After three hours, the victim became giddy and then unconscious. Consciousness was regained about an hour later. There were multiple episodes of vomiting. Hypotension and bradycardia were observed and there were widespread ST-T wave abnormalities and nodal escape beats. The physical and laboratory examinations otherwise were normal. The patient recovered with treatment in 48 hours.

Management: The therapy employed in this case included atropine to manage the conduction defects and bradycardia. Fluids and vasopressors were given to support blood pressure.

References:
Raghuraman V, Raveendran M: Mahogany seeds--an unusual poison. *J Indian Med Assoc* 78:186-188, 1982.

Symphoricarpos species
Family: Caprifoliaceae

S. albus (L.) S.F. Blake (= *S. racemosus* Michx.)
S. occidentalis Hook.

Trivial Names: Snowberry, Belluaine (Canada), Buck Brush, Waxberry

Description: This deciduous shrub grows to about 3 feet and has simple, opposite, oval leaves up to 2 inches long. The small bell-shaped flowers are pink and grow in small clusters along the main stem. The fruit is a white berry. Figure 376

Distribution: Snowberry grows in woods and open slopes in southeastern Alaska (but not in the Yukon), Alberta to Quebec, south to California, Colorado, Nebraska, and Virginia.

Toxic Part: The berries are toxic if ingested in quantity.

Toxin: Unidentified (contains small quantities of chelidonine)

Symptoms: Emesis and catharsis result from ingestion of berries.

Management: Fluid replacement may be required to prevent dehydration, particularly in young children.

See also *Chelidonium majus*.

References:

Amyot T: Poisoning by snowberries. *Br Med J* 1:986, 1885.

Chavant L, et al: *Symphoricarpus racemosus* Michaux, Phytochemical research and study of the toxicity of the fruit. *Plantes Med Phytothérap* 9:267-272, 1979. (In French)

Lewis WH: Snowberry (*Symphoricarpos*) poisoning in children. *JAMA* 242:2663, 1979.

Szaufer M, et al: Chelidonine from *Symphoricarpos albus*. *Phytochemistry* 17:1446-1447, 1978.

Symplocarpus foetidus (L.) Nutt.
Family: Araceae

Trivial Names: Skunk Cabbage, Polecat Weed, Chou Puant or Tabac du Diable (Canada)

Description: The flowering spathe appears before the leaves in the spring. The spathe is 3 to 6 inches long and may be green, purple, or brown and striped or spotted. The leaves eventually reach 3 feet in length and 1 foot in width. All parts of this plant have an unpleasant odor. Figure 377-378

Distribution: Skunk cabbage grows from Quebec to Nova Scotia to North Carolina and Iowa.

Toxic Part: The leaves are injurious.

166

Toxin: Raphides of calcium oxalate and questionable unidentified protein

Symptoms: Painful burning of the lips and oral cavity result from chewing of leaves. An acute inflammatory reaction develops with bullae and edema. Hoarseness, dysphonia, and dysphagia occur. Due to the rapid onset of pain, the plant is rarely swallowed.

Management: The pain and edema subside slowly without therapy. Cool liquids or demulcents held in the mouth may bring some relief. Analgesics may be considered. The insoluble oxalate in these plants does not cause systemic poisoning in man.

References:

Plowman T: Folk uses of New World aroids. *Econ Bot* 23:97-122, 1969.

Taxus species
Family: Taxaceae

T. baccata L.
T. brevifolia Nutt.
T. canadensis Marsh.
T. cuspidata Nutt. ex Chapman

Trivial Names: Yew, Ground Hemlock

T. canadensis: Buis de Sapia (Canada)

Description: *Taxus* are evergreen trees and shrubs with alternate branchlets and reddish brown, thin, scaled bark. The flat, needle-like leaves are about 1 inch long and grow in opposite pairs along the twigs. The hard seeds are green to black and partially exposed in a fleshy red cup (aril). Figure 381-382

Distribution: *T. baccata* (English Yew) is cultivated in the southern United States.

T. brevifolia (Western Yew) grows from Alaska south along coastal British Columbia to western Washington,

167

Oregon, northern California, Idaho, and Montana and southern Alberta.

T. canadensis (Canada Yew) grows in Pennsylvania, West Virginia to Iowa north to southeastern Manitoba to Nova Scotia.

T. cuspidata (Japanese Yew) is cultivated in the north temperate zones.

Toxic Part: Most of the plant, including the seeds but *not* the red aril, is toxic.

Toxin: Taxine alkaloids

Symptoms: Dizziness, dry mouth, and mydriasis develop within one hour, followed by abdominal cramping, salivation, and emesis. A rash may appear; the face becomes pale and the lips are cyanotic. There is generalized weakness and the patient may become comatose. Bradycardia and other arrhythmias, hypotension, and dyspnea may be observed. Death is due to cardiac or respiratory failure. Allergic anaphylactoid-like reactions may result from chewing the needles.

Management: The stomach should be evacuated and a slurry of activated charcoal should be administered orally. Monitor the electrocardiogram. A temporary pacemaker may be indicated. Respiratory support must be given as required. Anaphylactoid reactions are treated with epinephrine, fluids, and respiratory assistance.

References:

Bryan-Brown T: The pharmacological actions of taxine. *Quart J Pharm Pharmacol* 5:205-219, 1932.

Burke MJ: On the allergic properties of yew. *NY State Med J* 79:1576-1577, 1979.

Miller RW: Brief survey of *Taxus* alkaloids and other taxane derivatives. *J Nat Prod* 43:425-437, 1980.

Morton J: Poisonous and injurious higher plants and fungi, in Tedeschi C, et al (eds): *Forensic Medicine*. Philadelphia, WB Saunders Co, vol III, 1977, 1544-1545.

Schulte T: Fatal poisoning from yew needles (*Taxus baccata*). *Arch Toxicol* 34:153-158, 1975. (In German)

Senilh V, et al: Presenting evidence of new analogs of taxol from extracts of *Taxus baccata*. *J Nat Prod* 47:131-137, 1984. (In French)

Thevetia peruviana (Pers.) K. Schum.
(= *T. neriifolium* A. Juss. ex Steud.)
Family: Apocynaceae

Trivial Names: Yellow Oleander, Ahouai des Antilles,
Be-Still Tree, Cablonga, Flor del Perú, Lucky Nut,
NOHO-MALIE (Hawaii), Retama, Serpent

Description: This small tree is 10 to 20 feet tall with
leaves resembling those of the *Nerium oleander* but
Thevetia has a milky sap. Flowers are yellow with a
peach tinge. The small (about 1 inch), clam-shaped fruit
contains two to four flat seeds. Figure 383-384

Distribution: *Thevetia* grows in south Florida and the
southwestern United States, the West Indies, Hawaii,
and Guam.

Toxic Part: All parts of the plant, particularly the
seeds, are poisonous.

Toxin: Digitalis-like glycosides

Symptoms: Pain in the oral cavity, nausea, emesis,
abdominal pain, cramping, and diarrhea result from
poisoning. Digitalis glycoside toxicity has a variable
latent period, which depends on the quantity ingested,
and is usually expressed as conduction defects and sinus
bradycardia. Hyperkalemia may be present. Rhythm
disturbances other than escape beats are not necessarily
exhibited.

Management: Gastric lavage or induced emesis should
be performed. Activated charcoal may be given
repeatedly later. Saline cathartics also may be useful.
Electrocardiographic monitoring and measurement of
serum potassium should be performed frequently.

Conduction defects may require the use of atropine or
transvenous pacing. Phenytoin is the agent of choice for
rhythm disturbances. Dialysis and forced diuresis are
not useful.

The digitalis-specific antibodies, Fab fragments, may
become the management of choice for life-threatening
toxicity but are not generally available yet.

References:

Ansford AJ, Morris H: Fatal oleander poisoning. *Med J Australia* 1:360-361, 1981.

Dickstein ES, Kunkel FW: Foxglove tea poisonings. *Am J Med* 69:167-169, 1980.

Ekins BR, Watanabe AS: Acute digoxin poisonings: Review of therapy. *Am J Hosp Pharm* 35:268-277, 1978.

Morton J: Poisonous and injurious higher plants and fungi, in Tedeschi C, et al (eds): *Forensic Medicine*. Philadelphia, WB Saunders Co, vol III, 1977, 1479-1481.

Smith TW, et al: Treatment of life-threatening digitalis intoxication with digoxin-specific Fab antibody fragments. Experience in 26 cases. *N Engl J Med* 307:1357-1362, 1982.

Urechites lutea (L.) Britton
Family: Apocynaceae

Trivial Names: Yellow Nightshade, Babeiro Amarillo (Puerto Rico), Bejuco Ahoja Vaca (Dominican Republic), Catesby's Vine (Bahamas), Corne Cabrite (Haiti), Curamagüey (Cuba), Nightsage (Jamaica), Wild Allamanda (Florida), Wild Nightshade, Wild Unction (Bahamas)

Description: Yellow nightshade is a shrubby vine with milky sap. The opposite leaves are 2 inches wide and 3.5 inches long, obtuse at both the tip and base. The flowers grow in a cluster (cyme) and only a few are open at one time. There are five yellow petals, which may be marked with red on the inside. The fruit usually appears in pairs as thin, woody, slightly curved pods up to 8 inches long. The pod contains winged seeds. Figure 397-398

Distribution: This plant grows in Florida, the Bahamas, and the Greater and Lesser Antilles south to St. Vincent.

Toxic Part: The leaf is poisonous.

Toxin: Urechitoxin, a cardiac glycoside

Symptoms: Pain in the oral cavity, nausea, emesis, abdominal pain, cramping, and diarrhea develop after ingestion. Digitalis glycoside toxicity has a variable latent period that depends on the quantity ingested and is usually expressed as conduction defects and sinus bradycardia. Hyperkalemia may be present. Rhythm disturbances other than escape beats are not necessarily exhibited.

Management: Gastric lavage or induced emesis should be performed. Activated charcoal may be given repeatedly later. Saline cathartics also may be useful. Electro-cardiographic monitoring and measurements of serum potassium should be done frequently.

Conduction defects may require the use of atropine or transvenous pacing. Phenytoin is the agent of choice for rhythm disturbances. Dialysis and forced diuresis are not useful.

The digitalis-specific antibodies, Fab fragments, may become the management of choice for life-threatening toxicity but are not generally available yet.

References:

Adams D, et al: *Poisonous Plants in Jamaica*. Kingston, University of West Indies, Dept Extra-Mural Studies, 1963, 36.

Dickstein ES, Kunkel FW: Foxglove tea poisonings. *Am J Med* 69:167-169, 1980.

Ekins BR, Watanabe AS: Acute digoxin poisonings: Review of therapy. *Am J Hosp Pharm* 35:268-277, 1978.

Smith TW, et al: Treatment of life-threatening digitalis intoxication with digoxin-specific Fab antibody fragments. Experience in 26 cases. *N Engl J Med* 307:1357-1362, 1982.

Urginea maritima (L.) Bak.
Family: Liliaceae

Trivial Names: Red Squill, Sea Onion, Squill

Description: *Urginea* grows from an onion-like bulb. The leaves are 1.5 feet long and 4 inches wide. Whitish flowers appear at the stem tips in dense clusters.
Figure 400-401

Distribution: Red squill is native to Eurasia and South Africa. It is primarily in cultivation for commercial extraction of squill, mostly in California.

Toxic Part: The bulbs are poisonous.

Toxin: Digitalis-like glycosides

Symptoms: Pain in the oral cavity, nausea, emesis, abdominal pain, cramping, and diarrhea result from poisoning. Digitalis glycoside toxicity has a variable latent period that depends on the quantity ingested and is usually expressed as conduction defects and sinus bradycardia. Hyperkalemia may be present. Rhythm disturbances other than escape beats are not necessarily exhibited.

Management: Gastric lavage or induced emesis should be performed. Activated charcoal may be given repeatedly later. Saline cathartics also may be useful. Electro-cardiographic monitoring and measurement of serum potassium should be performed frequently.

Conduction defects may require the use of atropine or transvenous pacing. Phenytoin is the agent of choice for rhythm disturbances. Dialysis and forced diuresis are not useful.

The digitalis-specific antibodies, Fab fragments, may become the management of choice for life-threatening toxicity but are not generally available yet.

References:

Dickstein ES, Kunkel FW: Foxglove tea poisonings. *Am J Med* 69:167-169, 1980.

Ekins BR, Watanabe AS: Acute digoxin poisonings: Review of therapy. *Am J Hosp Pharm* 35:268-277, 1978.

Smith TW, et al: Treatment of life-threatening digitalis intoxication with digoxin-specific Fab antibody fragments. Experience in 26 cases. *N Engl J Med* 307:1357-1362, 1982.

Veratrum **species**
Family: Liliaceae

V. album L.
V. californicum Durand
V. viride Ait.

Trivial Names: False Hellebore, American White Hellebore, Corn Lily, Earth Gall, Green Hellebore, Indian

Poke, Itch Weed, Pepper-Root, Rattlesnake Weed, Skunk Cabbage, Swamp Hellebore, Tickle Weed, White Hellebore

Description: *Veratrum* are tall perennial herbs with alternate, pleated leaves. The flowers are white marked with green on the top portion of the stalk. The fruit is a small pod containing winged seeds. Figure 405-408

Distribution: *V. album* grows in the Aleutian Islands, Alaska.

V. *californicum* grows on the west coast from Washington to Baja California east to Montana, Colorado, and New Mexico.

V. *viride* grows in Alaska, the Yukon, British Columbia, Alberta, Oregon, Montana, Minnesota, and Quebec south to Tennessee and Georgia.

Toxic Part: All parts of this plant are poisonous.

Toxin: Veratrum alkaloids

Symptoms: A burning sensation and pain in the upper abdominal area are followed by salivation, nausea, and episodes of vomiting. Sweating, blurred vision, and confusion may develop. Bradycardia and hypotension occur. Symptoms have been described as "having a heart attack." Even in severe intoxications, symptoms usually disappear within 24 hours.

Management: Severe hypotension is managed by fluid replacement, positioning, and administration of ephedrine if needed. Bradycardia responds to atropine. Ingestion of large quantities produces central respiratory depression that requires ventilatory support.

References:

Benforado J: The veratrum alkaloids, in Root W, Hofmann F (eds): *Physiological Pharmacology*. New York, Academic Press, vol 4, 1967, 331-398.

Hruby K, et al: Poisoning with *Veratrum album*. *Wien Klin Wschr* 93:517-519, 1981. (In German)

Kupchan SM: Hypotensive veratrum alkaloids. *J Pharm Sci* 50:273-287, 1961.

Nelson DA: Accidental poisoning by *Veratrum japonicum*. *JAMA* 156:33-35, 1954.

Viscum album L.
Family: Loranthaceae

Trivial Names: (European) **Mistletoe**

Description: This parasite grows primarily on the trunks of deciduous trees, particularly the apple. Stems are much branched and the leaves are 2 to 3 inches long, thick, leathery, and usually a pale yellowish green. The fruit is a sticky white berry. Figure 409

Distribution: This European plant was introduced into Sonoma county California.

Toxic Part: Only the leaves and stems are toxic. The berries are presumed to be harmless.

Toxin: Viscumin, a toxic lectin (toxalbumin), inhibits protein synthesis. Related lectins, collectively the viscotoxins, are present but activity following oral administration has not been reported.

Symptoms: The toxin is similar in action to the lectins contained in *Abrus precatorius* and *Ricinus communis* but is less potent. Following a latent period of many hours, abdominal pain and diarrhea occur. Necrotic lesions may be produced along the entire gastroenteric tract.

Management: Severe poisoning is rare. Therapy should be as for severe gastroenteritis. Loss of bowel function may occur after massive overdose, eg, ingestion of tea made from a large quantity of mistletoe leaves. Despite parenteral alimentation, such an intoxication may be irreversible.

References:

Anderson LA, Phillipson JD: Mistletoe--the magic herb. *Pharm J* 229:437-439, 1982.

Olsnes S, et al: Isolation and characterization of viscumin, a toxic lectin from *Viscum album* L. *J Biol Chem* 257:13263-13270, 1982.

Stirpe F, et al: Inhibition of protein synthesis by a toxic lectin from *Viscum album* (mistletoe). *Biochem J* 190:843-845, 1980.

Stirpe F, et al: Action of viscumin, a toxic lectin from

mistletoe, on cells in culture. *J Biol Chem* 257:13271-13277, 1982.

Wisteria species
Family: Leguminosae (Fabaceae)

W. floribunda (Willd.) DC.
W. sinensis (Sims) Sweet

Trivial Names: Wisteria or **Wistaria,** Kidney Bean Tree

Description: These woody vines bear masses of sweetpea-like flowers, which are usually blue, but pink and white varieties also exist. The pods of *W. floribunda* are smooth; those of *W. sinensis* are covered with velvety down. The pods persist through winter. Figure 412-414

Distribution: Wisterias are hardy in the north but are most common in the southeastern United States as far west as Texas.

Toxic Part: All parts of this plant are toxic. Statements in the literature that the flowers are nontoxic are in error.

Toxin: An uncharacterized glycoside, wistarine, and a lectin

Symptoms: Nausea, abdominal pain, and repeated emesis occur. Diarrhea is slight or absent. Ingestion of massive amounts (from chewing the bark) have produced fluid loss sufficient to cause hypovolemic shock.

Management: Antiemetics are useful. Fluid replacement should be instituted if indicated. Patients are usually asymptomatic within 24 hours.

References:

Jacobziner H, Rabin HW: Briefs on accidental chemical poisonings in New York city. *NY State J Med* 61:2463-2466, 1961.

Kurokawa T, et al: Purification and characterization of a lectin from *Wistaria floribunda* seeds. *J Biol Chem* 251:5686-5693, 1976.

Materazzi G: Contribution of clinical cases and studies on poisoning by the seeds of glicine (*Wistaria chinensis* Curt). *Minerva Ped* 22:1754-1756, 1970. (In Italian)

Ventura R: On two cases of Wistaria (*Wistaria chinensis* Curt) poisoning. *Minerva Medicolegale* 76(4):180-181, 1956. (In Italian)

Verhulst HL: Wisteria. National Clearinghouse For Poison Control Centers Bulletin, July-August, 1961.

Xanthosoma species
Family: Araceae

Trivial Names: Blue 'APE or Blue Taro (Hawaii), Caraïbe (Haiti), Malanga (Cuba), Yautía (Puerto Rico)

Description: *Xanthosoma* resemble caladium, but the leaves are more spear shaped. The tubers or rhizomes are thick, and the sap is milky. Figure 415-416

Distribution: This plant is in cultivation in the southern United States, Hawaii, the West Indies, and Guam.

Toxic Part: The leaves are injurious. Some species are grown for their edible tubers.

Toxin: Raphides of calcium oxalate and questionable unidentified protein

Symptoms: Intense burning in the mouth and lips usually prevents swallowing of significant amounts. Inflammation occurs, sometimes with bullae and edema. Direct irritant dermatitis also has been observed.

Management: Pain and swelling recede slowly without therapy. Holding a cool liquid or demulcent in the mouth may bring relief.

References:

Mitchell J, Rook A: *Botanical Dermatology*. Vancouver, Greengrass, 1979.

Plowman T: Folk uses of New World aroids. *Econ Bot* 23:97-122, 1969.

Sakai WS, Hanson M: Mature raphid and raphid idioblast structure in plants of the edible Aroid genera *Colocasia*, *Alocasia*, and *Xanthosoma*. *Ann Bot* 38:739-748, 1974.

Zamia pumila L.

(All formerly named species of *Zamia* have been consolidated as *Zamia pumila*.)

Family: Zamiaceae

Trivial Names: Coontie, Bay Rush (Bahamas), Comptie, Guayiga (Dominican Republic), Florida Arrowroot, Marunguey (Puerto Rico), Palmita de Jardín (Puerto Rico), Sago Cycas, Seminole Bread, Yuguilla (Cuba)

Description: The short trunk of the *Zamia* may be entirely underground and a few (rarely more than 12) leaves emerge directly from it. The leaves are pinnate, somewhat palm-like, and about 2 feet long. Both male and female cones are produced. Figure 417-418

Distribution: *Zamia* grows on the southeastern coast of Georgia, throughout Florida, the Bahamas, the northwestern coast of Jamaica, the Dominican Republic, and Puerto Rico. It is absent from Haiti, the Virgin Islands, and the remainder of the West Indies.

Toxic Part: The roots and trunk are poisonous. The toxin can be removed from the grated root by water; treated plant material was a commercial source of starch in Florida until the 1920s.

Toxin: Cycasin, methylazoxymethanol-glucoside

Symptoms: The most common response is vomiting, which may be persistent. Other symptoms may include diarrhea, colic, depression, and muscular paralysis.

Management: Other than fluid replacement and symptomatic care, no specific therapy can be recommended.

References:

Second Conference on the Identification of Toxic Elements of Cycads. National Institutes of Health, (Aug 17) 1962.

Proceedings of the Third Conference on the Toxicity of Cycads. National Institutes of Health, (Apr 17) 1964. *Fed Proc* 23:1337-1388, (Nov-Dec) 1964.

Fifth Conference on Cycad Toxicity. National Institutes of Health, (Apr 24-25) 1967.

Sixth International Cycad Conference. *Fed Proc* 31:1465-1546, (Sept-Oct) 1972.

Dossaji SF: The distribution of azoxyglycosides, amino acids, and bioflavinoids in the order Cycadales: Their taxonomic, phylogenetic, and toxicological significance. PhD dissertation, University of Texas (Austin), 1974.

Kurland LT (ed): Conference on the Identification of Toxic Elements of Cycads. National Institutes of Health, (Feb 28) 1962.

Morton JF: Poisonous and injurious plants and fungi, in Tedeschi CG, et al (eds): *Forensic Medicine*. Philadelphia, WB Saunders, vol 3, 1977, 1456-1567.

Whiting MG: Toxicity of cycads. *Econ Bot* 17:271-302, 1963.

Whiting MG (ed): Conference on the Toxicity of Cycads (Fourth). National Institutes of Health, (Apr 15) 1965.

Zantedeschia aethiopica (L.) Spreng.
Family: Araceae

Trivial Names: Calla, Calla Lily, Lirio Cala (Spanish)

Description: This is the calla of gardeners, not the true calla (*Calla palustris*). This plant has smooth-edged arrowhead-shaped leaves that are sometimes mottled with white and grow on long, stout stalks. The showy flowering spathe flares out like a lily. It is white or green in this species but may be pink or yellow in others. Figure 419

Distribution: *Zantedeschia* is grown outdoors in mild climates and as a greenhouse or house plant elsewhere.

Toxic Part: The leaves are injurious.

Toxin: Raphides of calcium oxalate and possible unidentified protein

Symptoms: Intense burning of the lips and mouth usually prevents swallowing of significant amounts. Inflammation and sometimes bullae and edema develop.

Direct irritant dermatitis also occurs. These insoluble oxalates do not produce systemic poisoning in man.

Management: No treatment is required. Holding cool liquids or demulcents in the mouth may bring some relief. Analgesics may be given in severe cases.

References:

Mitchell J, Rook A: *Botanical Dermatology*. Vancouver, Greengrass, 1979.

Plowman T: Folk uses of New World aroids. *Econ Bot* 23:97-122, 1969.

Zephyranthes atamasco (L.) Herb (= *Amaryllis atamasco* L.)
Family: Amaryllidaceae

Trivial Names: Atamasco Lily, Fairy Lily, Rain Lily, Zephyr Lily

Description: The grassy leaves of *Zephyranthes* emerge from the ground and grow to a length of 1 foot. The flowers form on a hollow, leafless stalk and are usually white but may be tinged with purple. The plant is propagated by bulbs.

Distribution: *Zephyranthes* grow in wet areas from Virginia to Florida west to Alabama. Figure 420

Toxic Part: The bulb is poisonous.

Toxin: Lycorine

Symptoms: Ingestion of large quantities may produce nausea and persistent emesis with diarrhea.

Management: Human poisonings are infrequent because of the small concentration of alkaloids. Fluid replacement may be required if dehydration develops. See *Narcissus*.

References:

Jasperson-Schib R: Toxic Amaryllidaceae. *Pharm Acta Helv* 45:424-433, 1970. (In German)

Zigadenus species (sometimes written *Zygadenus*)
Family: Liliaceae

Trivial Names: Death Camas, Alkali Grass, Hog's
Potato, Myster Grass, Poison Sego, Sand Corn, Soap
Plant, Squirrel Food, Water Lily, Wild Onion

Description: These perennial herbs have grass-like
leaves up to 1.5 feet long. The flowers form along the top
of the central stalk and are usually yellow or whitish
green. Most species of *Zigadenus* have an onion-like
bulb, but none have the characteristic onion odor.
Figure 421-422

Distribution: *Zigadenus* species are found throughout
the United States except the extreme southeast and Hawaii;
it also is found across Canada and in Alaska.

Toxic Part: All parts of the plant, including the flowers,
are toxic.

Toxin: Zygadenine, zygacine, iso- and neogermidine,
protoveratridine

Symptoms: Burning in the mouth, thirst, persistent
emesis, headache, dizziness, bradycardia, hypotension,
and convulsions result from poisoning.

Management: Fluids, atropine, and positioning of the
patient may be required. If hypotension does not respond
to these measures, ephedrine may be given.

References:

Catterall WA: Neurotoxins that act on voltage-sensitive
sodium channels in excitable membranes. *Ann Rev
Pharmacol Toxicol* 20:15-43, 1980.

Krayer O, et al: Pharmacological and chemical relation
between the veratrum alkaloids and the zygadenus
alkaloids. *Fed Proc* 11:364, 1952.

Spoerke DG, Spoerke SE: Three cases of *Zigadenus*
(death camas) poisoning. *Vet Hum Toxicol* 21:346-347,
1979.

Yaffe S, Kupchan SM: Veratrine-like properties of the
alkaloidal fractions from *Zygadenus venenosus*.
Fed Proc 9:326, 1950.

II.

Plant Dermatitis

II.

Plant Dermatitis

The most common adverse reactions to plants are cutaneous injuries. These can result from simple mechanical or chemical trauma, a photochemical response to psoralens contained in some species, or sensitization to plant allergens. Some plants produce cutaneous damage by more than one mechanism (eg, carrots are phototoxic and allergic sensitizers). Certain dermal reactions, such as contact urticaria, may be nonimmunologic, immunologic, or both. The diagnosis and treatment of plant dermatitis may be complicated further by secondary infection, id reactions, excoriation from scratching, or improper therapy. Identification of the responsible plant is important to prevent repeated exposure.

The discussion in this section is concerned with plant dermatitis *per se*. Dermatitis from plant derivatives, such as lacquers, sawdust, essential oils, perfumes, or flavorings, is not discussed. See Table 1 for a list of common dermatitis-producing plants.

Mechanical Or Irritant Chemical Injury

Contact with plants having thorns, bristles, spines, barbs, or sharp serrated edges can cause lacerations or puncture wounds often embedded with plant particles. These injuries are rarely complicated, but cutaneous penetration by plant parts may introduce opportunistic bacteria or fungus. The fine stiff hairs (glochids) of cactus in the genus *Opuntia* often produce an aseptic granulomatous condition resembling scabies. Embedded thorns have produced more serious problems, such as osteoblastic or osteolytic changes in bone, synovitis in joints, or soft tissue granulomas. Plants with irritant hairs or detachable needles are listed in Table 2.

Plants of the family Araceae, eg, dumbcane (*Dieffenbachia*), and certain palms, eg, fishtail palm (*Caryota mitis*), contain bundles of needle-like, water-insoluble crystals of calcium oxalate. When the plant cell is disrupted, these needles (raphides) are ejected from the bundles. Cutaneous exposure to the juice from fresh cuttings produces intense, painful itching. This is probably a mechanical rather than chemical response since a similar effect is produced by fibers of glass wool having the same diameter. A list of plants containing irritant raphides is given in Table 3.

In the case of lacerations or punctures, simple cleansing of the wound to remove dirt and plant material is usually adequate. Antibiotic therapy should be reserved for secondary infections. Deeply embedded thorn fragments should be excised, and tetanus prophylaxis should be administered if indicated. Raphides or glochids may be removed by placing adhesive tape lightly over the surface and gently lifting it away. The application of petrolatum also may provide some relief.

Many plants contain substances that produce direct irritation of the skin and mucous membranes. These chemicals affect most, if not all, persons, and the individual's allergic tendencies have no influence on the response. The skin reaction usually takes place shortly after exposure, which distinguishes it from allergic contact dermatitis; however, these reactions cannot be differentiated readily by examination of the skin. The extent of trauma is determined by the potency of the irritant, its concentration, and the duration of contact. The lesion is limited to the area exposed. Regions of the skin having a thickened horny layer (palms and soles) are less sensitive then areas where the stratum corneum is thin.

Although a number of plants, such as buttercup (*Ranunculus*), daphne (*Daphne mezereum*), and hot pepper (*Capsicum annuum*), contain potent irritants, most vesicant injuries are due to the terpene-containing latex of many members of the family Euphorbiaceae. This latex exerts a caustic action on the skin and causes keratoconjunctivitis with temporary blindness after corneal contact. See Table 4 for a list of plants containing irritant sap or latex.

The irritant sap or latex should be removed by flushing the skin with water. A mild soap may be needed to remove gummy plant residues. Cool, moist dressings may relieve pain and reduce swelling. In ocular exposures, the eye must be irrigated immediately. The pupil should be dilated with a cycloplegic agent and artificial tears may be instilled. Steroids should not be

used unless edema persists and secondary infection
has been ruled out.

Contact Urticaria

Contact urticaria is defined as a transient urticarial
reaction or, less frequently, a wheel-and-flare response
occurring within 30 minutes of cutaneous exposure. The
reaction may be nonimmunologic or allergic, but the
former is more common. Plants may produce both
reactions.

It is presumed that urticariants either cause the
release of histamine and other vasoactive substances
after cutaneous penetration or that they contain these
substances themselves and introduce them into the
skin by means of specialized hairs. Almost all individuals
are assumed to be vulnerable to nonimmunologic
contact urticaria following sufficient exposure. In the
northern hemisphere, members of the family, Urticaceae
(nettles), or species of *Cnidoscolus* are associated with
this type of response. See Table 2.

Typically, an almost instantaneous, intense, burning
sensation occurs on contact with the stinging hairs
followed by itching, which may last for a few hours.
Exposure to *Cnidoscolus* also may be associated with
ipsilateral swelling of more proximal lymph nodes.
Treatment usually is not required; however, if itching
is intense, antihistamines (eg, hydroxyzine,
cyproheptadine) may be given orally.

An immunologic basis for the urticarial response
to some plants can be demonstrated by the Prausnitz-
Küstner test (passive serum transfer). Atopic patients may
display immediate contact urticaria as an expression
of a cross-allergy. Contact urticaria associated with potato
peels, onion, garlic, apples, birch trees, and certain
spices may be associated with noncutaneous allergic
manifestations, including rhinoconjunctivitis,
angioedema, asthma, gastroenteric disturbances, or
anaphylaxis. There has been a recent report of
anaphylaxis secondary to the introduction of grass pollens
through abraded skin.

Photodermatitis

Psoralens (furocoumarins) in certain plant species
can sensitize the skin to ultraviolet light. The mechanism
is phototoxic rather than photoallergic. Moisture plays
a significant role in facilitating the transfer of psoralens

into the skin. Subsequent exposure of the affected area
to sunlight results in erythema ranging from mild sunburn
to severe secondary burn with enormous bullae. As the
inflammation resolves, hyperpigmentation develops. This
may persist for many months. Psoralen-containing
plants are listed in Table 5.

As with sunburn, inflammation can be suppressed
by the oral administration of prostaglandin inhibitors,
such as aspirin. Application of cold compresses may
ease the burning sensation during the acute phase. The
affected area should be protected from sunlight and
fluorescent lights for two weeks after exposure.

Allergic Contact Dermatitis

This allergic phenomenon requires previous
sensitization to the plant allergen before subsequent
cutaneous contact with the plant will result in
dermatitis. The sensitizing compound is usually a hapten,
which reacts with skin protein to form an antigen.
Allergic contact dermatitis is a cell-mediated immune
reaction effected by thymus-derived lymphocytes
(T-cells) and has no relationship to the patient's other
allergies (eg, hayfever, food allergy, asthma). In atopic
patients, allergic contact dermatitis may resemble atopic
eczema.

Plants of the poison ivy family (Anacardiaceae)
most commonly cause allergic contact dermatitis in
the western hemisphere. In the United States, poison ivy
(*Toxicodendron radicans*) and western poison oak
(*T. diversilobum*) are responsible for more clinical cases
than all other plant, household chemical, and industrial
chemical sensitizers combined. The economic impact of
dermatitis produced by these plants is considerable;
poison oak is responsible for over 50% of the workmen's
compensation cases in California. The sensitizer in
these plants (various unsaturated, long-chain, substituted
catechols) is contained in special channels. Contact
with the intact plant does not produce sensitization or
dermatitis.

A genetic, antigen-specific tolerance to the sensitizer
in the Anacardiaceae appears to exist in 15% to 30% of
the population. Race, age, and sex are of minor importance
in the proclivity for becoming sensitized. One or more
contacts with the plant allergen may be necessary before
the individual becomes sensitized. An incubation period
of 5 to 21 days is needed after initial contact to produce

the immunologic changes required to elicit a clinically evident cutaneous response. Once established, sensitivity to the Anacardiaceae usually persists for decades and any part of the body surface may react.

The severity of the response varies greatly among patients. In studies utilizing a measured quantity of allergen, some patients experienced a disabling reaction while others displayed only mild erythema. The response also is determined by the amount of allergen, the size of the exposed area, and the thickness of the stratum corneum at the exposure site. Following contact, 12 to 48 hours or more elapse before a cutaneous response becomes evident. This latent period is important to determine the mechanism of the reaction. Erythema develops initially, frequently with edematous swelling. Rash usually is limited to the area of contact, but previous reaction sites, including patch test areas, may flare. During the following 24 hours, blisters (vesicles or bullae) form containing nonallergenic serous fluid, which cannot spread the dermatitis. Exudation may be marked. Intense itching is a prominent and consistent feature of allergic contact dermatitis. Crusting and scaling begin within a few days and, in the absence of complications or continued exposure, the dermatitis rarely lasts longer than ten days. Allergic contact dermatitis affecting the eyelids or scrotum is usually expressed as diffuse edematous erythema. The soles, palms, and hairy scalp are rarely affected.

Immediate recognition of exposure permits prompt removal of the allergen and may avoid dermatitis. About ten minutes are required for cutaneous penetration of the allergen. Washing with running water is recommended, but the use of soap is discouraged because it removes protective skin oils and may increase penetration of the allergen. Organic solvents, such as alcohol, should be employed with care to avoid spreading the allergen over a wider area. Early application of topical steroids minimizes the severity of dermatitis. Systemic steroids given during the first six hours after exposure are maximally effective. Patients with severe disabling dermatitis (face, genitals, or over 25% of the body surface) should receive large doses, eg, a single 40 mg IM dose of methylprednisolone or an oral dose of 15 mg dexamethasone taken in 4 or 5 divided doses during the first two days. Potent topical steroids also have been employed during the acute phase.

Adjunctive therapy is directed at reducing pruritus and discomfort and protecting against excoriation. Cool, moist compresses may be applied. Various shake lotions, such as calamine, are useful, but products containing local anesthetics (eg, benzocaine), irritants (eg, phenol, camphor), or metals (eg, zirconium, iron) should be avoided. Systemic antihistamines are ineffective against the rash, but their sedative action may promote sleep.

The only effective prophylaxis is to avoid contact with the offending plant or fomites carrying the allergen (animal fur, contaminated tools and clothing, camping gear, and smoke containing unburned plant particles). Individuals with occupations or recreations in which contact is likely should wear as much protective clothing as practical and avoid touching the face or genitals with unwashed hands. The allergen may be removed from clothing or contaminated equipment by washing with water.

No cream, lotion, or spray has been found to exert surface protection against the allergen, although some promising polymeric compounds are being studied. Attempts at desensitization also have been disappointing. These have ranged from the folk practice of eating the newly formed leaves in the spring to the oral and systemic administration of allergen extracts. The degree of hyposensitization is limited and usually of short (less than one season) duration. The adverse reactions reported include pruritus, dermatitis, gastroenteric disturbances, inflammation at the site of injection, fever, glomerulonephritis, nephrotic syndrome, and death. Convulsions have occurred in children following oral administration of plant extract. The risk:benefit ratio should be assessed carefully and these procedures reserved for occupationally exposed individuals and those whose sensitivity and probability of exposure place them at high risk of experiencing severe debilitating dermatitis.

Allergic contact dermatitis from plants other than those in the poison ivy family occurs. Individuals sensitive to one species of the Anacardiaceae react to another (see Table 6), but cross sensitivity does not extend to allergens in other plant families. The potency of the allergens present in these families varies, but they are generally weaker sensitizers and multiple, prolonged, massive exposures are necessary for sensitization.

Many species of the families Compositae (Asteraceae), Magnoliaceae, and the Jubulaceae (liverworts) contain sensitizing sesquiterpene lactones in all plant parts except the pollen. Rashes appearing in late summer on exposed body surfaces (so-called "ragweed pollen dermatitis") should be attributed to airborne plant fragments rather than pollen.

Some members of the Orchidaceae and Liliaceae contain allergenic quinones and lactones that produce chronic eczematous dermatitis in occupationally exposed patients ("tulip fingers," "lily rash"). Typically there is hyperkeratosis, painful fissures of the fingertips, and onycholysis. Agricultural workers, food handlers, and chefs often develop sensitivity to allergens in a number of vegetables. Patch testing may be needed to identify the offending material.

RECOMMENDED FOR FURTHER READING

Cronin E: *Contact Dermatitis*. Edinburgh, Churchill & Livingstone, 1980.

Fisher AA: *Contact Dermatitis*, ed 2. Philadelphia, Lea & Febiger, 1973.

Guin JD, Beaman JH: *Toxicodendrons* and *Toxicodendron* dermatitis. *Contin Educat Fam Phys* 14:23-32, June, 1981.

Hausen BM: *Woods Injurious to Human Health*. New York, Walter de Gruyter, 1981.

Lampe KF: Contact dermatitis and other types of plant dermatitis, in Drill VA, Lazar P (eds): *Cutaneous Toxicity*. New York, Raven Press, 1984.

Mitchell J, Rook A: *Botanical Dermatology*. Vancouver, Greengrass, 1979.

Sakai WS, et al: Study of raphide microstructure in relation to irritation. *Scanning Electron Microscopy* 2:979-986, 1984.

Stoner B, Rasmussen JE: Plant dermatitis. *J Am Acad Dermatol* 9:1-15, 1983.

Storrs FJ (ed): Symposium on contact dermatitis. *Dermatol Clinics* 2:521-660, 1984.

Woods B, Calnan CD: Toxic woods. *Br J Dermatol* 95(suppl 13):1-97, 1976.

Table 1.
Representative Plants Causing Contact Dermatitis

Botanical Name	Trivial Name	Figure
Amaryllidaceae		
Narcissus species	Daffodil, Narcissus, Jonquil	272
Anacardiaceae		
See Table 6		
Annonaceae		
Asimina triloba (L.) Dunal.	Pawpaw	55
Apocynaceae		
Allamanda cathartica L.	Allamanda, Canario	25-26
Nerium oleander L.	Oleander	273-275
See Table 4		
Araceae		
See Table 3		
Araliaceae		
Hedera canariensis Willd.	Alegerian Ivy	189
H. helix L.	English Ivy	190-191.
Aristolochiaceae		
Aristolochia elegans M.T. Mast	Calico Flower	50
A. gigantea Mart. & Zucc. non Hook.		51-52
A. grandiflora Swartz	Pelican Flower	
Asclepiadaceae		
See Table 4		
Bignoniaceae		
Campsis radicans (L.) Seem.	Trumpet Creeper	81
Bromeliaceae		
Ananas comosus (L.) Merrill	Pineapple	
Chenopodiaceae		
Sarcobatus vermiculatus (Hook.) Torr.	Greasewood	
Commelinaceae		
Rhoeo spathacea (Swartz) Stearn	Moses-in-a-Boat,	335
(= *R. discolor* (L'Her.) Hance)	Oyster Plant	
Setcreasea pallida Rose cv.	Purple Queen	356
'Purple Heart' (= *S. purpurea* Boom)		
Compositae (Asteraceae)		
Ambrosia species	Ragweed	
Artemisia species	Mugwort	
Aster species	Aster, Daisy	
Chrysanthemum species	Chrysanthemum, Daisy,	101-104
	Feverfew, Marguerite	
Erigeron species	Fleabane	162
Franseria acanthicarpa (Hook.)	Poverty Weed	
Coville (= *Ambrosia acanthicarpa*		
Hook.)		
Gaillardia species	Gaillardia	
Helenium autumnale L.	Sneezeweed	

Table 1. (cont.)
Representative Plants Causing
Contact Dermatitis

Botanical Name	Trivial Name	Figure
H. microcephalum DC.		
Iva species	Marsh Elder	
Lactuca sativa L.	Lettuce	
Oxytenia acerosa Nutt.	Copper Weed	
(= *Iva acerosa* (Nutt.) R.C. Jackson)		
Parthenium argentatum Gray	Guayule	
P. hysterophorus L.	Parthenium	
Rudbeckia hirta L.	Black-eyed Susan	
(= *R. serotina* Nutt.)		
Soliva pterosperma (Juss.) Less.		
Tanacetum vulgare L.	Tansy	380
Tagetes minuta L.	Mexican Marigold	
Xanthium species	Cocklebur	
See Table 5		
Convolvulaceae		
Dichondra repens J.R. and G. Forst.		
Cornaceae		
See Table 2		
Euphorbiaceae		
Hura crepitans L.	Monkey Pistol, Sandbox Tree, Javillo	205-207
Ricinus communis L.	Castor Bean, Higuereta, Ricino	336-337
See Table 4		
Fumariaceae		
Dicentra spectabilis (L.) Lem.	Bleeding Heart	
Gingkoaceae		
Gingko biloba L.	Gingko, Maidenhair Tree	184
Gramineae (Poaceae)		
Oryza sativa L.	Rice	
Panicum glutinosum Sw.	Sticky Grass	287
Secale cereale L.	Rye	
Hydrophyllaceae		
Phacelia campanularia Gray	California Bluebell	294
P. crenulata Torr. ex S. Wats.	Scorpion Flower	295
P. minor (Harv.) Thell. ex F. Zimm.	Whitlavia	
(= *P. whitlavia* A. Gray; *Whitlavia grandiflora* Harv.)		
P. parryi Torr.		
P. viscida (Benth. ex Lindl.) Torr.		
See Table 2		
Juglandaceae		
Juglans nigra L.	Black Walnut	

Table 1. (cont.)
Representative Plants Causing Contact Dermatitis

Botanical Name	Trivial Name	Figure
Leguminosae (Fabaceae)		
Prosopis glandulosa Torr.	Mesquite	317
(= *P. juliflora* (Sw.) DC. var.		
glandulosa (Torr.) Cockerell)		
See Table 2		
Liliaceae		
Allium cepa L.	Onion, Cebolla	29
A. sativum L.	Garlic, Ajo	
Hyacinthus species	Hyacinth	208
Tulipa species	Tulip	
Loranthaceae		
Phoradendron serotinum (Raf.) M.C.	(American) Mistletoe	302
Johnst. (= *P. flavescens* (Pursh)		
Nutt.)		
Magnoliaceae		
Magnolia grandiflora L.	Magnolia, Bull Bay	249
Moraceae		
Maclura pomifera (Raf.) C.K. Schneid.	Osage Orange	248
See Table 5		
Myrtaceae		
Eucalyptus globulus Labill.	Blue Gum, Eucalyptus	165
Orchidaceae		
Cypripedium species	Lady's Slipper	141-142
Palmae (Arecaceae)		
See Table 3		
Pinaceae		
Abies balsamea (L.) Mill.	Balsam Fir	
Primulaceae		
Primula farinosa L.	Birdseye Primrose	
P. obconica Hance	Primula, German Primrose	316
Proteaceae		
Grevillea banksii R. Br.	KAHILI Flower	
G. robusta A. Cunn.	Silk(y) Oak	186
Ranunculaceae		
See Table 4		
Rosaceae		
Agrimonia species	Agrimony	19
Rosa odorata (Andr.) Sweet	Tea Rose	
See Table 5		
Rutaceae		
See Table 5		
Saxifragaceae		
Hydrangea species	Hydrangea	209
Solanaceae		
Lycopersicon esculentum Mill.	Tomato	

Table 1. (cont.)
Representative Plants Causing Contact Dermatitis

Botanical Name	Trivial Name	Figure
Solanum carolinense L.	Horse Nettle	362
S. tuberosum L.	Potato	367
Thymelaeaceae		
See Table 4		
Ulmaceae		
Ulmus glabra Huds.	Wych Elm, Scotch Elm	
U. procera Salisb.	English Elm	396
Umbelliferae (Apiaceae)		
See Table 5		
Urticaceae		
See Table 2		
Vitaceae		
See Table 3		
Zygophyllaceae		
Larrea tridentata (Sesse & Moc. ex DC.) Coville (= *L. glutinosa* Engelm.)	Creosote Bush	234

Table 2.
Representative Plants with External Irritant, Stinging Hairs, or Detachable Needles

Botanical Name	Trivial Name	Figure
Cactaceae		
Opuntia species (eg, *O. microdasys* (Lehm.) Pfeiff.)	Bunny Ears	281-282
Cannabidaceae		
Humulus lupulus L.	Hops	204
Cornaceae		
Cornus sanguinea L.	Bloodtwig Dogwood	130
Euphorbiaceae		
Acidoton urens Sw.	Mountain Cowitch	
Cnidoscolus chayamansa McVaugh	Chaya	116
C. stimulosus (Michx.) Engelm.	Tread Softly, Bull Nettle	117
C. texanus (Muell. Arg.) Small		
C. urens (L.) Arth. (= *Jatropha urens* L.)		
Dalechampia scandens L.	Liane Gratté	
Platygyne hexandra (Jacq.) Muell. Arg.	Pringamosa	
Tragia volubilis L.	Pringamosa	395
Hydrophyllaceae		
Phacelia imbricata Greene		
P. malvifolia Cham.	Stinging Phacelia	
Wigandia caracasana H.B.K.		
W. urens (Ruiz & Pav.) H.B.K.		410-411
Leguminosae (Fabaceae)		
Lupinus hirsutissimus Benth.	Stinging Lupine	
Mucuna deeringiana (Bort) Merrill (= *Stitzlobium deeringianum* Bort)	Velvet Bean	266
M. pruriens DC. (= *Stitzlobium pruriens* (L.) Medik.; *Dolichos pruriens* L.)	Cowhage, Cowitch, Pica-Pica, Pois Gratté, Vine Gungo Pea	267-269
M. urens (L.) DC.	Bejuco Jairey, Ox-Eye Bean, Yeaux Bourrique, Torteza	
Malpighiaceae		
Malpighia polytricha A. Juss.	Touch-Me-Not	250
M. urens L.	Cowitch Cherry	251-252
Sterculiaceae		
Sterculia apetala (Jacq.) Karst. (in exposed fruit)		372
Urticaceae		
Laportea aestuans (L.) Chew (= *Fleurya aestuans* (L.) Guad.)	Pica-Pica	
L. canadensis (L.) Weddell	Wood Nettle	233
Urera baccifera (L.) Weddell	Ortiga Brava	399
Urtica dioica L.	Stinging Nettle	402-403
U. urens L.	Stinging Nettle	404

Table 3.
Representative Plants Containing Irritant Raphides

Botanical Name	Trivial Name	Figure
Araceae		
Alocasia species (eg, *A. macrorrhiza* (L.) G. Don)	Elephant's Ear, Taro	32-33
Anthurium andreanum Linden.	Flamingo Lily	42
Arum italicum Mill.	Italian Arum	53
A. maculatum L.	Cuckoopint	54
Caladium bicolor (Ait.) Venten.	Caladium	70
Calla palustris L.	Water Arum	71
Colocasia species (eg, *C. esculenta* (L.) Schott)	Elephant's Ear	119
Dieffenbachia species	Dumbcane	152-154
Epipremnum aureum Bunt. (= *Pothos aureus* Linden & Andre; *Raphidophora aurea* Birdsey; *Scindapsus aureus* Engl.)	Pothos	161
Philodendron scandens C. Koch & H. Sello ssp. *oxycardium* (Schott) Bunt.	Heartleaf Philodendron	296
P. selloum C. Koch		297
Palmae (Arecaceae)		
Caryota mitis Lour.	Fishtail Palm	85
Vitaceae		
Parthenocissus quinquefolia (L.) Planch.	Virginia Creeper	288
P. tricuspidata (Siebold & Zucc.) Planch.	Boston Ivy	289

Table 4.
Representative Plants Containing an Irritant Sap or Latex

Botanical Name	Trivial Name	Figure
Agavaceae		
Agave species (eg, *A. americana* L.)	Century Plant, Maguey	17-18
Apocynaceae		
Acokanthera oblongifolia (Hochst.) Codd (= *A. spectabilis* (Sond.) Hook. f.)	Bushman's Poison, Wintersweet	4
Plumeria species	Frangipani	311-312
Asclepiadaceae		
Calotropis gigantea (L.) Ait. f.	Crown Flower	74
C. procera (Ait.) Ait. f.	Algodón de Seda	

Table 4. (Cont.)
Representative Plants Containing an Irritant Sap or Latex

Botanical Name	Trivial Name	Figure
Euphorbiaceae		
Euphorbia cotinifolia L.	Poison Spurge, Carrasco	
E. gymnonota Urb.		170-171
E. lactea Haw.	Candelabra Cactus	172-173
E. lathyris L.	Caper Spurge, Mole Plant	174
E. marginata Pursh	Snow-on-the-Mountain	175
E. milii Ch. des Moulins	Crown-of-Thorns	176
E. myrsinites L.	Creeping Spurge	177
E. tirucalli L.	Pencil Cactus	179
Excoecaria agallocha L. var. *orthostichalus* Muell. Arg.	Blinding Tree	
Grimmeodendron eglandulosum (A. Rich.) Urb.	Poison Bush	187
Hippomane mancinella L.	Beach Apple, Manzanillo	202-203
Pedilanthus tithymaloides (L.) Poit.	Slipper Flower	291-292
Sapium hippomane G.F.W. Mey.		
S. laurocerasus Desf.	Hinchahuevos	348
Stillingia sylvatica Gard.	Queen's Delight	
Synadenium grantii Hook. f.	African Milkbush	379
Ranunculaceae		
Anemone patens L. (= *Pulsatilla patens* (L.) Mill.)	Pasque Flower	40
Caltha palustris L.	Marsh Marigold	76
Clematis species (eg, *C. virginiana* L.)	Virgin's Bower	109-111
Ranunculus species (eg, *R. acris* L.)	Buttercup, Crowfoot	322-325
Thymelaeaceae		
Daphne mezereum L.	Daphne	143-144
Dirca palustris L.	Leatherwood, Wicopy	156

Table 5.
Representative Plants Producing Phytophotodermatitis

Botanical Name	Trivial Name	Figure
Compositae (Asteraceae)		
Achillea millefolium L.	Yarrow, Milfoil	3
Anthemis cotula L.	Dog Fennel, Mayweed	
Moraceae		
Ficus carica L.	Fig	180
F. pumila L. (= *F. repens* Hort. non Willd.)	Creeping Fig, Creeping Rubber Plant	181

Table 5. (Cont.)
Representative Plants Producing Phytophotodermatitis

Botanical Name	Trivial Name	Figure
Rosaceae		
Agrimonia eupatoria L.	Agrimony	19
Rutaceae		
Citrus aurantiifolia (Christm.) Swingle	Lime	108
Dictamnus albus L.	Gas Plant, Burning Bush	150-151
Pelea anisata H. Mann	MOKIHANA	
Ruta graveolens L.	Rue	341
Umbelliferae (Apiaceae)		
Ammi majus L.	Bishop's Weed	36
Anthriscus sylvestris (L.) Hoffman		
Daucus carota L. var. *Carota*	Queen Anne's Lace	149
Daucus carota var. *sativus* Hoffm.	Carrot	
Heracleum lanatum Michx.	Cow Parsnip	196
H. mantegazzianum Sommier & Levier	Giant Hogweed	197
H. sphondylium L.	Cow Parsnip	198-199
Pastinaca sativa L.	Parsnip	290

Table 6.
Anacardiaceae Producing Allergic Contact Dermatitis

Botanical Name	Trivial Name	Figure
Anacardium occidentale L.	Cashew, Marañón	37-38
Comocladia species (eg, *C. dodonaea* (L.) Urban)	Guao	120-123
Cotinus coggygria Scop. (= *Rhus cotinus* L.)	Smoke Tree	133-134
Mangifera indica L.	Mango	253-254
Metopium toxiferum (L.) Krug & Urban	Poisonwood, Cedro Prieto	261-262
Schinus terebinthifolius Raddi	Brazilian Pepper Tree, Florida Holly	350
Toxicodendron diversilobum (Torr. & A. Gray) Greene (= *Rhus diversiloba* Torr. & A. Gray)	Western Poison Oak	385-386
T. radicans (L.) Kuntze (= *Rhus radicans* L.)	Poison Ivy	387-390
T. rydbergii (Small ex Rydberg) Greene		
T. toxicarium (Salisb.) Gillis (= *Rhus toxicodendron* L.; *R. quercifolia* (Michx.) Steudel)	Eastern Poison Oak	391-392
T. vernix (L.) Kuntze (= *Rhus vernix* L.)	Poison Sumac	393-394

Mushroom Poisoning

III.
Mushroom Poisoning

Mushroom poisoning differs from other forms of plant poisoning in two important features: (1) Plant poisoning occurs primarily in children under age 5 years who have ingested plant material as mouth-texturing, out of curiosity, or while "playing house"; mushroom poisoning is more common in adults who ingest them as a source of food or for their psychic effect. In mushroom poisonings, therefore, it usually is easier to obtain a history of the ingestion. (2) Unlike plant intoxication, botanic identification of mushrooms during an emergency may be impossible, Fig. 423-437. Since there are a small number of distinct toxic syndromes produced by mushrooms, it is possible to determine the type of poisoning, evaluate its potential seriousness and prognosis, and outline a course of management based solely on the history and symptoms.

Differential Diagnosis of Mushroom Poisonings

Mushroom intoxications can be classified on the basis of the following questions:

1. **When were the mushrooms eaten and when did the first symptoms occur?**
   When symptoms develop within two hours of ingestion, they rarely are severe and require conservative management only. Poisonings characterized by a latent period of six hours or more are associated with severe and sometimes life-threatening consequences.

2. **What were the initial symptoms?**
   Mushroom intoxications characterized by rapid development of symptoms may be divided further as follows: (a) primarily nausea and abdominal discomfort sometimes with vomiting and/or diarrhea; (b) primarily sweating; (c) primarily inebriation or hallucinations without drowsiness or sleep; or (d) primarily delirium associated with sleepiness or coma.

   Mushroom intoxications of delayed onset may be divided into those producing: (a) a feeling of abdominal fullness and severe headache about six

203

hours after ingestion; (b) persistent emesis and watery diarrhea beginning about 12 hours after ingestion; or (c) polydipsia and polyuria about three days after ingestion.

3. **Was more than one kind of mushroom eaten?**
   If more than one kind of mushroom was eaten, two different types of toxicity may occur, which necessitates a longer period of observation.

4. **Did anyone who did not eat mushrooms become sick?**
   If similar symptoms are observed in a member of the group who did not ingest mushrooms, one should consider bacterial food poisoning from some other source or, in a wild-food foraging party, the possibility of vascular plant poisoning, eg, pokeweed, should be entertained.

5. **Did everyone who ate the mushrooms become sick?**
   If a single member of a mushroom-eating group becomes ill, one should consider food sensitivity, since mushrooms can produce allergic sensitization. Another possibility is the genetic deficiency of one or more enzymes required to metabolize the unusual sugars, eg, trehalose, associated with mushrooms; this is expressed as a bloated feeling and diarrhea.

6. **Was an alcoholic beverage consumed within 72 hours after the mushroom meal?**
   Some otherwise edible mushrooms interfere with the metabolism of alcohol resulting in a disulfiram-like reaction due to the accumulation of acetaldehyde. Extreme nausea, vomiting, and headache then occur shortly after consumption of the alcoholic beverage.

Management of Mushroom Intoxications

Mushrooms Producing Gastroenteric Discomfort of Rapid Onset

A number of mushroom species produce various degrees of gastroenteric discomfort, which may be associated with vomiting and/or diarrhea. Some of those that cause severe reactions are listed in Table 1, Mushrooms Producing Gastroenteritis. Treatment is as for gastroenteritis of any etiology. Some mushrooms may cause emesis and/or diarrhea that lasts for several days and replacement of fluids and electrolytes is necessary to prevent severe dehydration and hypovolemic shock.

Mushrooms Producing Sweating

Mushrooms that cause sweating contain the parasympathetic stimulant, muscarine, which is not affected by cooking. These mushrooms are of the genera, *Clitocybe* and *Inocybe*.

The ingestion of small concentrations of muscarine is associated with sweating and sometimes abdominal discomfort. Larger amounts may produce abdominal pain, emesis, blurred vision, and other parasympathetic responses. The intoxication usually subsides in two hours. When the patient experiences severe discomfort or anxiety, symptoms may be abolished by atropine in a dose sufficient to produce dryness of the mouth.

Mushrooms Producing Inebriation or Hallucinations Without Drowsiness

Mushrooms containing psilocybin are members of the genera, *Psilocybe*, *Panaeolus*, *Copelandia*, *Gymnopilus*, *Conocybe*, and *Pluteus*.

The clinical response of adults is determined by the quantity of toxin ingested, the mood and personality of the patient, the setting of the experience, and, if the effect is sought deliberately, the drug sophistication of the patient. Accidental poisoning in adults resembles alcoholic inebriation, and treatment is not required. The effects usually dissipate within two hours but may be more prolonged when large amounts were eaten. Effects lasting longer than 24 hours are not due to a natural toxin but should be ascribed to the consumption of a mushroom "doctored" with a hallucinogen, usually phencyclidine (PCP).

In young children exposed to large doses of toxin in mushrooms consumed as food, hallucinations may be accompanied by hyperthermia, tonic-clonic convulsions, coma, and death. External cooling and respiratory support are required. The decision to administer diazepam to control convulsions should be based on their persistence.

Mushrooms Producing Delirium Associated with Drowsiness or Coma

Amanita muscaria (L. ex Fr.) Hooker and *Amanita pantherina* (DC. ex Fr.) Secr. exert this effect. Despite its species name, *A. muscaria* usually contains only clinically insignificant quantities of muscarine. The toxins producing delirium are ibotenic acid and its decomposition product, muscimol, the active substance. Muscimol acts as a GABA agonist on bicuculline-reactive postsynaptic receptors in the central nervous system.

Symptoms usually appear within two hours. There may be abdominal discomfort initially, but this may be minimal or absent. Drowsiness and dizziness develop and may be accompanied by sleep. This is succeeded by increased motor activity, illusions or delirium, and sometimes manic excitement. Episodes of alternating drowsiness and excitement may persist for a few hours. Poisoning is rarely severe in adults, but patients may require protection against injury during the manic phase.

In preadolescent children, ingestion of large quantities of these mushrooms as food may result in convulsions, coma, and complex neurologic signs persisting for up to 12 hours. Respiratory support should be given if indicated; otherwise, therapeutic intervention is not necessary.

Mushrooms Provoking a Disulfiram-Like Effect

Only a small number of mushrooms exert this action, which is encountered most frequently after ingestion of *Coprinus atramentarius* Fr. It should be stressed that the mushroom itself is edible. It contains an amino acid, coprine, which is converted to cyclopropanone hydrate in the body. This metabolite inhibits acetaldehyde dehydrogenase, and the consumption of alcoholic beverages up to 72 hours after ingestion of the mushroom may result in headache, nausea and vomiting, flushing, and cardiovascular disturbances. These reactions persist for two to three hours. No therapeutic intervention, except for reassurance, is indicated.

Mushrooms Inducing Abdominal Discomfort and Severe Headache About Six Hours After Ingestion

Gyromitra esculenta (Pers. ex Fr.) Fr. is associated most often with this type of intoxication. It contains a number of hydrazones, gyromitrin and its homologues, which are hydrolyzed to the active toxin, monomethylhydrazine. This toxin is volatile and water soluble; thus, the mushroom may be rendered edible by air drying or extraction of the toxin with boiling water. Monomethylhyrazine inactivates pyridoxine.

The onset of symptoms is characteristically sudden and may result from ingestion of the mushroom or inhalation of the vapor during cooking. Emesis may occur but diarrhea is absent. Recovery usually is complete within two to six days, but fatalities have occurred.

Medical management is identical to that for

overdosage of isoniazid: correction of acidosis and intravenous administration of pyridoxine.

Mushrooms Causing Emesis and Profuse, Watery Diarrhea About 12 Hours After Ingestion

Most of the fatalities from mushroom poisoning are caused by *Amanita phalloides* (Fr.) Secr. and its relatives (see Table 2, Mushrooms Containing Amatoxin). Amatoxins are cyclic octapeptides, which selectively enter the hepatocyte where they bind to and inhibit RNA polymerase II. This prevents protein synthesis and results in cellular death. Occasionally, the kidney also is affected. The initial symptoms are due to an action of amatoxins on the intestine, but this is not responsible for the ultimate outcome. Apparently other cell types cannot be penetrated by the toxin. The amatoxins are not affected by cooking or drying and cannot be extracted by boiling water.

After a latent period of about 12 hours, persistent nausea, vomiting, intestinal pain, and profuse watery diarrhea occur. After a few hours, regardless of therapeutic intervention, a symptom-free period of variable duration (up to three to five days) follows, succeeded by hepatic insufficiency indistinguishable from acute viral hepatitis. Increased levels of serum transaminases are the most sensitive indicators of hepatic damage. Blood glucose and clotting factors of hepatic origin decrease.

During the initial gastroenteric phase of intoxication, fluids and electrolytes should be supplied. An adequate urine flow should be maintained because amatoxins are eliminated partially by the kidney and also to reduce the duration of exposure of renal cells to the toxin. When tolerated, repeated oral administration of activated charcoal with water interrupts the enterohepatic cycling of the toxins. Treatment therafter does not differ from that for acute viral hepatitis. If management is successful, the patient recovers rapidly in about one week. The return toward normal of factor V and fibrinogen levels is prognostic of recovery. Despite intensive care, the fatality rate remains 10% to 15%.

Various additional therapeutic agents are employed in European protocols including high-dose vitamins, corticosteroids, sex hormones, high-dose glucose, high-dose penicillin G, and thioctic (alpha-lipoic) acid. The value of these measures has not been established experimentally.

Mushrooms Causing Polydipsia and Polyuria Three or More Days After Ingestion

Certain species of the large genus *Cortinarius* cause this type of poisoning. After a latent period of 3 to 17 days, the patient develops polydipsia and may consume several liters of fluid daily. This may be accompanied by nausea, headache, muscular pains, and chills. After the initial polyuria, renal failure associated with severe tubular necrosis may develop. Postmortem examination reveals fatty degeneration of the liver and severe inflammatory changes in the intestine. Beyond management for severe renal failure, no specific intervention can be recommended. Institution of hemodialysis or hemoperfusion with XAD-4 Amberlite resin as soon as possible after ingestion may reduce the risk of severe, irreversible renal damage.

Recommended for Further Reading

Faulstich H, et al (eds): *Amanita Toxins and Poisoning*. New York, Witzrock, 1980.

Holmdahl J, et al: Acute renal failure after intoxication with *Cortinarius* mushrooms. *Human Toxicol* 3:309-313, 1984.

Lampe KF: Toxic fungi. *Ann Rev Pharmacol Toxicol* 19:85-104, 1979.

Lampe KF: Mushroom poisoning, in Rechcigl M Jr (ed): *Handbook of Naturally Occurring Food Toxicants*. Boca Raton, CRC Press, 1983, 193-212.

Lincoff G, Mitchel DH: *Toxic and Hallucinogenic Mushroom Poisoning*. New York, Van Nostrand Reinhold, 1977.

Rumack BH, Salzman E (eds): *Mushroom Poisoning: Diagnosis and Treatment*. Boca Raton, CRC Press, 1978.

Schumacher T, Høiland K: Mushroom poisoning caused by species of the genus *Cortinarius* Fries. *Arch Toxicol* 53:87-106, 1983.

Tebbett IR, Caddy B: Mushroom toxins of the genus *Cortinarius*. *Experientia* 40:441-446, 1984.

Wieland T, Faulstich H: Peptide toxins from *Amanita*, in Keeler RF, Tu AT (eds): *Handbook of Natural Toxins*. New York, Marcel Dekker, vol I, 1983, 585-635.

Table 1.
Mushrooms Producing Gastroenteritis

Mushrooms that may cause severe intoxication:

Chlorophyllum molybdites (Meyer ex Fr.) Mass. (= *Lepiota morgani* Sacc.)

Entoloma lividum (Bull. ex St-Amans) Quél. (= *Rhodophyllus lividus* Quél.; *R. sinuatus* Sing.)

Tricholoma pardinum Quél.

Omphalotus olearius (DC. ex Fr.) Sing. (= *Clitocybe illudens* (Schw.) Sacc.; *Pleurotus olearius* (DC. ex Fr.) Gill.)

Paxillus involutus (Batsch ex Fr.) Fr.

Mushrooms that produce mild or transient intoxication:

Agaricus arvensis Schaeff. ex Secr. var. *palustris* A.H. Smith

Agaricus hondensis Murr.

Boletus luridus Schaeff. ex Fr.

Boletus pulcherrimus Thiers & Halling (= *B. eastwoodiae* (Murr.) Sacc. & Trotter)

Boletus satanas Lenz

Gomphus floccosus (Schw.) Sing. (= *Cantharellus floccosus* Schw.)

Gyromitra ambigua (Karst.) Harmaja

Hebeloma crustuliniforme (Bull. ex St-Amans) Quél.

Lactarius torminosus (Schaeff. ex Fr.) S.F. Gray

Pholiota aurea (Fr.) Kummer (= *Togaria aurea* W.G. Smith; *Phaeolepiota aurea* Marie ex Konr. & Maubl.)

Ramaria formosa (Fr.) Quél.

Russula species

Tricholoma irinum (Fr.) Kummer (= *Clitocybe irina* (Fr.) Bigelow & A.H. Smith)

Verpa bohemica (Kromb.) Schroet.

Table 2.
Mushrooms Containing Amatoxin

Amanita bisporigera Atk.

Amanita ocreata Peck

Amanita phalloides (Fr.) Secr.

Amanita suballiacea Murr.

Amanita verna (Bull. ex Fr.) Vitt.

Amanita virosa Secr.

Galerina autumnalis (Pk.) A.H. Smith

Galerina marginata (Batsch. ex Secr.) Kühner

Galerina venenata A.H. Smith

Lepiota josserandii Bon & Boif.

Mushrooms presumed to contain amatoxins:

Conocybe filaris Fr.

Lepiota brunneoincarnata Chodat & Martin

Lepiota helveola Bres.

Lepiota subincarnata Lg.

1   ROSARY PEA *Abrus precatorius*

2   ROSARY PEA *Abrus precatorius*

3 YARROW *Achillea millefolium*

4 BUSHMAN'S POISON *Acokanthera oppositifolia*

5 MONKSHOOD *Aconitum columbianum*

6 MONKSHOOD *Aconitum napellus*

7 WHITE BANEBERRY *Actaea pachypoda*

8 WHITE BANEBERRY *Actaea pachypoda*

9 **RED BANEBERRY** *Actaea rubra*

10 **DESERT ROSE** *Adenium obesum* ssp. *multiflorum*

11 **PHEASANT'S EYE** *Adonis vernalis*

12   HORSE CHESTNUT *Aesculus hippocastanum*

13   HORSE CHESTNUT *Aesculus hippocastanum*

14   CALIFORNIA BUCKEYE *Aesculus californica*

15   CALIFORNIA BUCKEYE   *Aesculus californica*

16   FOOL'S PARSLEY   *Aethusa cynapium*

17 CENTURY PLANT *Agave americana*

18 CENTURY PLANT *Agave americana*

19 AGRIMONY *Agrimonia eupatoria*

20 TUNG NUT *Aleurites fordii*

21   CANDLENUT *Aleurites moluccana*

22   CANDLENUT *Aleurites moluccana*

23   *Aleurites trisperma*

24 *Aleurites trisperma*

25 ALLAMANDA *Allamanda cathartica*

26 ALLAMANDA *Allamanda cathartica*

27   **BUSH ALLAMANDA**   *Allamanda neriifolia*

28   **BUSH ALLAMANDA**   *Allamanda neriifolia*

29   **ONION**   *Allium cepa*

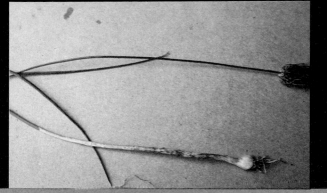

30 FIELD GARLIC *Allium vineale*

31 FIELD GARLIC *Allium vineale*

32 ELEPHANT'S EAR *Alocasia macrorrhiza*

33 ELEPHANT'S EAR *Alocasia watsoniana*

34 ALOE *Aloe barbadensis*

35 BELLADONNA LILY *Amaryllis belladonna*

36   BISHOP'S WEED   *Ammi majus*

37   CASHEW   *Anacardium occidentale*

38 CASHEW *Anacardium occidentale*

39 WINDFLOWER *Anemone canadensis*

40 PASQUE FLOWER *Anemone patens*

41 PASQUE FLOWER *Anemone pulsatilla*

42 FLAMINGO LILY *Anthurium andraeanum*

43 *Anthurium cordifolium*

44 *Anthurium cubense*

45 PIGTAIL ANTHURIUM *Anthurium scherzeranum*

46 GREEN-DRAGON *Arisaema dracontium*

47 JACK-IN-THE-PULPIT *Arisaema triphyllum*

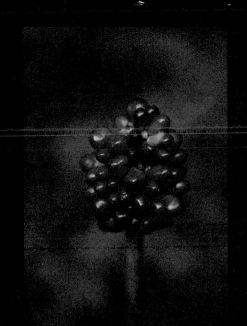

50 CALICO FLOWER *Aristolochia elegans*

51 *Aristolochia gigantea*

52 *Aristolochia gigantea*

53 ITALIAN ARUM *Arum italicum*

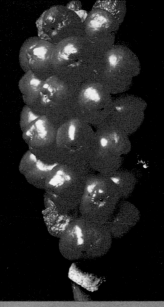

54   CUCKOOPINT *Arum maculatum*

55   PAWPAW *Asimina triloba*

56 DEADLY NIGHTSHADE *Atropa belladonna*

57 DEADLY NIGHTSHADE *Atropa belladonna*

58 JAPANESE AUCUBA *Aucuba japonica*

59 PRAIRIE FALSE INDIGO *Baptisia leucantha*

60 PRAIRIE FALSE INDIGO *Baptisia leucantha*

61 ACKEE *Blighia sapida*

62 ACKEE *Blighia sapida*

63 RED ANGEL'S TRUMPET *Brugmansia sanguinea*

64 RED ANGEL'S TRUMPET *Brugmansia sanguinea*

65 ANGEL'S TRUMPET *Brugmansia suaveolens*

66 *Caesalpinia mexicana*

67 BARBADOS PRIDE *Caesalpinia pulcherrima*

68 *Caesalpinia vesicaria*

69 *Caesalpinia vesicaria*

70   CALADIUM   *Caladium bicolor*

71   WATER ARUM   *Calla palustris*

72 MASTWOOD *Calophyllum inophyllum*

73 MASTWOOD *Calophyllum inophyllum*

74 CROWN FLOWER *Calotropis gigantea*

75 *Caltha leptosepala*

76 **MARSH MARIGOLD** *Caltha palustris*

77 CAROLINA ALLSPICE *Calycanthus floridus*

78 CAROLINA ALLSPICE *Calycanthus floridus*

79   CAROLINA ALLSPICE *Calycanthus floridus*

80   *Calycanthus occidentalis*

81   TRUMPET CREEPER *Campsis radicans*

82   HOT PEPPER *Capsicum annuum* cv. 'Scotch Bonnet'

83   HOT PEPPER *Capsicum annuum* cv. 'Scotch Bonnet'

84 TABASCO PEPPER *Capsicum frutescens*

85 FISHTAIL PALM *Caryota mitis*

86 GOLDEN SHOWER *Cassia fistula*

87   **GOLDEN SHOWER**   *Cassia fistula*

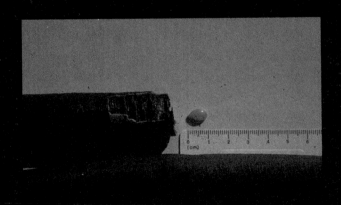

88   **GOLDEN SHOWER**   *Cassia fistula*

89 COFFEE SENNA *Cassia occidentalis*

90 BLUE COHOSH *Caulophyllum thalictroides*

91   BLUE COHOSH *Caulophyllum thalictroides*

92   ORIENTAL BITTERSWEET *Celastrus orbiculatus*

93   BITTERSWEET *Celastrus scandens*

94 BITTERSWEET *Celastrus scandens*

95 *Cestrum aurantiacum*

96 DAY BLOOMING JESSAMINE *Cestrum diurnum*

97 DAY BLOOMING JESSAMINE *Cestrum diurnum*

98 *Cestrum elegans*

99 NIGHT BLOOMING JESSAMINE *Cestrum nocturnum*

100   CELANDINE   *Chelidonium majus*

101   MARGUERITE   *Chrysanthemum frutescens*

102 CRYSANTHEMUM *Chrysanthemum indicum*

103 CRYSANTHEMUM *Chrysanthemum* sp.

104 CRYSANTHEMUM *Chrysanthemum* sp.

105 *Cicuta bulbifera*

106 **WATER HEMLOCK** *Cicuta douglasii*

107   **WATER HEMLOCK**   *Cicuta maculata*

108   **KEY LIME**   *Citrus aurantiifolia*

109   **VIRGIN'S BOWER**   *Clematis integrifolia*

110   VIRGIN'S BOWER *Clematis integrifolia*

111   CLEMATIS *Clematis patens* cv. 'Nelly Moser'

112 KAFFIR LILY *Clivia* sp.

113 KAFFIR LILY *Clivia miniata*

114 BALSAM APPLE *Clusia rosea*

115 BALSAM APPLE *Clusia rosea*

116 CHAYA *Cnidoscolus chayamansa*

117 TREAD SOFTLY *Cnidoscolus stimulosus*

118   AUTUMN CROCUS   *Colchicum autumnale*

119   ELEPHANT'S EAR   *Colocasia gigantea*

120   GUAO   *Comocladia dodonaea*

121 GUAO *Comocladia dodonaea*

122 GUAO *Comocladia glabra*

123 GUAO *Comocladia velutina*

124 POISON HEMLOCK *Conium maculatum*

125 POISON HEMLOCK *Conium maculatum*

126 POISON HEMLOCK *Conium maculatum*

127 LILY-OF-THE-VALLEY *Convallaria majalis*

128   LILY-OF-THE-VALLEY   *Convallaria majalis*

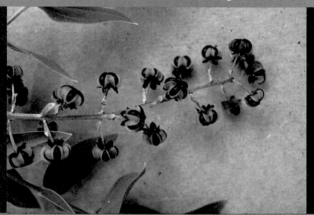

129   *Coriaria myrtifolia*

130   BLOOD-TWIG DOGWOOD   *Cornus sanguinea*

131 *Corynocarpus laevigatus*

132 *Corynocarpus laevigatus*

133 SMOKE TREE *Cotinus coggygria*

134 SMOKE TREE *Cotinus coggygria*

135 POISON BULB *Crinum asiaticum*

136 RATTLEBOX *Crotalaria spectabilis*

137 RATTLEBOX *Crotalaria spectabilis*

138   **RUBBER VINE**   *Cryptostegia grandiflora*

139   **RUBBER VINE**   *Cryptostegia grandiflora X madagascariensis*

140   **RUBBER VINE**   *Cryptostegia grandiflora X madagascariensis*

141 PINK LADY'S SLIPPER *Cypripedium acaule*

142 SMALL YELLOW LADY'S SLIPPER *Cypripedium calceolus* var. *parviflorum*

143 FEBRUARY DAPHNE *Daphne mezereum*

144 FEBRUARY DAPHNE *Daphne mezereum*

145 JIMSON WEED *Datura stramonium*

146 JIMSON WEED *Datura stramonium*

147 JIMSON WEED *Datura stramonium* var. *tatula*

148 JIMSON WEED *Datura stramonium* var. *tatula*

149 QUEEN ANNE'S LACE *Daucus carota*

150 GAS PLANT *Dictamnus albus*

151 GAS PLANT *Dictamnus albus*

152   DUMB CANE *Dieffenbachia maculata*

153   DUMB CANE *Dieffenbachia maculata* cv. 'Tropic Snow'

154   DUMB CANE *Dieffenbachia* cv. 'Mary Lou'

155 FOXGLOVE *Digitalis purpurea*

156 LEATHERWOOD *Dirca palustris*

157 *Duranta lineata*

158 GOLDEN DEWDROP *Duranta repens*

159 GOLDEN DEWDROP *Duranta repens*

160 VIPER'S BUGLOSS *Echium vulgare*

161 POTHOS *Epipremnum aureum*

162 FLEABANE *Erigeron philadelphicus*

163 LOQUAT *Eriobotrya japonica*

164　LOQUAT *Eriobotrya japonica*

165　BLUE GUM *Eucalyptus globulus*

166　STRAWBERRY BUSH *Euonymus americana*

167   EUROPEAN SPINDLE TREE   *Euonymus europaeus*

168   EUROPEAN SPINDLE TREE   *Euonymus europaeus*

169 FIRE-ON-THE-MOUNTAIN *Euphorbia cyathophora*

170 *Euphorbia gymnonota*

171 *Euphorbia gymnonota*

172   CANDELABRA CACTUS *Euphorbia lactea*

173   CANDELABRA CACTUS *Euphorbia lactea*

174 MOLE PLANT *Euphorbia lathyris*

175 SNOW-ON-THE-MOUNTAIN *Euphorbia marginata*

176   CROWN-OF-THORNS   *Euphorbia milii* var. *splendens*

177   CREEPING SPURGE   *Euphorbia myrsinites*

178   POINSETTIA *Euphorbia pulcherrima*

179   PENCIL CACTUS *Euphorbia tirucalli*

180   FIG *Ficus carica*

181 CREEPING FIG *Ficus pumila*

182 SNOWDROP *Galanthus nivalis*

183 YELLOW JESSAMINE *Gelsemium sempervirens*

184 MAIDENHAIR TREE *Gingko biloba*

185 GLORY LILY *Gloriosa superba*

186 SILKY OAK *Grevillea robusta*

187 POISON BUSH *Grimmeodendron eglandulosum*

188 KENTUCKY COFFEE BEAN *Gymnocladus dioicus*

189 ALGERIAN IVY *Hedera canariensis* cv. 'Glorie de Marengo'

190 ENGLISH IVY *Hedera helix*

191 ENGLISH IVY *Hedera helix*

192   HELIOTROPE   *Heliotropium amplexicaule*

193   *Helleborus foetidus*

194 *Helleborus foetidus*

195 CHRISTMAS ROSE *Helleborus niger*

196   COW PARSNIP *Heracleum lanatum*

197   GIANT HOGWEED *Heracleum mantegazzianum*

198   COW PARSNIP *Heracleum sphondylium* ssp. *montanum*

199   COW PARSNIP *Heracleum sphondylium* ssp. *montanum*

200   AMARYLLIS   *Hippeastrum* sp.

201   *Hippobroma longiflora*

202 MANCHINEEL *Hippomane mancinella*

203 MANCHINEEL *Hippomane mancinella*

204 HOPS *Humulus lupulus*

205 SANDBOX TREE *Hura crepitans*

206 SANDBOX TREE *Hura crepitans*

207 SANDBOX TREE *Hura crepitans*

208   **HYACINTH**   *Hyacinthus orientalis*

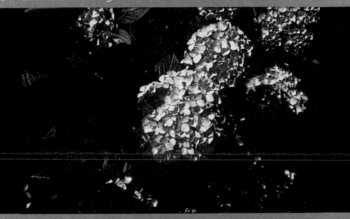

209   **HYDRANGEA**   *Hydrangea* sp.

210   **SPIDER LILY**   *Hymenocallis fragrans*

211   SPIDER LILY *Hymenocallis speciosa*

212   SPIDER LILY *Hymenocallis speciosa*

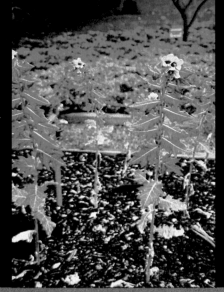

213 **BLACK HENBANE** *Hyoscyamus niger* var. *agrestis*

214 **ENGLISH HOLLY** *Ilex aquifolium*

215 AMERICAN HOLLY *Ilex opaca*

216 YAUPON *Ilex vomitoria*

217 **ORRIS** *Iris X germanica* var. *florentina*

218 **YELLOW FLAG** *Iris pseudacorus*

219 PHYSIC NUT *Jatropha curcas*

220 PHYSIC NUT *Jatropha curcas*

221   BELLYACHE BUSH *Jatropha gossypiifolia*

222   PEREGRINA *Jatropha integerrima*

223 JICAMILLA *Jatropha macrorhiza*

224 CORAL PLANT *Jatropha multifida*

225 GOUT STALK *Jatropha podagrica*

226 MOUNTAIN LAUREL *Kalmia latifolia*

227   COYOTILLO *Karwinskia humboldtiana*

228   GOLDEN CHAIN *Laburnum anagyroides*

229 GOLDEN CHAIN *Laburnum anagyroides*

230 GOLDEN CHAIN *Laburnum anagyroides*

231 LANTANA *Lantana camara*

232 LANTANA *Lantana camara*

233 WOOD NETTLE *Laportea canadensis*

234 CREOSOTE BUSH *Larrea divaricata*

235 *Leucaena leucocephala*

236 SWEETBELLS *Leucothoe racemosa*

237 PRIVET *Ligustrum japonicum*

238 PRIVET *Ligustrum obtusifolium* var. *regelianum*

239 CARDINAL FLOWER *Lobelia cardinalis*

240 *Lobelia kalmii*

241　GREAT LOBELIA　*Lobelia siphilitica*

242　TATARIAN HONEYSUCKLE　*Lonicera tatarica*

243   TATARIAN HONEYSUCKLE *Lonicera tatarica*

244   MATRIMONY VINE *Lycium carolinianum*

245   SPIDER LILY *Lycoris radiata*

246 MAGIC LILY *Lycoris squamigera*

247 FETTER BUSH *Lyonia elliptica*

248 OSAGE ORANGE *Maclura pomifera*

249 BULL BAY *Magnolia grandiflora*

250 TOUCH-ME-NOT *Malpighia polytricha*

251 COWITCH CHERRY *Malpighia urens*

252   COWITCH CHERRY   *Malpighia urens*

253   MANGO   *Mangifera indica*

254 MANGO *Mangifera indica*

255 CASSAVA *Manihot esculenta*

256 CHINABERRY *Melia azedarach*

257 CHINABERRY *Melia azedarach*

258 MOONSEED *Menispermum canadense*

259 MOONSEED *Menispermum canadense*

260 MOONSEED *Menispermum canadense*

261 POISONWOOD *Metopium toxiferum*

262 POISONWOOD *Metopium toxiferum*

263   BALSAM PEAR   *Momordica charantia*

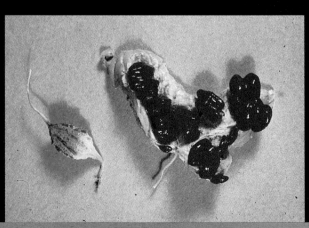

264   BALSAM PEAR   *Momordica charantia*

265 SPLIT-LEAF PHILODENDRON *Monstera deliciosa*

266 VELVET BEAN *Mucuna deeringiana*

267 COWITCH *Mucuna pruriens*

268   COWITCH   *Mucuna pruriens*

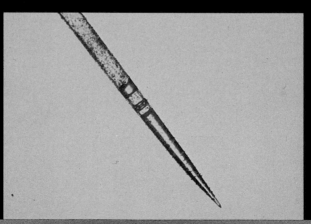

269   COWITCH   *Mucuna pruriens*

270 *Myoporum laetum*

271 *Myoporum laetum*

272 DAFFODIL *Narcissus* cv. 'Mary Bohannon'

273 OLEANDER *Nerium oleander*

274 OLEANDER *Nerium oleander*

275 OLEANDER *Nerium oleander*

276 TREE TOBACCO *Nicotiana glauca*

277   TOBACCO   *Nicotiana tabacum*

278   TOBACCO   *Nicotiana tabacum*

279 WATER DROPWORT *Oenanthe crocata*

280 *Oenanthe sarmentosa*

281 BUNNY EARS *Opuntia microdasys*

282   BUNNY EARS *Opuntia microdasys*

283   WONDER FLOWER *Ornithogalum thyrsoides*

286 YAM BEAN *Pachyrhizus erosus*

287 STICKY GRASS *Panicum glutinosum*

288   VIRGINIA CREEPER *Parthenocissus quinquefolia*

289   BOSTON IVY *Parthenocissus tricuspidata*

290 WILD PARSNIP *Pastinaca sativa* var. *pratensis*

291 SLIPPER FLOWER *Pedilanthus tithymaloides*

292   SLIPPER FLOWER   *Pedilanthus tithymaloides*

293   *Pernettya mucronata*

294   CALIFORNIA BLUEBELL   *Phacelia campanularia*

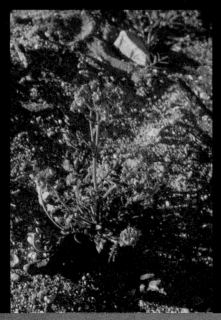

295   SCORPION FLOWER   *Phacelia crenulata*

296   HEART-LEAF *Philodendron scandens* ssp. *oxycardium*

297 *Philodendron selloum*

298   *Philodendron speciosum*

299   *Philodendron speciosum*

300 *Phoradendron rubrum* on *Swietenia mahagoni*

301 *Phoradendron rubrum*

302 (AMERICAN) MISTLETOE *Phoradendron serotinum*

303 JAPANESE LANTERN PLANT *Physalis alkekengi*

304 JAPANESE LANTERN PLANT *Physalis alkekengi*

305 CLAMMY GROUNDCHERRY *Physalis heterophylla*

306 CLAMMY GROUNDCHERRY *Physalis heterophylla*

307   POKEWEED   *Phytolacca americana*

308   POKEWEED   *Phytolacca americana*

309   *Pieris formosa*

310 *Pieris formosa*

311 FRANGIPANI *Plumeria rubra*

312   FRANGIPANI *Plumeria rubra*

313   MAYAPPLE *Podophyllum peltatum*

314   MAYAPPLE   *Podophyllum peltatum*

315   TRIFOLIATE ORANGE   *Poncirus trifoliata*

316   GERMAN PRIMROSE   *Primula obconica*

317 WESTERN HONEY MESQUITE *Prosopis glandulosa var. torreyana*

318 BLACK CHERRY *Prunus serotina*

319 CHOKECHERRY *Prunus virginiana*

320 CHOKECHERRY *Prunus virginiana*

321 WESTERN CHOKECHERRY *Prunus virginiana*
var. *melanocarpa*

324 BUTTER DAISY *Ranunculus repens*

325 CURSED CROWFOOT *Ranunculus sceleratus*

326   COFFEEBERRY   *Rhamnus californica*

327   COMMON BUCKTHORN   *Rhamnus cathartica*

328   ALDER BUCKTHORN   *Rhamnus frangula*

329 RHUBARB *Rheum rhabarbarum*

330 CAROLINA RHODODENDRON *Rhododendron carolinianum*

331 WESTERN AZALEA *Rhododendron occidentale*

332 *Rhodendron triumphans* X *javanicum* X *leucogigas*

333 JETBEAD *Rhodotypos scandens*

334 JETBEAD *Rhodotypos scandens*

335 OYSTER PLANT *Rhoeo spathacea*

336 CASTOR BEAN *Ricinus communis*

337 CASTOR BEAN *Ricinus communis*

338   ROUGE PLANT *Rivina humilis*

339   BLACK LOCUST *Robinia pseudoacacia*

340   BLACK LOCUST *Robinia pseudoacacia*

341   RUE   *Ruta graveolens*

342   BLUE ELDERBERRY   *Sambucus caerulea*

343 (AMERICAN) ELDERBERRY *Sambucus canadensis*

344 *Sambucus mexicana*

345 EUROPEAN RED ELDERBERRY *Sambucus racemosa*

346 SOAPBERRY *Sapindus saponaria*

347 SOAPBERRY *Sapindus saponaria*

348   HINCHAHUEVOS   *Sapium laurocerasus*

349   PEPPER TREE   *Schinus molle*

350   FLORIDA HOLLY   *Schinus terebinthifolius*

351   SQUILL   *Scilla peruviana*

352   GROUNDSEL   *Senecio vulgaris*

353   SCARLET WISTARIA TREE   *Sesbania grandiflora*

354   *Sesbania punicea*

355   *Sesbania vesicaria*

356 PURPLE QUEEN *Setcreasea pallida* cv. 'Purple Heart'

357 CHALICE VINE *Solandra grandiflora*

358 CHALICE VINE *Solandra grandiflora*

359 CHALICE VINE *Solandra grandiflora*

360 NIGHTSHADE *Solanum americanum*

361 NIGHTSHADE *Solanum americanum*

362   HORSE NETTLE *Solanum carolinense*

363   HORSE NETTLE *Solanum carolinense*

364   BITTERSWEET *Solanum dulcamara*

365 NIPPLEFRUIT *Solanum mammosum*

366 JERUSALEM CHERRY *Solanum pseudocapsicum*

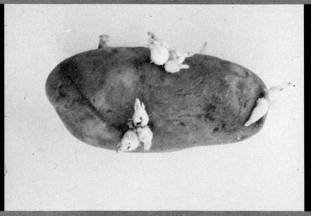

367 POTATO *Solanum tuberosum*

370 WHITE ANTHURIUM *Spathiphyllum* cv. 'Clevlandii'

371 PINKROOT *Spigelia marilandica*

372 *Sterculia apetala*

373 STRYCHNINE *Strychnos nux-vomica*

374 MAHOGANY *Swietenia mahagoni*

375   MAHOGANY   *Swietenia mahagoni*

376   SNOWBERRY   *Symphoricarpos albus*

377   SKUNK CABBAGE   *Symplocarpus foetidus*

379   AFRICAN MILKBUSH *Synadenium grantii*

378   SKUNK CABBAGE *Symplocarpus foetidus*

380 TANSY *Tanacetum vulgare*

381 ENGLISH YEW *Taxus baccata*

382 JAPANESE YEW *Taxus cuspidata*

383 YELLOW OLEANDER *Thevetia peruviana*

384 YELLOW OLEANDER *Thevetia peruviana*

385 WESTERN POISON OAK *Toxicodendron diversilobum*

386 WESTERN POISON OAK *Toxicodendron diversilobum*

387 POISON IVY *Toxicodendron radicans*

388 POISON IVY *Toxicodendron radicans*

389 POISON IVY *Toxicodendron radicans*

390 POISON IVY *Toxicodendron radicans*

391 EASTERN POISON OAK *Toxicodendron toxicarium*

392 EASTERN POISON OAK *Toxicodendron toxicarium*

393 POISON SUMAC *Toxicodendron vernix*

394 POISON SUMAC *Toxicodendron vernix*

395 PRINGAMOSA *Tragia volubilis*

396 ENGLISH ELM *Ulmus procera*

397 WILD ALLAMANDA *Urechites lutea*

398 WILD ALLAMANDA *Urechites lutea*

399 ORTIGA *Urera baccifera*

400 RED SQUILL *Urginea maritima*

401 RED SQUILL *Urginea maritima*

402   STINGING NETTLE   *Urtica dioica*

403   STINGING NETTLE   *Urtica dioica*

404   STINGING NETTLE   *Urtica urens*

405   CORN LILY   *Veratrum californicum*

406 CORN LILY *Veratrum californicum*

407 WHITE HELLEBORE *Veratrum viride*

408 WHITE HELLEBORE *Veratrum viride*

409 (EUROPEAN) MISTLETOE *Viscum album*

410 *Wigandia urens*

411 *Wigandia urens*

412 CHINESE WISTERIA *Wisteria sinensis*

413   CHINESE WISTERIA   *Wisteria sinensis*

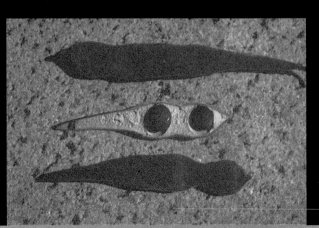

414   CHINESE WISTERIA   *Wisteria sinensis*

415   MALANGA   *Xanthosoma violaceum*

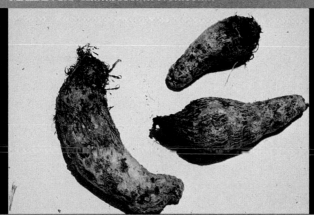

416   MALANGA   *Xanthosoma violaceum*

417   COONTIE   *Zamia pumila* ssp. *pumila*

418   COONTIE   *Zamia pumila* ssp. *pumila*

419   CALLA LILY   *Zantedeschia aethiopica*

420 ATAMASCO LILY *Zephyranthes atamasco*

421 DEATH CAMAS *Zigadenus paniculatus*

422　DEATH CAMAS　*Zigadenus paniculatus*

423　*Amanita muscaria*

424 *Amanita pantherina*

425 *Amanita phalloides*

426 *Amanita phalloides*

427 *Amanita verna*

428 *Chlorophyllum molybdites*

429 *Coprinus atramentarius*

430 *Cortinarius speciosissimus*

431 *Gymnopilus spectabilis*

432 *Gyromitra esculenta*

433 *Inocybe* sp.

434 *Omphalotus olearius*

435 *Paxillus involutus*

436　*Psilocybe cubensis*

437　*Russula emetica*

Index of Plants

400

417